Helen M. Young
April 27, 1999

FOREVER YOUNG

THE LIFE AND TIMES
M. NORVEL YOUNG &
HELEN M. YOUNG

FOREVER YOUNG

THE LIFE AND TIMES
M. NORVEL YOUNG &
HELEN M. YOUNG

21ST CENTURY CHRISTIAN

Copyright © 1999
21st Century Christian

Published by 21st Century Christan
2809 Granny White Pike
Nashville, TN 37204

Printed and Bound in the
United States of America
All Rights Reserved

All Scripture quotations are from the Holy Bible,
New International Version. Copyright © 1973, 1976, 1984
by International Bible Society. Used by permission of
Zondervan Publishing House. All rights reserved.

ISBN # 0-89098-167-1

CONTENTS

Some of Them Do Sparkle!

Many people vividly remember the popular Broadway musical, *Camelot*. The songs were inspiring. The story of Lancelot and Guenevere was enchanting. Some may recall that the armies of King Arthur and Lancelot eventually engage in battle against one another. But probably few remember how the story ends . . .

A boy of 14 is discovered behind Arthur's tent on the battle-field where a conflict soon will spell the end of Camelot. The boy admits he is a stowaway but quickly explains that he has come to fight for the Round Table. He hopes someday to be a knight, even though he has never even seen a knight in his village of Warwick. "I only know *of* them," he says, "the stories people tell."

A strange light comes into the king's eyes. "What do you think you know of the Knights and the Round Table?" asks Arthur.

"I know everything, Milord," the boy enthuses. "Might for right! Right for right! Justice for all! A Round Table where all Knights would sit. Everything!"

As Arthur excitedly talks with the boy, he finally orders, "Kneel, Tom. Kneel. With this sword, Excalibur, I knight you Sir Tom of Warwick. And I command you to return home and carry out my orders." With that, he sends the boy back to tell everyone, "There was one brief shining moment that was known as Camelot."

"Who is that, Arthur?" asked the king's faithful knight, Pellinore, as he watches the boy disappear into the night.

And King Arthur replies, "One of what we all are, Pelly. Less than a drop in the great blue motion of the sunlit sea." Then he smiles and says jubilantly, "But it seems some of the drops sparkle, Pelly. Some of them do sparkle! Run, boy!" And so the legend of Camelot lives on.

In a sense, this book is the story of a couple of drops in time that sparkle. Especially, it is the story of two people who embraced high ideals and also accomplished wonderful deeds. And yes, who also had to deal with the failings of others, as well as their own shortcomings. Still, their lives sparkle. They do sparkle!

The remarkable individuals about whom we write are actually two intertwining strands, often appearing as one. Such is the magnitude of the accomplishments of Matt Norvel and Helen Mattox Young that each of them deserves a thick volume or two of their own. However, we shall endeavor to briefly tell their stories between the covers of this one book. Perhaps one book is the only way their common tale can be told.

We begin by examining the strands individually, before they were inseparably woven together. And we do that by alternately presenting the narratives of their individual forebears and their early lives. But then quickly we turn to their life together, their work together. For more than a half century, their love and partnership produced not only four wonderful children, but also a multitude of good works and a timeless legacy of hope and faith.

As Norvel Young reminded us, there are givers and there are takers. Norvel and Helen lived their lives as givers. They were, in fact, the embodiment of giving and sacrificing. Despite the evil, pain and despair we encounter in this world, these two will remain for us examples of goodness, wholeness and hope.

1

FROM THE SOIL
OF TENNESSEE

*It was a time of "innocence," in the view
of our age. A time of honor, in their view,
when people believed that work should
be earnest, love should be true and
trust should be forever.*

A journey backward to the middle of the nineteenth century is needed in order to understand the life of M. Norvel Young – a journey back into the lives and times of his forebears. Because those hardy ancestors, especially his maternal grandparents, had a profound influence on Norvel. Their deep faith and basic decency, their simple nobility and principled work ethic were passed on to their children and grandchildren, almost as a part of the family DNA.

When we catch a glimpse of the Morrows and the Youngs we begin to see what moved Norvel, what made him the remarkable person he was. "The acorn doesn't fall far from the oak tree" can be a positive as well as a negative proverb. For if the oak tree grows strong and tall and gives shade to many, it is likely that the acorn it produces shall grow in the same way, perhaps blessing even more. These were not the days when it was common for son to rise up against father and daughter to rise up against mother. It was a time before the decline of heroes, a time when son honored father and daughter honored mother. It was a time of "innocence," in the view of our age. A time of honor, in their view, when people believed that work should be earnest, love should be true and trust should be forever.

THE MORROWS

Stephen Franklin Morrow was born in the town of Oakwood in Montgomery County, Tennessee, on September 7, 1857, as the sabers of the Civil War were starting to rattle. S. F., as he was always called, never knew his father, Randall Morrow, who died when S. F. was a baby.

His earliest memories, as a boy of seven or eight, were of the war. And yet the war was a distant thing, for the most part, consisting mainly of the stories and hushed discussions of worried adults. S. F.'s more vivid memories were shaped by the days of Reconstruction following the Civil War. It was a time when a cadre of vindictive politicians in Washington, D.C., wanted to punish the South for its attempt to secede. And times became very difficult.

S. F. was raised by his mother, Harriet Tyree Morrow, in Clarksville, Tennessee, northwest of Nashville near the Kentucky border. It was a typical small town, the kind in which most people lived in those days before the rise of twentieth century urbanization. As the boy grew into young adulthood, he might have been expected to travel down the Cumberland River to the big city of Nashville to seek his fortune, as many others were doing. Instead, S. F.'s interests were drawn in the opposite direction, back up the Cumberland River a short distance to the little village of Big Rock.

Big Rock held no small attraction for S.F. because of a family by the name of Lyle. The Lyles operated a store in the village, and S.F. had met and fallen in love with one of the Lyle daughters. Emily Prince Ella Lyle – or Ella, as she was known –

was born near Palmyra, Tennessee, perhaps 20 miles west of Clarksville, on December 9, 1857. The young Mr. Morrow courted and then won Ella's hand in marriage.

He was 22 years old, and she would turn 22 in less than two months after their wedding on October 19, 1879, at Oakwood. They were wed by Benjamin Franklin Coulter, an entrepreneur and church leader who was also an occasional preacher. Coulter had recently returned from Los Angeles, California, where he had helped to establish a local Church of Christ in 1874.

As the young couple settled into their new life together, S. F. worked hard to buy a piece of land for the raising of tobacco. He had decided to become a farmer, the most common occupation at the time, and tobacco seemed like a prime cash crop. But after clearing the land, and before he had time to plant his tobacco, someone came along and offered to buy the seed-ready property. Open to the idea of cash-in-hand, he accepted the opportunity. And he made a decent profit from that first season of hard work.

The prudent young man did not rush out and squander his money. Instead, he soon bought another piece of land and started over. But once again, after he had labored to remove the trees and brush and prepared the property, he found an anxious buyer for the cleared land. An astute S. F. Morrow quickly found that clearing and selling farmland was not only more enjoyable to him than farming, it was also more profitable than farming itself. He often sought out and hired freed slaves to help him clear the fields and ready the property for sale. Interestingly, at a time when most people thought owning land was the epitome of security and independence, S. F. discovered that land development was potentially far more profitable.

But he also had a second business that added to his net worth: he raised mules. According to stories that have been passed down, S. F. Morrow was quite a "judge of horse flesh," as they said in those days. He sold the mules to the United States Army and also to the companies that were engaged in building the transcontinental railroad. Good mules were in great demand in those days, strangely enough, because the crossbred animals were stronger and better workers than high-spirited, swift horses.

Early in his life, S. F. was converted to Christ and baptized by B. F. Coulter, who would later perform his wedding ceremony. Coulter at that time owned and operated the local mercantile in Clarksville. When he moved to Los Angeles permanently, he established the Coulter Dry Goods Company, which became the largest store of its kind in Los Angeles.

After S. F. and Ella were married, he taught her the Bible and she decided to become a Christian. Increasing years would reveal that S. F. was an extraordinary man of faith who was ready for every good Christian work.

As time went by, S. F.'s hard work in land development and animal breeding began to pay off, and he became financially successful. His own property holdings were also substantial, and he leased his land out to "sharecroppers." Still, because of his Christian faith, he managed to avoid the materialism that so often accompar es newfound wealth. He and Ella refused to live an extravagant lifestyle. When he was not developing land, he was organizing Bible schools in his region of Tennessee. He also befriended and financially supported a number of preachers of the gospel of Jesus Christ.

THE BIRTH OF RUBY

Despite their faith and success, like Job of old, tragedy struck the Morrows when their firstborn child, a son, accidentally drowned in a pond on the farm when he was four years old. Then, the next two children, also sons, were stillborn. But after these terrible heartbreaks, the fourth child proved to be a healthy baby girl. They named her Mary Ruby. Very early she began to be called by her middle name only. Perhaps they realized that she was, indeed, a beautiful and rare gem. After Ruby was born,

God blessed the Morrows with three more daughters and one son, all born on their farm near Dyers Creek.

Ella Morrow realized that little Ruby would not have much opportunity for education if the family stayed in the small community of Clarksville and its vicinity. So she persuaded S. F. to promise her that, when Ruby reached the age of 12, they would move to the state capital to be closer to Nashville Bible School, a preparatory school established and supported by members of the Church of Christ. There, Ruby could receive the training her mother had never been privileged to know.

Ruby was a typical "daddy's girl." She loved to be around S. F. As she grew, she found various tasks that would allow her to work beside him. A bright girl, she wrote letters for her father and also kept his books. She also enjoyed helping him with his project of furnishing tents for area-wide "gospel meetings," that is, preaching campaigns that lasted for several days, sometimes weeks. And she helped him with a myriad other church-related activities.

S. F. was interested in sharing his faith in Christ with everyone he contacted. For example, he encouraged his sharecroppers to come to Bible class at church. But they often excused their lack of attendance because their children did not have shoes to wear. So he made Ruby and his other children go to Bible School barefooted, so the poorer people without shoes would not be embarrassed. However, this became a source of embarrassment for Ruby, though later, she came to understand and appreciate her father's motivation.

At the relatively young age of 45, S. F. retired from land development and farming in the Clarksville area, selling all his holdings for the grand sum of $50,000. It was a very sizeable amount at that time. He invested the money in home mortgages, earning six-percent interest – which some thought was risky business in those days. Most important, he kept his promise to Ella: the family packed up and headed for the metropolis of Nashville.

THE MOVE TO NASHVILLE

Traveling down the Cumberland River from Clarksville on a boat, the Morrows arrived at the barge landing at the end of Broad Street in Nashville. Hand in hand, they walked up the busy thoroughfare, filled with excitement. They were in the "big city" now! There were buildings of three and more stories here! There were more people, buggies and stores than they had ever seen. And in front of many of the stores along the street, new furniture was on display. The children eagerly walked from store to store, sampling the comfortable chairs.

They soon found a home to rent on 8th Avenue, close to Nashville Bible School so Ruby and the other children could attend school there. Later, S. F. and Ella bought a farm adjoining the farm of David Lipscomb where the school would eventually be relocated. Their decisions concerning where to live indicate both their interest in their children's education and their insistence that the education be based in Christian principles.

In time, S. F. convinced his brother to also buy a home in the newly developing area near the Bible school. His interest in Christian education as well as Christian evangelism would become an integral part of S. F.'s life during the remainder of his years.

Ruby did, in fact, enroll and attend Nashville Bible School as her father had promised. Though the school would one day become a junior college and then a respected Christian university, at that time it was much like a high school or a college preparatory academy. Ruby studied art, music, literature and other liberal arts subjects. And she took to her studies with enthusiasm. At her new school in Nashville, she learned the value of education, a lesson she one day would pass on to her son, M. Norvel Young.

THE YOUNGS

Norvel never knew his paternal grandfather, William Starr Young, but he did remember his grandmother Emily Young. In the 1940s, when Norvel and Helen would have their first child, that beautiful daughter would be named for Grandmother Young. Norvel remembered that Grandmother Young died while staying in his parents' home when he was perhaps eight years old. Both William and Emily Young were members of the Church of Christ, as were S.F. and Ella Morrow, so M. Norvel Young's religious heritage was set solidly in many decades of faithfulness to the American Restoration Movement, dating from the early 1800s.

Granddad and Grandmother Young had 12 children, and the eldest was a daughter named Mallie. The family lovingly called her "Sister." With the early death of William Starr Young, his eldest daughter would become like a second parent, helping her mother to raise the other 11 children. She eventually taught school in the town of Gallatin and vicinity, northeast of Nashville, for more than 25 years.

One of the other 11 children was Norvel's father, Matt Norvel Young, Sr. Matt Norvel was always called "Matt," and so in later years, to differentiate between him and his son and namesake, the younger Matt Norvel was known by his middle name.

As Matt reached his early teens, he was able to attend Nashville Bible School because sister Mallie taught school not far away, and she helped the younger children, especially the boys, to get an education. Somewhere along the line, Mallie had become good friends with David Lipscomb, legendary publisher and leader in Churches of Christ, who was one of the founders of Nashville Bible School – and for whom the school would later be renamed.

It was at Nashville Bible School that Matt Young encountered that precious – and precocious – gem, Ruby Morrow. Thus it was, with the intersection of the lives of Matt and Ruby, that two venerable Tennessee families would eventually produce *one new life* that was destined to effectively advance Christian education, as well as profoundly influence a distinctive American religious tradition.

THE COURTING OF RUBY

In their late teens as they were courting, Matt Young would come calling on Ruby at the Morrow home in Nashville. As the evening wore on and the 9:00 o'clock hour arrived, Ruby's father, S. F., would signal that it was time for Matt to leave. He did this by dropping his heavy shoe on the floor upstairs above the parlor where Matt and Ruby sat. If Matt delayed his leaving by more than a few minutes, S. F. would drop his other shoe. That sound would be quickly followed by the closing of the front door behind the love-struck young man.

Matt had some stiff competition as he vied for the hand of Ruby. It seems that a young preacher also was determined to marry her. And as the day for lovers rolled around, the preacher bought her a very elaborate Valentine to impress her. But Matt was not to be outdone. He searched for an even better Valentine. When he found it, the price tag was five dollars – a huge amount of money at the turn of the century, especially for a young man just beginning his adult life. He purchased it anyway, "and it seemed to turn the trick with Ruby," Norvel said many years later. "Dad told me, 'I outdid my competition.' And he always said that it was the best investment of his life." As he remembered the words he had heard from his father, tears filled Norvel's eyes. The love of his parents continued to warm his heart.

S. F. Morrow, though a man of wisdom and love for God, did not have much faith in this young man who was courting his daughter. Matt Young was not only small in stature, but he also had little money or promise of gaining any, in the estimation of Ruby's father. Like many other patriarchs, S. F. was concerned about the ability of the young man to take care of this beloved daughter after they were married. But two of Matt's greatest attributes were that he was not afraid of hard work and he had confidence that he would succeed.

The couple waited four long years while Matt worked to have enough money to offer a respectable living for his treasure. "Dad told me that he worked very hard to win Mother. The reason it was so difficult was that the Morrows were well-to-do, but Dad was basically a poor boy," said Norvel. Matt Young diligently worked wherever he could earn a dollar, and he saved every penny beyond the meager allowance he gave himself.

The glorious day in 1906 finally arrived. The great evangelist T. B. Larimore married Matt and Ruby. The wedding took place in the beautiful new two-story brick home of the Morrows. Years later, that same Morrow home would be donated to their beloved Nashville Bible School, or David Lipscomb College, as the school was renamed.

Before the wedding began, Ruby nervously asked Brother Larimore to make the ceremony as brief as possible. Early in her life Ruby was timid, and she was worried about standing before the guests for a long time. Apparently she had heard that Larimore could be quite long-winded. So she pleaded for briefness, and he agreed to her request to shorten the ceremony. In the end, it was so short that it seemed to be over before it began. Ruby and Matt later lamented that request for brevity.

After the wedding, S. F. Morrow, in his stern and sometimes condescending tones, said to his new son-in-law, "Well, that's the best day's work *you'll* ever do."

Not to be intimidated, the new son-in-law Matt quickly replied, "You didn't do so bad yourself!"

BECOMING A FAMILY

The happy couple took up residence in Nashville and settled into building a home. After about three years Ruby and Matt had their first child, a boy whom they named Stephen Franklin Young, after Ruby's father. Six years later, on October 5, 1915, a second son was born. They named him Matt Norvel Young, after his father.

Like most babies in the early days of the twentieth century, both boys were born at home. Ruby (who would be known by her children as "Mommie" – with the emphasis on the "-mie") had a difficult time with the first baby. But the delivery of her second baby was especially hard. She was not in a hurry to have a third child. And in fact, she would have only the two sons.

In those first few years of marriage, Matt tried his hand at different businesses. He started a grocery that delivered customers' food orders to their homes, but soon found that the city wasn't quite ready for that innovation. He worked for the railroad for awhile. But finally he entered the real estate business, and that career proved to be his forte.

In a relatively short time, he became a successful land developer, with several subdivisions and more than a hundred single-family houses to his credit. It seems he had taken a page out of his father-in-law's career book – the father-in-law who was convinced the young man would never amount to much.

Like S. F. Morrow, Matt did not begin his business with a large capital investment. Instead, he would build a house and sell it quickly, then build and sell again. Ruby, too, became involved in the planning. In the beginning, while the boys were still young, the family would move into the new house and give it a homey feel in order to help it sell faster. When Matt completed the sale of the house, they would move on to another new home. Moving at least once a year was not easy, but it did help launch a new career.

Contrary to S. F. Morrow's fears, Matt Young was more than an adequate provider – he was quite successful, and he lived a long and fruitful life. As for S. F., he lived to see the birth of his little great-granddaughter, Emily, Helen and Norvel's firstborn. But ironically, he died on October 19, the day that his second great-grandchild, Matt Norvel Young, III, was born.

The year was 1947, and S. F. Morrow had reached the ripe old age of 91. As he slipped beyond this world, his great-grandson made his debut at the very same time. S. F. Morrow's legacy of hard work, love for family and intense devotion to God remained as a paradigm for Norvel throughout his life.

A CHURCH-CENTERED LIFE

Matt and Ruby Young's eldest son, Stephen Franklin, grew to be a very handsome young man. For six years he had been an only child, and this may have contributed to some attitudes he would have to outgrow. Somehow Franklin always thought his parents had more money than they actually had. This created problems and he worried the Youngs through his early years. Perhaps because of that, Norvel decided as a boy that he would try not to trouble his parents when he was older. He would try to make them proud of him.

As Franklin grew to manhood, his attitude and his life became exemplary. He attended David Lipscomb College and Abilene Christian College. He then taught school in Spring Hill, Tennessee, and later joined his father in the real estate office. He always had an artistic bent to his life, loving art, literature and travel. He and his wife, Anne, collected antiques, especially pre-Civil War furniture. They also cherished their nieces and nephew until Franklin's untimely death in 1968 at the relatively young age of 59.

Franklin and Norvel were very different in temperament. The difference in their ages made them both somewhat like "only children." But they were devoted to one another, with no signs of jealousy or envy between them.

Church was always central to the lives of Matt and Ruby Young, so naturally it also was an important backdrop for the lives of their two sons as they grew up. Norvel was just a child when the family moved from the Lawrence Avenue Church of Christ in Nashville to the Belmont Church of Christ. But Norvel never forgot the large clock that hung in the back of the building on Lawrence Avenue. In fact, he remembered standing up in the pew, as a little tot, and staring at the seemingly motionless clock and wondering, "When is this preacher gonna quit?" Many years later he would remember those words as he listened to preachers and regretted that he had sometimes made his own sermons too long. He hoped his listeners did not think, "When is this preacher gonna quit?"

Growing up in Nashville where there were about 100 Churches of Christ, Norvel remembered some of the legendary preachers from his childhood days. H. Leo Boles was a well-known speaker, for example, along with F. D. Syrgley, who wore a patch over one eye and was a great debater. Norvel also remembered attending many of the N. B. Hardeman "tabernacle meetings" in Ryman Auditorium, which later became the home of the "Grand Ole Opry." However, his attendance was not necessarily voluntary! The year was 1921, and he was only six years old at the time.

As a boy, Norvel was fun loving but also had a very serious side. He said that his questions and thoughts at the age of 12 were as deep as many he had when he was 40. In his twelfth year he was buried with Jesus Christ in baptism. The year was 1927. He was immersed by the famous scholar-preacher Dr. Hall L. Calhoun, who was the minister for the Central Church of Christ in Nashville. Calhoun, with his Ph.D. in Biblical Studies from Harvard University, would always be both a hero and mentor to Norvel and other young men of that era, such as Howard A. White and Frank Pack.

About the same time in his life, Norvel met another person who was to play an important role in many of his greatest endeavors. That person was J. P. Sanders. When they first met, neither could have imagined how their lives would intertwine in so many ways as they devoted themselves to serving God. In his book, *J. P. Sanders: A Champion of Christian Education*, Morris M. Womack quotes Sanders' recollection of that first meeting:

> The first time I met Norvel was in 1927 when he was just 12 or 13 years of age. It was fall of 1927 that I preached over at the Belmont Church where his dad was an elder. His grandfather had preached the first sermon at Hillsboro ... I knew several of his kinfolk

around there, but I didn't really get acquainted with Norvel until after he had finished his degree at Abilene Christian College and returned to Nashville. He had made a trip around the world after he got his master's degree at Vanderbilt, and during that year, I got better acquainted with him.

Following in the steps of many of his heroes who were preachers of the gospel, Norvel tried his hand at preaching very early. He was only about 15 when he delivered his first sermon at Nashville's Harpeth Hills Church of Christ in 1931. But in those mid- and late-teen years, Norvel discovered an important truth about himself. He wanted to preach, but he had so many other interests that he didn't think he would want to preach full time. Even later, when he attended college, he decided not to make preaching his primary career. He actually turned down ministerial scholarships at both David Lipscomb and Abilene Christian colleges because he would not take the money under false pretenses. At one point, his father told him, "I think you are the only man at Abilene who is paying his own way!"

Norvel graduated from Nashville's only high school at the time, Hume-Fogg High. One of his high school classmates, Dinah Shore, went on to Vanderbilt University and then became a well-known singer and entertainer. Norvel studied Latin and other college preparatory subjects, hoping that he too would be able to attend the respected Vanderbilt. But his father would not hear of Norvel attending anything but a Christian college. He assured Norvel that he would help him attend David Lipscomb College – otherwise, he was on his own. Although later attaining university status, Lipscomb was at that time a junior college, offering only a two-year degree. It would be more than a decade before the school would move to senior college status under the deanship of Norvel's friend, young J. P. Sanders.

Because of declining health, his grandparents S. F. and Ella Morrow lived in the home of Norvel's parents for awhile. As

Norvel pictured in his mind S. F.'s stern Victorian look, his tall, thin stature and his white mustache and goatee, Norvel said, "I remember that Granddad reminded me of Kaiser Wilhelm." Sadly, when Norvel was about 17 and attending David Lipscomb College, Grandmother Morrow died.

S. F. decided to move back to his own home, and Norvel went to live with his grandfather for about a year. "One reason I stayed with Granddad was that the Morrow family home was not too far from the Lipscomb campus," said Norvel. "However, all of us felt sad about his losing my grandmother, and I thought I might be of some comfort to him."

Those were difficult days. It was in the midst of the Great Depression, and in addition to Norvel, S. F. Morrow also had one of his daughters and her husband, Norvel's aunt and uncle, living with him.

But the days were also filled with excitement and preparation. Norvel's world would be widening in the next few years.

NORVEL ON HIS OWN

But even more, the experience caused him
to see himself as more than simply a Tennessean
or a Southerner or even an American.
He realized that he was also
a citizen of the world.

With all the connections of the Morrow and Young families to David Lipscomb College, attending there was a foregone conclusion for Norvel Young. And he was so familiar with the school that it was nearly like being at home. But Lipscomb was still a junior college at the time. Therefore, at most, Norvel would be at home only two more years. Before long, he truly would be on his own.

LIPSCOMB DAYS

While he was at David Lipscomb College, M. Norvel Young studied under professors like R. C. Bell, Hall L. Calhoun, H. Leo Boles, S. P. Pittman, and E. H. Ijams. Norvel especially remembered that in his second year at Lipscomb, he was greatly assisted in his speech preparation by Professor Ijams. Norvel had entered the big annual oratorical contest where he was, in his words, the "dark horse candidate" to win. Also participating in the contest were students like Frank Pack (who won the following year), Howard White (who came in second), and J. C.

Moore. But it was "Dark Horse" Norvel Young who walked away with first place! The subject of his winning speech was "Eternal Principles in a World of Change," an amazingly current subject even today.

Realistically, no one should have considered Norvel the dark horse. He was very bright and studious. He had performed admirably in various school plays, including Oscar Wilde's *The Importance of Being Earnest* – so he was no novice to the limelight. He had poise and timing as a presenter. And these traits served him well in public speaking.

Sara Whitten, who would one day become chairperson of her alma mater's foreign language department, was a fellow student with Norvel at David Lipscomb College. She remembered talking and laughing with him and a couple other students during S. C. Boyce's history classes. Apparently, Boyce's unusual lecture style included "talking to the ceiling, the doors, and the windows more than to the students," according to Whitten.

Norvel fondly remembered one of his Lipscomb teachers, the legendary Miss Ora Crabtree, who taught public speaking and drama for more than 30 years at the college. Miss Crabtree never preached a single sermon, but she profoundly influenced scores of men who went on to become prominent preachers. Norvel Young was only one of those who benefited from her training in verbal expression.

Norvel was developing many lifelong friends at Lipscomb. He remembered one of his classmates, the brilliant young Frank Pack, as a student. How could either of them know that one day Dr. Pack would serve as an honored faculty member under Norvel's presidency at Pepperdine? When Pack was a student at Lipscomb, he was considered something of a child prodigy.

But it was Batsell Barrett Baxter who was Norvel's best friend at college. Batsell Barrett was one year behind Norvel, but their families, their professions, their goals and faith – their very lives – would be linked forever.

STUDENT LEADER AT ABILENE

When it was time to transfer to a senior college, Norvel chose Abilene Christian College. One reason for that choice was that his aunt, Ora McFarland, was a dormitory supervisor at Abilene. "She ran the dorm like a Marine barracks sergeant," he laughed.

Norvel remembered preaching at Olden, Texas, a small oil town near Ranger, during the 1934-35 school year. He would sometimes take another aunt, his Aunt Mallie Webb, with him on these preaching assignments. She was a capable Bible student who would offer keen insights to him. But of course, she was extremely proud of her nephew. For his part, Norvel liked to preach, but he remembered with a chuckle, "The thing I dreaded was having to spend all Sunday afternoon talking with the brethren!" It was undoubtedly a natural feeling for an energetic young 20-year-old, who would have much preferred to spend the time reading a good book or being with his peers.

In June 1935, Norvel boarded a train and headed home to Nashville for a summer visit. Being short of money, he previously had been unable to spend Christmas with his parents, so now he anxiously counted every mile between Abilene and central Tennessee. It was good to be home and with his beloved family, but his vacation was short. He had to be on his way quickly to his summer job to earn money for college expenses.

Something else happened in 1935 that basically went unnoticed by Norvel, but which, in retrospect, turned out to be crucially important to his later life. Back in Nashville, Norvel's father, Matt Young, went to the railroad station and picked up a man from Los Angeles. The man had traveled to Tennessee to take a closer look at David Lipscomb College because he was being urged to build a Christian college similar to Lipscomb in California. Since Matt Young was secretary of the board of trustees of Lipscomb, it fell to him to entertain visiting dignitaries, including this legendary Christian man who was known to have single-handedly supported missionaries and started good works, such as a home for unwed mothers. Matt Young, who himself would later become chairman of the board of the Fanning Orphans' Home, immediately liked the humble man of commitment and they become steadfast friends. The name of the transplanted Kansan from Los Angeles was George Pepperdine.

Best friends M. Norvel Young and Batsell Barrett Baxter sold Bibles during their summer break of 1935. The Bible sales team was led by Otis Gatewood, who was a little older than Norvel and was "quite a promoter." He later became a missionary in Europe, then president of Michigan Christian College and then president of European Christian College.

For some reason that was lost to Norvel, Gatewood took the team to the plains of Kansas. To begin with, the plains of Kansas are not what you would call an area of "high density population." You had to go a long way between prospects. But even more disheartening, not only was it the middle of the Great Depression, but the Kansas wheat farmers had had a crop failure that year, which made sales seem even more impossible. In later years, Norvel kidded Gatewood about that Kansas decision, claiming that the reason he chose the state as a sales region was that Gatewood had preaching meetings scheduled throughout that part of the country. Whatever his reason, Gatewood's choice turned out to be not so bad after all. It was a good experience for Norvel and Batsell Barrett, because over the summer the two enterprising marketers made $150 each – a sizeable amount in the mid-1930s.

With some of their earnings, the two invested in an Essex automobile. Each of the young men paid half of the $100 purchase price. The car was quite flashy and boasted a rumble seat (a seat that opened up from where the car trunk would normally be). But what the car possessed in sportiness, it lacked in mechanical condition. Norvel and Batsell bought nearly as much oil for the car as they did gasoline. They would purchase the oil two gallons at a time – that's two *gallons*, not quarts – for fifty cents a gallon. And every time they filled up with gas, they also filled up with oil. They named the car, aptly, "Petrolia."

In addition to their sales blitzing, Young and Baxter also had a little time for side adventures. When the summer job was finished, they took a few days and drove "Petrolia" to Colorado. High in the Rockies, they parked the car and determined to walk the tram path to the very top of Pike's Peak. They climbed all night to the "top of the world," as they put it, in order to watch the sunrise over the Rockies the next morning. To their dismay, when day dawned, the Rockies were fogged in and they couldn't see a thing.

Disappointed, they started back down the mountain to where they had parked their car. They hadn't gone far when they hitched a ride from a friendly gentleman. However, it was only after they were settled in the car's rumble seat and were careening down the mountain that they discovered the man was trying to set a new speed record for downhill descent of Pike's Peak. They skidded around hairpin curves, kicking rocks off into the abyss below, as their lives flashed before them! The Pike's Peak Adventure turned out to be more adventurous than the two shaken young men had bargained for.

The summer flew by, and as September arrived, Norvel returned to ACC for his final year. As a senior, he roomed with J. T. McClung in McDonald Hall. Norvel's friendliness, charisma and leadership were acknowledged as he was elected student body president. He also served on the senior debate team and his partner was Reuel Lemmons, whose friendship Norvel would treasure the rest of his life.

Each year in February, Abilene Christian College held its annual "Bible Lectureship," a gathering of several hundred Christians, including a large number of preachers. In the issue of the weekly student newspaper, *The Optimist*, that was published during the February 1936 Bible Lectureship, there was a small box of text that many readers could have missed. But it spoke volumes about how one generation viewed another. It was a statement written by student body president Norvel

Young and addressed to those veteran ministers who were returning to Abilene for fellowship and spiritual refreshment. The statement read, "We, the preacher students of ACC, salute you, older preachers of the gospel! We look upon you as sons to their fathers. We esteem you for your unconquerable spirit; we admire you for your never-ceasing courage; we respect you for your superior experience; we marvel at your scriptural knowledge; and we resolve to be imitators of you even as you are imitators of Christ."

When commencement time came in June 1936, he walked across the stage at Abilene Christian College and received his bachelor's degree, summa cum laude – with *highest honors*.

A YEAR AT VANDERBILT

Norvel's English professor at ACC, a Miss Jewel Watson, saw the young man's potential and urged him to continue his education and pursue a master's degree. Wisely, he followed her advice, deciding he could live at home in Nashville and avoid costly room and board expenses while attending Vanderbilt College (later University). Since he had not applied early enough, he did not go through the regular admission procedures and had to be admitted on probational status in the fall of 1936.

Norvel moved back to the Young family home in Nashville at 1904 Blakemore Avenue. The gray-stone, two-story house, built by Norvel's father in 1927, was always a meeting place for church and college people, and especially for youth. Matt and Ruby Young believed their possessions really belonged to God, and the house along with everything else ought to serve God's people. The residence is still standing and today is the headquarters of the Academy of Recording Arts and Sciences, which presents the Grammy Awards. (In 1994, Helen and Norvel returned to see the home, and at that time it was a coffee house. The owners gave them a table in a private dining room that had been Norvel's old bedroom. The two had a great time, and the owners would not hear of the Youngs paying their own fare.)

From fall 1936 to spring 1937, Norvel studied diligently and was able to complete the requirements for his master's degree at Vanderbilt in just two semesters. So, "A Year at Vanderbilt" should be understood as one *academic* year, or about nine months. He graduated with a master of arts degree in English, specializing in English and American literature.

As he received his graduate degree, Norvel looked back over five exciting, but also very grueling years of education. He had applied himself and accomplished his educational goals with single-mindedness. But one does not work through the summers, earn an undergraduate degree *summa cum laude* – receiving nearly straight A's – and also complete a master's degree in two semesters without tremendous personal costs. Norvel was very much in need of rest and recuperation. And his mother knew it. She had an idea.

BEGINNING OF AN ADVENTURE

It was June 1937. M. Norvel Young's master's degree from Vanderbilt College had just been placed into his hand. And on the very same day, he set out on an adventure that would be both character-forming and, ultimately, life-altering.

He began his first overseas odyssey. Before it was over, it would become his first trip around the world – but not his last. It would take him and his traveling companion, cousin James Baird, six and a half months to complete their circumnavigational journey, all without the advantage of air travel. Even by today's standards, it was a remarkable feat for the two young men – Norvel was 21 years old and his cousin was just 17.

Growing up, Norvel and James were more like brothers than cousins. So it was natural that before they faced the responsibilities of adulthood, they would enter upon a last great adventure as young men. As big as their dreams were in those days, they probably didn't guess that they both would become highly respected university presidents one day. For the moment, they were just two young men ready to follow the open road and the open sea before them.

There was not a question of the wisdom of such a trip, but only from where the finances might come. "We didn't think we could do it," Norvel remembered. "My mother deserves most of the credit." Yes, his mother had an idea.

Ruby Young loved to travel, and she envisioned what an extended trip to the British Isles and Europe could do for her son and James, how it could expand their horizons, give them a deeper view of life and help them mature as persons. She had traveled some herself before she was married. In particular, she had traveled to California with Dr. and Mrs. Grant in 1902 and had been very impressed with the Golden State. Now, the thought of her son having a graduation present of a trip to Europe excited her as much as it did him.

Ruby convinced her husband to give Norvel $500 for the trip. She also persuaded Dr. Baird to advance $500 for James. That may not seem a great deal of money in today's economy, but it was enough in that day to see the young men on their journey – or at least to see them on what turned out to be the first leg of the journey.

In retrospect, it was an unusual, even extraordinary time to be continent hopping. Black Monday, that terrible day in October when Wall Street's stock market crashed, was only eight years before. America and Europe were still mired in an economic depression that pulled many rich and powerful people down and tested the mettle of every last man and woman. But when you are young—in your late teens or passing that magical twenty-first year mark – you are invincible, life is filled with wonder and it's no time for timidity.

As they prepared to leave, they carefully planned and plotted. Friends and family advised them of all the possible challenges. Ruby Young, fearful of sending the young men off with so much cash in hand, literally sewed their money into their trousers. And to guard against pickpockets, Ruby put zippers on their back trouser pockets. They were walking armored cars!

Norvel and James boarded a bus in Nashville for the first part of the trip. Saying good-bye proved to be more difficult than they imagined. Both of their fathers were on hand, and it was a very emotional and tearful moment as they left home, even though they thought at the time that their trip would be a rather short one. Their plans were to travel to Europe and return within a month or so.

When the two young men arrived in New York City, they purchased an inexpensive deck passage on a Cunard Line oceanliner headed across the Atlantic Ocean, paying out $190 each for the round trip. In 1937 there were no intercontinental air routes except the Pan American Clipper, which was very expensive. They intended to correspond with their parents in Nashville often, using the American Express offices scattered across Europe for all their transactions and as postal will-call addresses.

THE BRITISH ISLES

The trans-Atlantic crossing deposited the young men in Glasgow, Scotland. Each of them sent one large suitcase on ahead to London. So as they went ashore, they had little more than the clothes they were wearing. These were the days before the popularity of carrying backpacks – and they would have difficulty carrying around their large suitcases. So they traveled light, planning to cover the territory from Scotland to London fairly quickly, pick up their suitcases and move on to the Continent.

They excitedly explored the old Scottish city of Glasgow, and when Sunday came, they planned to go to church. They found a local Church of Christ but were surprised at how elaborate the interior was. All the members were very formal, and everyone was dressed in a suit or a fine dress. When the services began and they heard the organ and piano, they knew they were not in the kind of *acappella* Church of Christ they were used to in Nashville and Abilene! They discovered that, in the British Isles, the churches known in America as Disciples of Christ had never changed their original name:

Churches of Christ. After the services, Norvel and James stayed and chatted with the people, telling them about their American cousins, the Churches of Christ.

As the two traveled, they would find inexpensive hostels or bed-and-breakfast homes in which to stay, sometimes paying only a shilling for their lodging. At that time, a shilling was worth perhaps 25 cents in American money, as Norvel recalled.

In order to conserve their cash, they rejected the idea of traveling by train in favor of buying bicycles. They even risked the prospect of becoming objects of an occasional joke or scorn and purchased *women's bikes* – for $7.50 each – because they were slightly cheaper than men's bikes. So off they peddled to see Scotland and England. They did receive taunts at times from some of the English children. "Hey, what are you doing with those sissy-bikes?" the kids would shout. Norvel and James just peddled on. They never had been too swayed by public opinion.

They rode by Scotland's famous Loch Lomond and on to Edinburgh. They turned south and headed into England, through valleys and moors, through the legendary forests of Nottingham and through bustling cities and countless picturesque villages.

When Sundays came, the young men always found a place to worship. They hunted first for a Church of Christ. But if one could not be found, then they would find a church that looked interesting and attend the services. No matter where they went, they never failed to enjoy themselves and to make new friends. The things that seemed to interest the English churchgoers whom they met were that the two young men were Americans, yet they didn't smoke or drink – and they were interested in religion!

Never known for his shyness, Norvel had written ahead and asked for an appointment with the legendary C. S. Lewis. This was during the rising fame of the great Christian writer in England. When Norvel and James came peddling into venerable old Oxford, they fit in well – they looked like the hundreds of other young adults riding to their studies (except, of course, that they were young men riding women's bicycles!). They asked directions for and finally found Magdalen College. But Lewis had come down with the flu and could not receive the young Americans. Disappointed, they headed on to London after seeing the sights of perhaps the most famous university town in the world.

Finally they arrived in the City on the Thames. It had been a fabulous beginning for their adventure. They had ridden their bicycles over 500 miles of British roads and highways!

In London, the pair found an interesting place to stay. The hotel was within their limited budget, comfortable enough and the price of the room included breakfast – which was served with the *Daily Worker*, a noted communist newspaper. "Apparently, they were recruiting!" Norvel remarked. The paper's propaganda was wasted on the two young capitalists, except to further entertain them with new experiences.

After touring the city, Norvel and James sold their bicycles for five dollars each. Subtracting the five-dollar sales price from the original price of $7.50 that each of them paid for their bikes meant that their British transportation had cost them the grand total of $2.50 each to that point. They were learning something of economics, as well as geography.

THE CONTINENT

It was time to press on, so they took a train to the English Channel and caught a ship headed for the Netherlands. They arrived at The Hague and traveled by train across the windmill-dotted country and into Germany. This was only two years before Europe erupted into war, and the young men noticed rumblings of militarism in Frankfurt, Heidelberg and Munich. They saw and heard Nazi propaganda set against the beautiful backdrops of the Rhine and Neckar valleys and the lush hills and mountains of Bavaria. But though they heard his lieutenants spouting the hateful rhetoric, they never heard Hitler himself speak.

Norvel and James particularly liked Heidelberg. In fact, Norvel was so enamored with the city that he led the way as Pepperdine College began a "Year-in-Europe" program there 26 years later while Norvel was president. Perhaps it was the intoxicating beauty of Heidelberg that motivated the two young travelers to wire home at that point and ask for more money. Whatever their reasons, it was in Heidelberg that they decided to try to travel beyond Europe. Perhaps they could make it all the way around the world, they thought!

They asked their parents for $500 more apiece; "Send it to American Express in Rome," they wrote. After all, each of the frugal travelers had spent only $200 of their original $500. At that rate, they might just make it through the Middle East and Asia, across the Pacific Ocean and on to the West Coast if they could add a few hundred dollars to what they had.

In Germany, they saw Hitler's troops moving along the autobahn. Even when they caught a train across a national border, they saw German troops marching in Austrian streets. But the two young Americans were not particularly disturbed. They told themselves, "We beat Germany once, 20 years ago. They are not a wealthy nation, and they can't stand up to the United States and the rest of the world. They would be foolish to go to war." The adventurers didn't realize that they were traveling through a part of the world that would soon come apart at the seams. Terrible danger was just over the horizon.

They crossed the Alps from Austria into Italy and caught a train to Rome. As soon as they pulled into the station in the ancient city, they rushed to the American Express office. Had their parents been successful in finding enough money for them to carry on around the world? The money wasn't there. So they went sightseeing. And waited.

Days passed, and still there was no word from Nashville. This was before the time of swift overseas mail delivery by airplanes. Their request for money had been sent from Heidelberg a couple of weeks earlier. Now, after a week in Rome, they disappointedly prepared to pack up and head home. With hope seriously waning, they went to the American Express office one last time – and the money was there! Ruby Young had come through again.

About three months into their journey Norvel and James got a letter from Granddad S. F. Morrow. It read:

> Dear James & Norvel
>
> I keep up with you all through Ruby. Glad you are both doing well and having a good time. And I hope you are learning many good and valuable lessons that will help you through life and be a blessing to others in your teachings. Jesus is the only perfect being that ever lived. He has left us an example that we should follow in his footprints. Read your Bibles daily and don't fail to pray often. . . .

PRESSING ON

With money so tight during the Depression, one wonders what made Norvel think his parents could pull together another $500. "I just hoped they could," he later remembered. "I had confidence in Mother." And Helen added, "Mother Young was pretty successful in encouraging Dad." Dr. Baird had also managed to find the money for James.

Norvel and James had been so careful with their money that they each had $200 left at this point. Now, with both of them receiving additional money, they started off on their long second lap through the Middle and Far East with $700 each.

From Italy they caught a ship to Greece. The young Bible scholars were fascinated with the ancient places that figured so prominently in New Testament stories and in pre-Christian history. Autumn was setting in as they left Greece and sailed across a cold Mediterranean Sea to Alexandria. There, they came in contact with large numbers of the poorest of the poor for the first time in their lives. The people crushed in around them, trying to carry their suitcases in order to get money. It would not be the last time they saw the destitute masses of the earth.

From Alexandria, they pressed on to Cairo, then found a train that took them up the Nile to the early Egyptian ruins at Thebes. History swirled around them in the desert winds.

They caught a bus from Egypt into Palestine that made Greyhound look like a luxury yacht. The only seats left were far in the back, and Norvel and James had to put up with the seeds their fellow travelers were spitting from their watermelons. The young men were quite sure that the driver sought and hit every pothole along the 30-hour trip.

Once in the Holy Lands, however, they were awe-struck. They spent an amazing 30 days of adventure in the great places they had only studied about in Sunday school and college Bible classes! These were the days of British control of the region, a full ten years before Israel would become an independent Jewish state. In most places, there were no "bed and breakfast" inns. So in Galilee, for example, they stayed with a British high commissioner for the area. In other places, they were hosted by various kibbutz (Jewish communes), where they learned to live like the local residents. It was a month in the land of Jesus that they never forgot.

They traveled on to Damascus, then to Baghdad – near ancient Babylon – in Iraq. From there they went through the Shah's Iran. Then the young men were ready to press on beyond the Middle East, which meant making it to the Persian Gulf where they knew they could catch a ship headed for Pakistan. They bargained hard with a taxi driver to take them to the coast, and finally they were speeding across a seemingly endless desert. But suddenly the taxi driver stopped the car in the middle of nowhere. He said he would not budge without more money. It took a half-hour of shouting and a small bit of intimidation by six-footer James Baird to persuade the unhappy driver to resume the trip. But by the time they reached the coast, the delay had caused them to miss the ship, which sailed only once a week. Fortunately for Norvel and James, they met some officials of the British American Oil Company who had some employee housing available. Apparently, the clean-cut appearance of the young men impressed the officials, so the traveling duo spent a leisurely week on the gulf coast.

CROSSING INTO ASIA

The coal-burning ship arrived on schedule, and the young men boarded her and set out to sea again. One kind gentleman lent them blankets for the night crossing, but they were covered with coal soot by the time they landed in Pakistan. They traveled by train to Bombay, India, and tried to arrange a meeting with Mahatma Gandhi. However, the great man was occupied in organizing strikes against the salt producers of India, and they could not get near him.

They traveled across the sub-continent by night aboard the British trains, using the time for rest. They would climb up on top of the baggage compartments and sleep in the cool open air. They usually were not alone. Indians would crowd around them, because they were "objects of considerable curiosity," Norvel remembered.

Though the beauty was unforgettable, their visit to the magnificent Taj Mahal was marred by swarms of mosquitoes. The insects turned out to be more than merely a nuisance – Norvel came down with malaria. He was quite ill for about two weeks. But finally, they were able to move on.

In New Delhi, their parents, the Youngs and Dr. Baird (James' mother had passed away earlier), wired them some news that, though exciting, was not fully appreciated by the young men for the impact it would have one day. They informed Norvel and James that George Pepperdine had opened his college in Los Angeles on schedule. It was September 1937.

After what seemed like months, the travelers crossed the border into Burma. In all, their trek across India had taken them more than 2,000 miles. Now they were moving into the lush Orient and another entirely different culture. They spent several days in this beautiful but strange environment. Norvel remembered seeing, for the first time in his life, women sitting along the boulevards, smoking cigars. It was an unusual sight for a couple of Bible Belt American boys in the 1930s!

They journeyed south into Thailand, and after a few days in Bangkok, moved on down the Malay Peninsula to Singapore. They visited a week in that important city-state, though their meager means forced them to stay in a "seedy" hotel. Then they sailed to Saigon, Vietnam. From there they sailed across the South China Sea to the British colony of Hong Kong where, again, their accommodations were less than acceptable. From Hong Kong, the ship traveled north along the China coast to Shanghai. There, they were surprised to see large numbers of Japanese troops in and around the city.

As they approached the Japanese islands, Norvel and James knew they were on the last leg of their long adventure. The ship landed at Kobe, and the two became even more aware of the international tensions that existed in Asia, as well as in Europe. Since the vessel had arrived from Shanghai, China, watchful Japanese intelligence personnel were quite interested in the Americans travelers. Norvel and James boarded a train headed for Tokyo, but officials stopped the train for 20 minutes or so while they confronted the two. The officials, suspicious that the Americans might be spies, made the young men undress as they sifted through every piece of clothing and luggage. Finding nothing illegal, they finally allowed the train to leave the station.

In Tokyo, the travelers found the welcome faces of some American missionaries: O. D. Bixler, Elbridge Linn, Lillie Cypert, Hettie Lee Ewing and Sarah Andrews. They stayed with the Bixlers for several days and saw the sights of Japan's major city. By this time, autumn was becoming a memory, and pleasant weather, like their adventure, was nearly gone. Back in Kobe, Norvel and James were feeling winter's chill. They had no choice but to purchase some heavy overcoats for 12 dollars each. And with that, they boarded the ship headed for Seattle, Washington, U.S.A.

HOMEWARD BOUND

That winter of '37, Norvel Young and James Baird had two Christmases. It so happened that they sailed across the International Dateline exactly on December 25. So they were able to celebrate the holiday two days in a row! The crossing took two long weeks in the North Pacific Ocean. Finally, just before New Year's, they reached Seattle. It was good to be home.

Norvel's parents and brother had decided to drive to California and meet the world travelers. So when Norvel and James arrived in Seattle, they called and informed the parents that they were back in the United States. Then they hopped on a bus – it was the cheapest means of transportation at the time – and started for Los Angeles.

They had left their homes in mid-June, and now it was the end of December. Their around-the-world trip had taken them six and a half months. The journey had cost each of them about $975. And they had spent about $100 on souvenirs.

It is difficult to accurately assess the significance and impact of this early adventure in the life of M. Norvel Young. It certainly would not be the last time he would see the world. Ocean-hopping would one day be a common occurrence in his lifestyle. But even more, the experience caused him to see himself as more than simply a Tennessean or a Southerner or even an American. He realized that he was also a citizen of the world.

This new perspective would set him apart from many of his peers at that time and would ultimately lead to his influencing others to seek a broader view of their world. In the future, the effects of this personal paradigm shift would result in his leadership in post-war relief work in Germany, missionary work there and around the world, foreign campuses for Pepperdine University and in strong friendships with international leaders in politics, literature, business and religion.

By any standard, this experience at age 21 was profound. And the circumstances he encountered in Los Angeles turned out to be fortuitous, to say the least. Perhaps all the events of 1937 and 1938 are more appropriately viewed as *providential*.

BOY MEETS GIRL

*But no one, not even Norvel, knew how profoundly
he would be linked to the future of the institution. Nor
how profoundly the school would affect his life ... beginning
with the beautiful young Pepperdine senior who would
change everything for him.*

*A*n exhausted but elated Norvel Young and cousin James Baird arrived in Los Angeles after a grueling 48-hour bus ride from Seattle. It was the next to the last lap of their journey. The very last lap would be the long automobile trip back to Nashville.

But before that final trek, they had the opportunity of enjoying one more "exotic" place: Southern California. It was a bright January in 1938.

Norvel's brother, Franklin, had driven out with parents Matt and Ruby Young to meet the two world travelers. Franklin was genuinely pleased that his younger brother had been given the opportunity to circumnavigate the globe. "Franklin was always very magnanimous," remembered Norvel. "He was always proud of what I accomplished as the years passed by. Never jealous."

More than a half century later, Helen Young added, "Franklin was such a kind person – just like Norvel. Norvel was never jealous, either. He even hired people and paid them more than he made. It didn't bother him." Norvel then commented, "Well, a good leader has to get people who are smarter than he is! At Pepperdine, our greatest accomplishment was picking good people."

FIRST SIGHT OF A NEW COLLEGE

In January 1938, Norvel and James rolled into Los Angeles after the long bus ride, weary but impressed with the bustling city that flashed by their window. They had seen many cities: the capitals and world centers of Europe, the Middle East and Asia. But Los Angeles was different from them all. It was America, after all! And it was the home of Hollywood, Beverly Hills, the San Fernando Valley and so many storied towns. It buzzed with excitement.

They found their way from downtown to the new George Pepperdine College campus at 79th Street and Vermont Avenue in south-central Los Angeles. The sparkling school had opened with great fanfare on September 21, 1937, about three and a half months earlier. The governor of California had been on hand to welcome the new college, as had the mayor of Los Angeles and a crowd of about 2,000 well-wishers. The new sky-blue buildings gleamed in the California sun. And though the campus was fresh and exciting, in-process projects revealed that it was still somewhat in an embryonic stage when the two world travelers arrived. They could only imagine what it would be when it was finished. And right through the middle of the campus was a drive lined by exotic palm trees. It seemed like paradise.

Norvel returned to America sporting a dashing (he thought) mustache. But when mother Ruby Young got a look at it, she strongly suggested that he shave it off. He waited a while, showing it around campus and wearing it for his chapel speech, then he finally (and reluctantly) complied. After all, the entire family had received an invitation to stay in President and Mrs. Batsell Baxter's home on the Pepperdine campus. That was the beautiful mansion at the end of the palm-tree-lined drive. And Mother certainly did have a nose for what was proper – and in 1937 facial hair didn't fall into that elevated category.

Many years later, Norvel remembered his first impression of the Pepperdine campus. "I said, 'It is so beautiful!'" This from a young man who had just completed a trip in which he was treated to the wonders of the world! However, he was very familiar with the campuses of David Lipscomb College, Abilene Christian College and Vanderbilt College, and by comparison at that moment in time, the Pepperdine College campus was new and contemporary-looking, with "streamline-modern" style architecture. The clean lines and round corners were right in step with the art deco design of the '20s and '30s. Then there was the mystique of Southern California, with the palms and warm weather, about which Ruby had so often spoken to her son. What was more, Norvel had the impression that Mr. Pepperdine's wealth was unlimited. Who knew what great things would happen at this new school with the backing of such a rich and spiritual man?

At the president's home, the entire Young family renewed their long-standing friendship with Batsell and Fay Baxter, old Nashvillians. It was a double treat for Norvel, because he also got to visit with his great college friend, Batsell Barrett Baxter, son of the college's president. The younger Baxter was working on a master's degree at the University of Southern California and living with his parents on the Pepperdine campus.

During that first evening at the president's home, Norvel regaled everyone with stories of his and James Baird's worldwide exploits. In that era of economic blight, it was uncommon to find people who had just traveled to Europe – but here were two young men who had traversed both the Atlantic and the Pacific, not to mention the lesser bodies of water, on their way around the world. His enthusiasm spilled over onto everyone present. Eyes were wide. Ruby Young was beaming.

Enthralled by the narratives of the exciting journey, President

Baxter insisted that Norvel share some of the stories with the students and faculty in the college chapel service the next day. So, with members of the college's first faculty, such as Russel Squire, Hubert Derrick, Wade Ruby, Jay Thompson, Edward Petty, Miss Martha Middlebrooks and others, in attendance, Norvel addressed one of the earliest chapel assemblies of Pepperdine College. It was a memorable moment, for there were few world travelers in those days, because the Great Depression continued its grip on America. And the storm clouds of World War II were gathering over Europe.

In the audience at that January chapel service was a certain female student who thought the speech by Norvel Young was interesting. "He's a very good speaker," she thought, "and how unusual that he has a mustache." Beyond those observations, her mind quickly returned to her classes.

MR. YOUNG, MEET MISS MATTOX

During the week the Youngs were in Los Angeles, they were treated to a stay at the president's home on campus, a gracious mansion built in a Spanish Colonial architectural style. Norvel and Batsell Barrett Baxter caught up on one another's lives. Then one day, when it was time for a diversion, Batsell Barrett suggested to Norvel that they might play a little tennis. After all, there was a court just behind the president's home, a residual luxury from when the mansion was owned by a wealthy resident.

It was a lovely, sunny winter's day. And as they were swatting the ball around on the tennis court, two female students strolled up to play tennis. As they waited their turn to play, they watched Norvel and Batsell Barrett volley. But in a few moments, the two young men, understandably distracted by the women, paused so that Batsell Barrett could introduce his globetrotting friend to the young ladies.

One of the two students was an Oklahoman who had transferred as a junior to Pepperdine from Harding College in

Arkansas. Her name was Helen Mattox. She was a beautiful brunette with a sweet smile. It was a cordial meeting and conversational exchange, but neither the young Mr. Young nor the young Miss Mattox was struck with "love at first sight." Both were preoccupied with personal goals and plans at that point in their lives. Norvel was thinking of further educational preparation and good works that were buzzing in his mind. And Helen was thinking of how she had another three semesters to go in college before she would be able to help her parents financially. Neither could foresee how they would be drawn together with an unbreakable bond a little more than a year hence.

It may be quite significant that the two were not swept off their feet at first meeting. Many romances that were "love at first sight" have ended in separation. It was parents and friends who saw more clearly that Norvel and Helen had the same faith and values, the same heritage and the same optimistic view of life. They would need some nudges in order to "fall in love." They would get them. But after nearly six decades together, they were unconcerned that their first meeting didn't produce romantic sparks. It wasn't "first love" that made their marriage successful, it was "committed love," through-thick-and-thin love, that made the difference.

While Norvel was oblivious to his romantic future, his mother was not. Ruby Young's old friend from Nashville had been lured to Pepperdine College from Lipscomb College by President Baxter and Mr. Pepperdine. Martha Middlebrooks, former Lipscomb dean of women, was not only a wonderful dean of women, she was a skilled matchmaker as well. She pulled Ruby aside and informed her that she had found the perfect girl for son Norvel. That carefully chosen girl was none other than the brunette at the tennis court, Helen Mattox. Even though Helen and Norvel did not "fall in love at first sight" and would not meet again for another eight or nine months, history would prove Miss Middlebrooks to be exactly right.

After a wonderful week in sunny California, Matt, Ruby and Franklin Young piled into their Packard automobile with Norvel and James and headed back to a chilled, January-gray Nashville. It made Pepperdine's Los Angeles campus seem even more a paradise. But it was time to get back to work to pay for that fabulous round-the-world trip.

BACK HOME IN NASHVILLE

Norvel made plans to pursue a doctorate at George Peabody College in Nashville, and in the meantime he taught high school courses at David Lipscomb Academy and preached for the Belmont Church of Christ. However, he had not forgotten California and the beautiful new campus of Pepperdine College. He was excited when, within five months of his visit to Pepperdine, President Baxter asked him to come back to join the faculty in the fall semester of the college's second year.

Of course, there was one problem. Norvel's major field of study at his master's level was English, but Pepperdine College had Dr. Wade Ruby, an excellent scholar and professor of English, and others in that discipline. There was an opening, however, in the history department, and the job paid $150 a month. So, if he wanted the position, Norvel had only a few months to get ready for it.

He accepted the offer and began at once to study Latin-American History and Western Civilization at Peabody College to gain a sufficient background in those subjects to teach them. But that wasn't all he did in early 1938. As usual, Norvel Young was working on several things at one time. What was to become a lifelong pattern was emerging by this time: he had two or more good works in the hopper at all times.

During the spring and summer, he not only studied history, but he and his close friend, J. P. Sanders, also became involved in a new publication designed especially for Christian young people. James D. Bales, who would become a longtime professor at Harding College, recalled the events:

> The first few months of 1938, George W. DeHoff, Woodrow Whitten and I roomed together at Peabody College in Nashville. George was interested in starting a monthly magazine. Norvel Young's folks lived near the campus, and their home was open to us. J. P. Sanders preached at Hillsboro, and we generally attended there when we were not out preaching. It was natural for us to discuss this with Norvel and J. P. These two, along with J. C. Moore, as I recall, did almost all of the work in getting the magazine off the ground ... I was in on the starting but more as an interested bystander than of an actual help in starting it.

George DeHoff, who would become a widely known preacher, educator, and publisher in future years, also remembered those days:

> The germ idea of the *20th Century Christian* came out of Dr. George Benson's class, and it came from me. I had thought of the idea in Dr. Benson's class at Harding College that I wanted to start a magazine for young people in the church because we didn't have, at that time as far as I know, any young people's magazines. I discussed it then with M. Norvel Young and O. P. Baird, so we got the idea of starting it.

In late May or early June, the small group, which included Norvel, Whitten, and Bales, gathered at Norvel's parents home and planned the publication. J. P. Sanders wasn't involved in the earliest meetings. The group worked on an editorial philosophy, which specified that the magazine ought to appeal to college students and have a format similar to *Reader's Digest*. Most of the church journals at that time were for preachers and church leaders, and dealt with doctrinal and often controversial subjects. But this new publication would endeavor to develop and strengthen faith in young people and focus on positive, uplifting subjects. One suspects that this positive direction was due in large part to the influence of the optimism of Norvel Young.

Soon the group also selected others to help them on an editorial board. And they asked J. P. Sanders to lead the charge. Norvel recalled, "We all agreed that J. P. should be the man who would be the editor because he was recognized. He was a more mature man. We were all in our early twenties or less." J. P., who was 32 years old at the time, later remembered that "a few days later, Norvel came in and said to me, 'We elected you editor.' They felt that no one had the facilities available and that no one else had a stable job. But I was minister at Hillsboro, and we could use the Hillsboro church building as a base for our work."

The first editorial board consisted of J. P. Sanders, managing editor; M. Norvel Young; A. C. Pullias; George W. DeHoff; Hugh M. Tiner; Woodrow Whitten; James D. Bales; Seldon Collins, business manager; and J. C. Moore, Jr., circulation director. Collins soon resigned as business manager and J. C. Moore became business and circulation manager.

The publication was a bold move on the part of a group of recent college graduates in their early 20s. And they searched for a name to fit their dynamic vision. John R. Hovius suggested the name *20th Century Christian* magazine, which sounded exciting and encouraging to everyone, and which seemed to reflect their modern, forward-looking attitude. At this early point in the century, the future looked bright, and the term "twentieth century" stood for all that was advanced and on the cutting edge. The swift new locomotive that streaked across the landscape, for example, was called "The Twentieth Century Limited."

Editor J. P. Sanders approached William Stephens, Nile Yearwood and others for financial support and was able to raise enough to get the magazine under way. Interestingly, Dr. Hugh Tiner, dean of George Pepperdine's new college, was visiting in Nashville as early discussions about the magazine were going on. He met J. P. Sanders while attending services at the Hillsboro Church, and Sanders told him of their plans for the new publication. "He put down the first dollar [the cost of a yearly subscription] and became the first subscriber," said Sanders. Back in Los Angeles, Tiner apparently told George Pepperdine what the young men were up to, and Mr. Pepperdine volunteered to help the effort by eventually buying ten thousand copies of the magazine and mailing them to both Christian and state colleges. The young people in Sanders' Sunday School class at the Hillsboro Church in Nashville volunteered their time to address and prepare the magazines for distribution.

The first proud issue of *20th Century Christian* magazine rolled off the presses in August 1938. The editors were able to secure more than 11,000 paid subscribers. On the 24th of August, Dean Hugh M. Tiner at Pepperdine College wrote a letter to J. P. Sanders and Norvel Young. He began, "I think you fellows are doing an excellent job on the Twentieth Century Christian. The first issue is really a very excellent piece of work." Farther on in the letter he wrote, "I gave a copy of the first issue to Brother Pepperdine. He is carried away with it. ... Brother Pepperdine is so enthusiastic about the paper that he has asked me to contact you about the possibility of sending copies to every congregation in the brotherhood." Indeed, George Pepperdine's interests and financial contributions in the magazine helped make it an early success. With his help, the editors printed a total of 20,000 copies of the first issue.

Sanders recalled to Norvel many years later, "After loading your new Pontiac with the first issue and taking it to the post office, you soon headed for California." Norvel's Pontiac was bright red and he named it the "20th Century Limited." He was driving it to Los Angeles to begin his teaching career at George Pepperdine College. Because of Norvel's presence in California, a "branch office" was established at Pepperdine. The next year, when Sanders also moved to Los Angeles, the "managing office" moved along with him.

During the early years, the magazine would need a large number of volunteers and a huge dose of sacrifice. Phillip and Mary Margaret Morrison, students at the time, later mentioned to Norvel:

> We have indelible memories of that basement in Crisman Library on the Lipscomb campus where the magazine was bundled for mailing, and we could only imagine the power of the Word going out to all parts of the world.
>
> The power of your influence for good in Nashville, Lubbock, Los Angeles, Malibu, and many other places will stand forever as a monument to what God can do when people surrender to his will. In times of both success and adversity, your life stands as a model and inspiration.

J. P. Sanders was editor of *20th Century Christian* for about seven years, setting it on a solid footing in that time. Norvel believed that much of the success of the magazine could be credited to J. P. risking his reputation in a very conservative and cautious era. "We would never have started, I think," said Norvel, "without his willingness to stick his neck out." He referred to the fact that some of the older, established preachers in Nashville were critical of the young men and their exciting enterprise. Morris Womack wrote, "One well-known minister commented, 'We don't need a *20th Century Christian*. What we need is a First Century Christian.' Some thought it would fail, but in spite of all the criticism, it succeeded." By lending the name of the minister of the venerable Hillsboro Church of Christ to the magazine, J. P. Sanders increased it chances of survival. His work was indispensable. But in the long haul, it was M. Norvel Young and the young woman he met at Pepperdine College in 1939 who would deliver *20th Century Christian* into the waiting hands of a new century. Their hands would touch the helm of the publication in significant ways for more than 60 years.

Probably no one in 1938 imagined that the fledgling magazine would still be around long enough to require a name change. But sure enough, as the magazine approached the next century, indeed, the *next millennium*, Norvel and Helen Young led the way in changing the name to *Twenty-first Century Christian* magazine. For many decades it encouraged young people, then with a shift of editorial philosophy, it continued to reach a wider and more diverse readership. The magazine stands as the first of Norvel's good works that has blessed a very large number of people. It would not be the last.

RETURN TO THE GOLDEN STATE

At the same time that Hugh Tiner was writing to Norvel and J. P. Sanders, suggesting that Mr. Pepperdine had seen the first issue and was interested in supporting *20th Century Christian*, the legendary missionary J. M. McCaleb was finally getting around to responding to a letter from Norvel, written in July. From Tokyo, Japan, McCaleb wrote, "It may be that some other name for the paper would be more suitable than '20th Century Christian.' In the first place it is hardly correct according to good grammar to start a sentence with figures. Then if it is to be a paper, especially for young people, some name indicating the same might be more appropriate, such as Christian Youth, Our Young People or something on that order." McCaleb went on to counsel the young publishers that "it requires considerable outlay to publish a good paper and the greater the constituency the better the paper." But his prudent advice was too late: the magazine was already a success! And as it turned out, McCaleb's suggestion that the publication have a name more appropriate to high school- and college-aged young people was a moot point. Within a few years, the magazine would be refocused toward a general audience of readers.

By September 1938, Norvel Young was ready for California. As Indian Summer warmed the hills of Tennessee, he left *20th Century Christian* magazine in the able hands of J. P. Sanders and headed west to meet his destiny. When he arrived in Los Angeles, he rented a room from a woman who lived in the 1100 block of 80th Street, near the George Pepperdine College campus. And every day, he would walk down the streets and across the campus whistling. "He was always whistling," Helen later recalled with a smile. "And he whistled well!"

Everyone on campus knew that the bright, optimistic young whistler was Norvel Young, the new history professor. But no one, not even Norvel, knew how profoundly he would be linked to the future of the institution. Nor how profoundly the school would affect his life ... beginning with the beautiful young Pepperdine senior who would change everything for him.

A Woman Named
Helen Mattox

*To her it was an omen, a powerful message from God.
Such was the serious and pious disposition of the youthful
Helen Mattox that the incident set her on a course
that led always toward a mission of serving God.*

Helen Mattox's paternal grandfather, Perry Washington Mattox, was a Texas farmer who worked the land and raised a large family. At his death he left each of his two sons and four daughters a farm. One of those sons was Helen's father, Judge Perry ("J. P.") Mattox. Interestingly, "Judge" was not J. P.'s judicial title; it was his first name.

Though he had received a fine piece of land, farming was not for J. P. Mattox. Instead, he became a businessman and owned a men's store. On September 21, 1904 – at about the age of 35 – he married Irene Corinne Young in Greenville, Texas. After a few years, because of his health, J. P. and his bride left the area where both their parents lived. They moved to West Texas.

Helen's mother, Irene Young Mattox, was the eldest of the 13 children of Fountain Livingston ("F. L.") Young and Mattie Higgins Young. Helen explained with a smile, "I was a Mattox who married a Young, but my mother was a Young who married a Mattox!"

Helen's father, J. P. Mattox, had been converted to Christianity by a traveling evangelist. But her mother, Irene, had been raised in a devoutly Christian home. Irene's father, F. L. Young, was a preacher for Churches of Christ. He is remembered as a reasonable, loving and dignified man, unlike many of his generation who were "fire and brimstone" preachers. He was a man who especially hated division and the spirit of sectarianism.

Seven children would eventually be born to J. P. and Irene Young Mattox: Marguarite, Joe, Fount William ("Billy"), Paul, Kathryn, Helen and Frank. Helen was the next to the last of the seven children, so her father was already 50 years old by the time she was born. And by that time, the Mattoxes had established themselves in Oklahoma. Helen was born in Bristow, Oklahoma, on August 31, 1918.

Her father had poor health most of his life. For awhile, doctors thought J. P. had tuberculosis, and that, in part, prompted a move from Central Texas to West Texas and then to Oklahoma. But though he was not always healthy in body, his spirit was very strong. He loved the Bible and especially loved to memorize passages from it. He taught Helen to memorize scripture when she was young – she remembered memorizing from the Book of Isaiah, chapters 53 and 55 and many others. J. P. mixed a little profit motive with his spiritual discipline: he would give Helen and her younger brother, Frank, five or ten cents for every Psalm or chapter they memorized. Helen remembered, "Frank and I found all the short chapters in the Bible to memorize!"

THE IMPOSING FIGURE OF F. L. YOUNG

Maternal grandfather Fountain Livingston Young had a profound influence on Helen. Her paternal grandparents passed away before she could know them. And Grandmother Mattie Young had also died, leaving F. L. alone. So as Helen grew up, she had only one grandparent. But what a grandparent he was! When she was 11 years old, her parents sent her to spend the summer with her grandfather at his home in the Highland Park area of Dallas. She had two or three wonderful months with F. L. and an aunt who cared for him.

Though advanced in years, F. L. was still preaching. Helen can remember that, in his last years, he would be sitting down, speaking from a chair rather than standing at a pulpit. He was widely regarded as a great preacher who had memorized long portions of the New Testament and who stressed the love and grace of God. Helen basked in the glow of being F. L. Young's granddaughter.

F. L. Young was born in Concordia Parish, Louisiana, on November 29, 1855. His parents were Ezekiel and Minerva Campbell Young. When F. L. was only five years old, the family set out from their home in Louisiana to Texas territory where Ezekiel had purchased a farm. But tragedy struck near Alexandria, Louisiana. Ezekiel contracted pneumonia and died. Minerva was a strong and determined woman so she continued on the journey. With her children and a faithful African American family, she finished the migration to Trinity County, Texas, and settled on the farm her husband had purchased and dreamed about.

"Fount," as the family called F. L., worked with his brothers on the farm until he was 21. But he longed to become educated like his uncles in Louisiana. For a year, he searched for the right college and worked to have money to pay for his education. He tried to associate with men he considered "learned and traveled," to learn from them. Then he began his studies at Add-Ran College in Thorp Spring, Texas, which later became Texas Christian University. He completed the courses and earned a degree. But he also won the hand of Mrs. John Higgins' daughter, Mattie, who was a pretty coed at the college. They were married on December 2, 1880, by the college president, Addison Clark. F. L. was 25 and his bride was 18. The two began their adventure together by moving to Seymour, Texas, where F. L. taught school. The first of their 13 children was born there.

F. L. studied law while he taught school and was seriously considering law as a profession. But then he attended a series of sermons and they seemed to stir a fire inside him. He began to know in his heart that preaching the gospel would be life's greatest possible work for him. Many years later, his daughter, Irene (Helen Young's mother), wrote, "This meant a serious change in life plans. Long into the night, from my little trundle bed, I would hear Father and Mother talk about what this would mean to us. Then Father would pray and Mother sometimes would weep."

Irene recalled that, soon after the family moved to Whitewright, the local church invited the great preacher, T. B. Larimore, to preach in meetings that lasted several weeks. The messages deepened the resolve of F. L. to preach the gospel. A few years later, he was in Nashville and was able to meet legendary churchmen like David Lipscomb, J. W. McQuiddy and James A. Harding. Daughter Irene wrote:

> After a group of these consecrated preachers had discussed the difficulties facing the church and each had suggested a solution one said, "F. L., when we are gone what will become of the church?" After looking from one to another he turned to the questioner and with firmness answered, "If I did not know that God is able to raise up men better and wiser than we are, I'd be distressed!"

F. L. started the Church of Christ in Amarillo, Texas, and lived in and preached for churches in Cleburne, Paris and other Texas cities before settling in Dallas. His seven sons and six daughters were a remarkable group, being educated at Harvard, Bowdoin, the University of Chicago and other fine schools. Two were medical doctors, two were lawyers and several were teachers and business people. Their devotion to one another was remarkable.

F. L. Young was a widower for many years after his wife, Mattie, passed away. Though elderly, he was still a strikingly handsome man, and many people tried unsuccessfully to serve as match-maker for him through his later years. He had two great loves in life: the Lord and Mattie. And that was enough for him.

F. L.'S DAUGHTER

F. L.'s daughter Irene Corinne Young Mattox was a bright and energetic woman. She was very outgoing and self-confident, perhaps partly the result of being the first child of a prominent preacher. She had her father's intellect, moral strength and lead-ership qualities. And she seemed to have inherited his speaking ability as well.

Irene was not frightened or intimidated by people of rank or wealth. Her father, by his example, gave her and all the children confidence. "You are the child of a King," he would say, refer-ring to King Jesus, of course. The family was materially poor, yet they were rich in the things that counted: family solidarity, love, loyalty, goodness and faith.

She remembered her family's financial situation: "There were no church treasuries in those days. Father answered the call to help establish a church even though there was only one family or a zealous Christian woman praying that he would come. There were times when the little boys brought the money they earned from picking cotton to help with his railroad fare."

Those were the distant days when traveling evangelists were paid like country doctors, with a sack of potatoes or flour, or a bag of beans, whatever the rural people had. "Good health, fam-ily devotion, a job for each one and sharing the bounty as well as the lack, developed a rare 'togetherness' in the family," Irene remembered. "We didn't know about introverts or extroverts, and inferiority complexes were unheard of. Our attitude was, I'm just as good as you are and you're just as good as I am and they are just as good as we are. God bless us all."

Irene Young began teaching school at age 17 during a time and in a place where a college degree was not necessary. With her first paycheck of 31 dollars, Irene bought linoleum for her mother's kitchen and a big hat with a feather on it for herself. Those two purchases may have been symbolic, or even prophetic, of her future life: she would continue to be an activist who loved to help people (as symbolized by the gift of linoleum for her mother, the wife of an underpaid preacher), and she would remain a dynamic woman who gained much influence in a wide circle (thus the rather pretentious hat).

Before her marriage, Irene traveled to Hull House in Chicago, and there she received college level training under the famous pioneering social worker, Jane Addams. After she was married, and whenever the demands of her own children would allow, she would return to school teaching to supplement the family income.

Irene was a devout Christian and she was far from a shrinking violet. She worked for women's suffrage. And she was an active member of the Women's Christian Temperance Union and campaigned for moral uprightness. She probably hated alcohol because of her father's teaching; he told the children, "Don't touch it." Indeed, F. L.'s two aunts had suffered because their husbands, though good men, had become slaves to alcohol.

Irene was also the spark plug that initiated the Parent Teachers Association in the city. And she nearly single-handedly began the social welfare efforts in Oklahoma City during the Great Depression. Helen remembered accompanying her mother all over town – to markets, restaurants, bakeries, wholesale houses – picking up any gifts of food. Then they would drive to an area outside the city where homeless people were camped in makeshift shelters. Helen winced more than a half-century later at the memory of those images of poverty and suffering. She remembered that, as they drove into the shanty area by the Canadian River, the poor children would come running toward the car shouting, "Mrs. Mattox is here, Mrs. Mattox is here!" They knew that Irene Mattox would help them stave off hunger for one more day.

Helen remembered that her father, J. P., loved to "do things right." Like others of his generation, J. P. upheld excellence in his work ethic as a part of the fiber of his being. He was a very meticulous craftsman and also very talented and capable. When Helen was about one year old, the Mattoxes moved from Bristow, Oklahoma, where she was born, to Oklahoma City. J. P. bought a five-acre parcel of land in the northwest part of the city and, with only the help of his young sons, built the family home himself. He built part of the first floor and the family moved into it. Then, as he had time, he finished the first floor and the second floor.

J. P. owned a cotton gin at Moore, not far from Oklahoma City, and he bought and sold cotton. Though he worked hard all his life, J. P. struggled to make ends meet for his family of nine.

Helen greatly admired her father. She was especially moved by his moral strength and quiet spirituality. Perhaps her own spiritual tendencies and, to some degree, her early introversion can be traced to his influence. But her mother, Irene, had an even greater influence on her. As a child, Helen was somewhat intimidated by her talented mother, thinking herself inadequate when compared to her. And yet, as Helen matured, she took on many of the dynamic characteristics of her mother.

AN OKLAHOMA CHILDHOOD

Though the family had little money for luxuries, there was always plenty of love and plenty to eat at the Mattox place. The house on the edge of Oklahoma City, with its five acres, was large enough to have peach, apricot and cherry trees, a grape vineyard and a large vegetable garden. A cool cellar stored their home-canned goods, which were ready for the winter.

Helen recalled her childhood as happy days romping around the family acreage. She and her brother Frank, who was two and a half years younger, were about the same size. They played together often, so she learned to roughhouse with the neighborhood boys. She would enthusiastically join in playing "cowboys and Indians" with home-made wooden "guns." She and Frank would fashion the stock from a piece of wood, then cut circular strips from old rubber inner tubes. These large handmade rubber bands were then stretched over the "gun" and held fast with a clothespin affixed to the stock. Pushing on the clothespin "trigger" released the rubber band toward some "enemy." Helen remembered cowboy and Indian wars with half a dozen neighbor kids in and around the garage her father had built near the house. The garage had a large attached wash house, which contained the reliable Maytag wringer washer, and above the wash house was an interior balcony that looked down into the garage. The balcony and the various hiding places in the garage made for intriguing shoot-outs.

Helen also enjoyed playing games of strategy. She had the patience to sit and play chess and checkers with her father.

When she was about 10 years old, Helen contracted some sort of intestinal ailment that refused to clear up. Doctors were perplexed, and Helen got weaker and weaker. She missed an entire semester in elementary school and was frail for about a year. Years later, one of her clearest memories was of frequent visits to the doctor. Even after the illness finally left her, she was slow recuperating. That was when her mother suggested that she become involved in sports. Helen had always been agile and athletic, but now she applied herself to field hockey, softball and other sports. And her health returned.

Helen roomed with her older sister, Kathryn, on the second floor of their home. One evening when Helen was perhaps 11 or so, there was a violent storm that had the whole family frightened until it finally blew over. Helen went upstairs to her room alone and lay on her bed, looking out the window toward the rain-washed city at night. Earlier, she had had a dream or a premonition about the end of the world. Now the storm had shaken her nerves. What she saw next would remain vivid all her life. From her upstairs window, something caught her attention: across town she could see a strange light shining, forming a very large cross that slanted down from the night sky. The scene was so strange, frightening and awesome that it was never erased from her memory. As she reflected back, she considered whether it might have been a Christian symbol atop a church that caught her eye, yet it seemed far too large for that. To her it was an omen, a powerful message from God. Such was the serious and pious disposition of the youthful Helen Mattox that the incident set her on a course that led always toward a mission of serving God.

A girl named Billie South was perhaps Helen's best friend. Helen described Billie's mother as "a lovely Christian woman who was very hospitable." Helen and Billie lived only a few blocks from each other and attended the same church. They became friends as Helen recovered from her illness and got more involved in athletics. But they were also very different. While Helen's deepest motivations were spiritual, Billie was consumed with sports. Not only was she an avid fan, with the statistics of college and professional sports on the tip of her tongue, but she was a better athlete than Helen. Still, they were dear friends, and Helen always tried to influence Billie to become more involved in church activities.

The local church was always a central aspect of Helen's life, as it was for her parents. At the age of three and a half, she recited the 23rd Psalm from the rostrum. Her father was very strict when it came to church attendance. If, for example, there was a school or other function on Sunday evening, Helen knew she would be required to attend Sunday evening services at church rather than the other activity. But somehow Helen never developed a negative attitude toward her father's rules. She knew he loved God and wanted only the best for his family.

During her early years, Helen and her family attended the 10th and Francis Church of Christ in Oklahoma City. Her mother was a leader of women's activities, teaching a large weekly Bible class. When she was 10 years old or so, her parents decided to start a new congregation in their own neighborhood. It was not an unfamiliar venture for the Mattoxes. J. P. and Irene had been involved in building four or five churches in Texas, before moving to Oklahoma. The new congregation, composed of the Mattoxes and two or three other families, met in the living room of the Mattox home at first. But as it grew, Helen's father purchased a piece of property in a good location at 12th and Drexel streets. J. P. himself then built a small church building on the land. Later, they outgrew the white frame structure that seated perhaps 100 people. A larger, stone building was constructed using stones brought from western Oklahoma by rail. Gathering the large stones was a project of the church's young people, directed by the minister. The church was known as the 12th and Drexel Church of Christ. This was the church that Helen remembered as her home congregation while growing up and the church where she was married.

Irene Mattox always had things for her children to do that would broaden their minds and help them develop as young adults. Both in elementary school and junior high school, she arranged for private lessons for the children in "elocution" (public speaking) from a neighbor. She also supplemented their schoolwork with activities in art and music. A love of learning was always encouraged at the Mattox home.

Speaking and critical thinking skills were stimulated in a subtle way. Her mother and father would purposely create interesting conversation at the dinner table and at other times. Irene was very interested in politics, even helping to elect Oklahoma Governor Robert S. Kerr – so she would engage the children in challenging discussions on the political scene and other relevant subjects.

Added to this, Helen's mother enrolled her as a member of the Children of the Confederacy, an auxiliary of the Daughters of the Confederacy to which her mother belonged. Both of Helen's parents came from Southern states and were loyal to the South. They were not bitter about the Civil War, but were saddened by the tragedies the war had visited on both the South and the North. Helen doesn't remember any hatred of the North by her parents, simply feelings of loyalty toward the South. She remembers the meetings of the children's group as social events that often had speakers who lectured on the details of the "War Between the States," as they called the Civil War.

Helen was always a good student. Because of that, her principal in junior high asked her to do a reading at a school assembly. She quickly agreed, thinking that she would read a piece of poetry or prose to the student body. But to her horror, she later found that he wanted her to do a recitation from memory. Though she was terrified, she went through with the recitation, quoting the poem, "The Highwayman." When asked why she didn't simply tell the principal she couldn't do it, she said, "I was too embarrassed to admit that I didn't understand him!"

The elocution lessons and the recitation were steps that helped Helen overcome her shyness. She had always been rather timid. In fact, many years later, Helen Winters Wright just couldn't imagine "little Helen" being able to speak to crowds and be a public leader. Mrs. Wright herself was an educated, distinguished and dominant leader and one of Irene Mattox's best friends. They were both Bible teachers and active in helping Oklahoma Christian College in its early days.

Helen attended Classen High School in Oklahoma City (which counts among its alumni Ed Gaylord, the communications magnate). Helen's favorite subject was English literature, and she credits her English teacher with helping her develop a love for poetry. While she did a little writing in high school, she later wished that she had emphasized that more, as she began to have the opportunity to write as an adult. She did very little dating in high school. "I was not a socialite," she said, "but more studious." Indeed, Helen earned the right to be in the honor society at Classen High.

Many who knew Helen only as an adult woman might be surprised to hear that she was a "tomboy" in her early days. The elegance and grace that defined her as an adult seemed to disguise the rather remarkable physical abilities of her youth. Not only did she romp with the boys in her childhood, as mentioned earlier, but also in high school she played competitive sports on the field hockey team and on the softball team, which went to the state finals. One of her favorite people was Miss Hulett, the physical education teacher and coach for the field hockey team. She won the award for best female athlete in her high school. And while Helen didn't view herself as very popular in the social life of the school, she had many friends who have remained friends all her life. She was very much a leader in her church youth group, which was good preparation for the next phase of her life.

In addition to playing on the school teams, Helen played softball in a summer city league. But summers were remembered most as a time when the family went to Texas for family reunions of the F. L. Young family and the Mattox family.

COLLEGE DAYS IN ARKANSAS

When Helen graduated from high school, she applied for admission to Harding College in Searcy, Arkansas. Attending Harding had become something of a family tradition. The first two Mattox children, Marguerite and Joe, went to Abilene Christian College, but migrated to California and didn't get their college degrees until later. But F. W. "Billy" Mattox attended Harding, as did Paul (who stayed just a year). Then Kathryn followed and earned her degree at Harding – she was a senior when Helen was a freshman. The youngest, Frank, followed Helen when she transferred to Pepperdine, but eventually he graduated from California Polytechnic University, San Luis Obispo.

Helen laughingly said, "Billy, one of my older brothers, was the closest thing to a juvenile delinquent that the Mattox family had. Yet today he is the most Christ-like person I know." Early on, Billy thought education was a waste of time and dropped out of high school. He loved to raise and train dogs and he loved to hunt with his dogs. School took him away from the outdoors, which he enjoyed so much. Obviously, this was a concern to his parents, especially his mother, who was president of the PTA.

One day as he was working in the family garden, he looked up and saw his father coming toward him. He knew something important was on his mind. Father told Billy that he had discovered that Harding Academy in Searcy, Arkansas, enrolled boarding students and asked if he would like to attend high school there. Billy knew that Arkansas was green and beautiful. "There ought to be good hunting and fishing there," he thought. So he agreed.

In a relatively short time in Searcy, Billy was a changed young man. Contact with deeply spiritual men like J. N. Armstrong, B. F. Rhodes, Stanley Bell and others kindled his dormant faith. Not only did he finish high school, he went on to college at Harding, deciding he wanted to become a preacher of the gospel. Ultimately, this "closest thing to a juvenile delinquent that the Mattox family had" would earn a Ph.D. from Peabody College and become the founding president of Lubbock Christian University.

By 1935 when Helen was ready for college, Harding had become the family tradition. But summer came, and she still had not heard whether she would be able to attend. She and younger brother Frank had gone to Texas to help on their uncle and aunt's ranch. She remembered the happy day that the letter came notifying her that everything was in order – she would enter Harding in September. Money had been a problem, but arrangements were made for Helen to work in President J. N. Armstrong's office on campus to help with her expenses. It was Armstrong's last year as president. The next year, returning missionary George Benson would become Harding's chief executive officer.

Helen was elated to be on campus, especially since her sister, Kathryn, who was a senior, lived just down the hall in the dormitory. Helen's schedule was difficult, but she applied herself with diligence to her studies and worked 15 hours a week doing secretarial duties, such as shorthand and typing. J. N. Armstrong was one of brother Billy's heroes, and Helen quickly learned to love him, too. She worked in his office, but she also studied under him in one of his Bible classes. "He helped me gain a new allegiance to the Lord in that first year," she said. "He had us memorize scripture in his class, which was difficult, but he was a great teacher." All her life Helen would remember the sacrificial and faithful Dr. Armstrong as one of the most inspirational persons she had ever known.

Though she enjoyed college greatly, she was a typical freshman with opinions and complaints. In a letter to her family on October 12, 1935, she wrote, "I would also enjoy a letter from Joe, Daddy and Paul. All the boys here are so ugly, nice and boring. It would be grand to hear from somebody intelligent and good-looking. ... I must close and go to bed, they are very strict about all the rules, and I must turn out the light."

She was always conscious of the financial strain her education put on the family. In March 1936 of her second semester, she wrote to her parents and said, "My books are costing a lot: $.50 rent on psy. book, $1.00 trig book, .60 work book in psy., $3.00 Soc. book. Do you suppose I'm worth it?"

In the same letter, she told how she had her first opportunity to visit Little Rock when she went "shopping with Maurine Rhodes, Georgia Lou, Elaine, and Lois." "I got my sandals," she wrote. "They are very nice, not cut out hardly at all and have low leather heels. They were $2.76. I got us some inexpensive hose too and a few other things we thought we had to have. The way Georgia Lou and Elaine shop gets me. Here's what they got: a canary bird, guaranteed $1.00, $.80 worth of pansy plants, a flashlight, etc. I never heard of anything so perfectly silly. The canary and pansies will die within a week. ... Easter will be here in two more weeks. I shall wear my new shoes, clean my white felt hat, and clean my blue turquoise graduation dress. It will be fine."

After her freshman year, Helen did not have to work during the school year. Her older sister Kathryn, who had always looked after her, graduated and began teaching school. She told Helen she would pay Helen's expenses so she wouldn't have to work. It is an example of the kind of love and loyalty that flourished in the Mattox family.

And for Helen, there was always the homesickness. In her second year, she wrote, "I miss you all so much. I believe if I had a ticket I would head for Oklahoma City on the next train. I surely did hate to see Kate [her sister Kathryn] leave – now I won't see a Mattox for five and a half long months."

Helen made an important decision as she arrived at Harding College. She thought it was "time to grow up and to be taken seriously" – which, to her mind at that time, meant putting athletics behind her. Besides, she thought she wanted to marry a preacher, and she speculated that a preacher might not be attracted to a female athlete, perhaps thinking her too masculine to be a minister's wife in such a conservative time.

Helen's roommate was a girl from a wealthy Texas family. Those responsible for dormitory assignments had decided that Helen might be a good influence on the girl, whose parents thought perhaps Harding College could "straighten her out a little." Helen did her best to help, but the two were friendly yet not best of friends. Meanwhile, Helen's social life was a complete reversal from high school. She flourished in the environment of this Christian college. She was surrounded by friends. And one of her best friends was Avanelle Elliott, who later married Norvel Young's cousin, James Baird.

While most of her social activities in high school were limited to sports, in college Helen became involved in nearly every activity. She remembered participating in the wonderful May Day festivals on campus, for example, when the girls wore long formal dresses and circled the "May Poles." And everyone would wait for the dramatic moment when the May Queen would be announced. Of course, she was at the center of almost every religious activity, including various banquets and outings. She was also a member of the "Ju Go Ju" social club, which in her estimation (naturally), was the "best club on campus!"

On one particular all-day outing, Helen and her group had a delicious barbecue in the mountains. The fellowship and fun were delightful, and the scenery was inspiring. The students returned to campus with great memories. But Helen returned with something else as well: a severe case of poison ivy. Her skin condition was so bad that she had to go to a doctor in Little Rock and spend several days in the college infirmary.

One of the activities in which she participated was the Harding "Pep Squad." These students, numbering perhaps three dozen, committed themselves to attending as many athletic games as possible, especially "away" games, to support the teams. They wore Harding sweaters and colors, and often traveled hundreds of miles to help the cheerleaders spur their teams to victory. Helen remembered one particular trip to Nashville, Tennessee, where the Harding Bisons played a basketball game against David Lipscomb College. Although she didn't recall a great deal about the adventure, with a chuckle she remembered thinking at the time, "Harding is a much more spiritual place than Lipscomb."

Always deeply involved in spiritual activities on campus, at one point in early 1937, she wrote her family, "Last night I began my life as a Christian all over again, because I had made such a mess of it. There are so many students here that I need to be an example to in the next twelve weeks that I am with them, and I believe I can help some."

In her first two years, Helen majored in business administration. But she also majored in "saving backsliding boys," as she put it. She made it her secret mission to encourage students, especially male students, to be faithful to God. In her first year she didn't date anyone regularly. But in her sophomore year, she began dating one young man who was an outstanding athlete. He was from western Oklahoma and he seemed very taken with Helen. They dated for almost two semesters, and she felt that she was successful in getting him to recommit himself to God.

When summer came, the young man made several trips to Oklahoma City to visit Helen. But she wasn't sure that she felt as strongly about the relationship as he did. Finally, her mother stepped into the situation, perceptive as always.

GO WEST, YOUNG WOMAN

Irene Mattox worried that if her daughter continued to date one person regularly, she might get so involved that she would marry before graduation. So that summer, between Helen's sophomore and junior years, mother Mattox steered her in another direction. That direction was west – toward a new college in California that would open in September, just a couple of months away. "It will be a change and an adventure that will be good for you. It will broaden your world," her mother assured her. Neither she nor her mother could have known the full implications of this transfer.

Helen agreed to the suggestion. In addition to being unsure of her feelings for the young man at Harding, she also reflected on her commitment to marry someone who would give full time to Christian service. The more she thought about it, the more she became excited about the prospects of attending a new college in the Golden State. She applied for admission to the inaugural class of George Pepperdine College. Within weeks she was accepted, and she transferred as a junior to the California school as it opened its door in 1937. She took her place as one of the 167 pioneer students at the new college. It was one of those fateful events that changed everything …

But moving to California in 1937 wasn't as impetuous or strange a thing as it may seem for this Oklahoma girl. Her sister, Marguerite, who was 13 years older than Helen, was already living in California. In the summer of 1928, after her sophomore year at Abilene Christian College, Marguerite had left school and moved west. She wrote to her brother Joe about the beauty and opportunity of California, and he, too, left school for the Golden State. This was only a year before the defining moment of the early twentieth century: the stock market crash of October 1929.

But even before '29, times were tough for the Mattoxes. Helen's father was not in good health, and there seemed to be an ever-present stress on the family's financial situation. That reality probably contributed to Marguerite and Joe's leaving ACC. It was also a very real worry for Helen. So much so that she decided to major in business administration because she thought a job in that field after graduation would bring a better salary and she could help her family financially.

Not long after arriving in California, Marguerite met Wilford H. Long. And they soon decided to marry. Mother and Father Mattox were not happy about the situation because Wilford, though still a young man, was divorced. Nevertheless, they piled into the car with their four youngest children – Paul, Kathryn, Helen and Frank (Billy was away at college) – and set out for the Pacific coast. Though the idea of Marguerite's marriage made them uncomfortable, they decided to be supportive of the wedding. And to make the trip a family vacation as well.

Though only about 11 years old at the time, Helen remembers her introduction to California. "It was a taste of Paradise," she said. "We rented an upstairs apartment in Venice where we could walk to the beach. I remember the exotic palm trees, the orange juice stands along the roadsides and the lovely orange groves." Later, the family drove south and discovered the seaside village of San Clemente. This was considerably before the development of recent years, and they were entranced with the terra cotta tile-roofed homes and buildings of the pretty little town. They stayed a day or two and soaked in the charm.

While in the Los Angeles area, they attended church services at the Southwest Church of Christ (later renamed the Normandie Church of Christ) located on Normandie Avenue north of the future site of Pepperdine College. The whole family was impressed with the beauty of the building. After services, they met George Pepperdine and his wife, Lena (who would contract a rare disease and die the following year). The Pepperdines invited the Mattoxes home for Sunday dinner. The Oklahoma visitors were quite taken with the gracious Pepperdine mansion on West Adams in Los Angeles. It had its own tennis court amid beautifully manicured grounds. Helen remembered walking in the lovely rose garden; it all seemed like a fairy tale. Though there was some uncertainty and tension regarding the wedding, the Mattoxes managed to have a memorable California vacation.

Now, eight years later, Helen was returning to her "Paradise" to attend college. The memories of that vacation helped to explain why she was not only receptive to her mother's suggestion, but very excited about the new college – that, plus the fact that she, too, feared she might be moving too quickly toward a serious relationship at Harding. Once in California, rather than feeling nervous about a new school and new student body, she felt independent again. And the feeling was good.

Helen had boarded the Santa Fe Scout train ("It was a fine air-conditioned train," she wrote her father) and traveled the southern route to Los Angeles. She arrived the week before the college was dedicated. She stayed with Marguerite until the semester began. In fact, the first time she saw the campus was that dramatic day, Tuesday, September 21, 1937, when George Pepperdine dedicated his new college at 4 o'clock in the afternoon. There were 2,000 chairs set up in front of a specially built platform in front of the new administration building. Helen arrived early and excitedly walked down the palm tree-lined drive that soon would become known as the "Promenade." She toured the administration building and noticed that it and the cafeteria were completed, but the other buildings were still under construction. She strolled among the visitors' chairs, wondering who would be present for this historic ceremony. She savored her first impression of the school.

Word was out that the governor of California and the mayor of Los Angeles would be in attendance – the air was electric.

Indeed, the governor and mayor were there and spoke glowingly of the new venture, as did inaugural president Batsell Baxter and dean Hugh Tiner. But perhaps the most riveting moment came when Mr. Pepperdine approached the microphone and gave his dedicatory address.

Helen was among those pioneer students who were temporarily housed in Mr. Pepperdine's hotel, the William Penn, downtown Los Angeles. They were taken on tours of the sights of Los Angeles the first week; then they were transported to school every day for a few weeks until the men's and women's dormitories were finished. Every day was exciting as she met new friends from Abilene Christian College and David Lipscomb College. Interestingly, she was one of only two transfer students from Harding College (the other was senior Malcolm Hinckley, who would become one of only four graduates at the end of Pepperdine College's first year), so nearly every student was new to her. Soon they would be her extended family.

Martha Middlebrooks, who was dean of women, gave Helen a job in her office. Miss Middlebrooks wrote Irene Mattox and said, "When I tell you that I selected your little girl for my secretary, I think that will let you know the estimation in which I hold her. I feel that she is one of my very own. In fact, it is hard to think that she is among my newcomers. Instead it seems that she is one of my Lipscomb bunch. It is quite easy to tell the students who have been in our Christian colleges." She went on to thank Mrs. Mattox for sending Helen to Pepperdine and assuring her that she had a place to stay when she came to visit her daughter.

In a letter to her parents in January 1938, Helen acknowledged that she was glad to hear that her brother, Frank, was doing well in basketball. But she hoped he would be able to come to Pepperdine after his graduation from high school, and she wrote, "I don't mean to sound like I'm lecturing, but, honestly, the boys here do have to make their grades. Dean Tiner won't bring a boy here only because he is an athlete. Frank has always done so well, and I can hardly wait to have him here." As it turned out, Frank was able to attend Pepperdine shortly.

In the fall of 1938, Helen entered her senior year. She wrote to her family, "I must have the Dean go over my schedule with me this week. I am going to have to take a full and running-over course if I graduate because I am behind in number of hours. Oh, I will be so happy to graduate. Of course, I'll regret being through school, but I plan to come home and get my M.A. at O.U. [Oklahoma University] in 1940-41." But those plans would be changing – because a certain person had already entered her life, someone who would change everything for Helen Mattox.

LAYING
FOUNDATIONS

What a summer he had: New York,
Columbia University, an appendectomy,
and a wedding! It didn't help to crawl
through a window, either.

F rom her very first semester at Pepperdine College, Helen
Mattox believed that she was getting a first-rate
education. Whether the professors and the classes were,
in fact, better than her freshman and sophomore years or she
simply was more serious and studious, she was not sure. But
she was quite certain that the Pepperdine experience was a
challenging and positive one.

One of her favorite classes was the psychology course she had
with Dr. E. V. Pullias. And though it was a grueling experience,
she would come to be thankful for the English classes she had
with Dr. Wade Ruby. Ruby was well known on campus for the
"torturous" paces he put his students through, but years later
hundreds of students like Helen were grateful to him. In fact,
Helen confessed, "Wade Ruby was the best teacher I ever had."
Of course, she took business courses like marketing, account-
ing and insurance from the chairman of the Business Administration Department, Dr. Edward Petty, and other business
professors.

In addition to her schoolwork, Helen nearly always had a job
on campus to help pay for part of her education. She was ever

conscious of what she considered to be the "burden" of her education on her parents. And she was concerned about her father's health, as well as the financial problems the family faced because of it. She had first worked for Miss Martha Middlebrooks in the dean of women's office. In her senior year, she worked for A. J. Dumm, who was head of the George Pepperdine Foundation.

Somehow, in her "spare time" Helen joined several of her friends in working on Pepperdine's student newspaper, even though journalism was not her major. And every day she drew closer and closer to the students who were becoming like family to her. They would remain dear friends for years to come. These were exciting days when new traditions were being born – like choosing the name of the newspaper (the *Graphic*), and selecting the school colors (blue and orange) and finding a name for the athletic teams (the Waves).

Helen was also involved in campus organizations. In 1938 she was elected president of Alpha Gamma, a service club for female honor students. Fay Baxter, the president's wife, was the sponsor of Alpha Gamma, and as the months rolled by, Helen became very close to her. The candlelight initiation ceremony was so dramatic and moving that it was still vivid in Helen's memory decades later.

She was asked by Miss Middlebrooks to help establish and organize a new sorority. At first it was going to be a Zeta Kappa chapter, but for some reason the effort took a new direction, and the sorority became the Cailinns. On the lighter side, Helen was a member of the "Pep Squad" as she had been at Harding College. However, the "Pep" had a double meaning in this case (spirit and *Pep*-perdine). Members of the group sported flashy sweaters with a large "P" on them. They were the "truly committed supporters" of the Waves teams.

Perhaps Helen's best friend at Pepperdine was her roommate, Billie Craig. Billie was a native of Mississippi and had transferred to Pepperdine from David Lipscomb College. They lived in the women's dormitory on campus, Marilyn Hall, which was designed with two-room suites, connected by a bathroom. Helen and Billie were in one room and on the other side of the bathroom was Wanda Wiltze and Wilabeth Schmidt's room. "They were lovely girls," reminisced Helen. "We all got along well and had a wonderful time together."

Their rooms were strategically located, overlooking the entrance to Marilyn Hall—so they could see all the comings and goings (especially who was dating whom). "The rooms were new and attractive," said Helen. "There was a monogram GPC on the bedspreads, and Mrs. Pepperdine and Mrs. Baxter had personally chosen all the decor for the rooms."

Most of the time, Helen's life revolved around the Pepperdine campus and the host of activities in which she was engaged. She would spend at least every other weekend at her sister's home. Then there were the athletic events, especially the exciting basketball games, like the ones against USC.

A BLOSSOMING ROMANCE

Helen fondly remembered the daily chapel services that were conducted in the third-floor room of the Administration Building. The room was originally designed to be a drama department rehearsal room, with a small stage and seating for no more than 150. Later, as the student body grew and the campus was completed, chapel services were held in the auditorium. But early on, nearly 200 students and faculty would press into the small upper room to sing and pray and listen to chapel addresses. Helen recalled hearing Norvel Young in January 1938 as he spoke in chapel about his and James Baird's adventures around the world. At the time, she thought about how bright and articulate the young traveler was – and how interesting it was that he was sporting a mustache (hardly anyone at Pepperdine had one). But those were about the extent of her musings concerning the young man from Nashville.

A couple of days later, she met Norvel at the tennis court

behind the president's home. She discovered that Norvel was a dear friend of the president's son, Batsell Barrett Baxter. Of course, she knew the younger Baxter because he was living in the president's home at Pepperdine while earning his master's at USC. And Baxter was engaged to Wanda Roberts, a student friend of Helen's. It became clear to her that Norvel's parents were good friends with President Baxter and his wife and their son, with a connection through the Nashville churches and David Lipscomb College. Still, she could not quite understand why people kept saying, "You ought to meet Norvel Young." After the steady dating of her sophomore year at Harding, she was happy to be free and unattached.

Helen herself was fairly close to Pepperdine's president and first lady. Dr. Baxter was a good man, but not very outgoing, as far as Helen was concerned. "He was quite formal, and he was also strict regarding dress and so on," she said. But Fay Baxter was warm and kind to the students, and especially liked Helen. She asked Helen to help her in the kitchen for social events, something Helen enjoyed very much. It was a nice experience to be in a family kitchen for this homesick Oklahoma girl.

Meanwhile, in early September 1938, Norvel Young and his mother, along with Elizabeth McMillan (later Elizabeth Randolph), left Nashville headed for Los Angeles. Norvel was filled with excitement at the thought of his first permanent position on Pepperdine's faculty. Mother Young, with her sense of decorum, was going along to get her son well established in his distinguished new role. And Elizabeth was returning as a senior to Pepperdine.

They found a family, just a block or two from the campus, who rented a room and bath with a separate entrance for Norvel. Then Mrs. Young and Mrs. Baxter insisted that their sons go downtown to buy tuxedos. Their sons, Norvel and Batsell Barrett, may have been only 23 years old, but they were professors now, and with the opening of school there would be formal affairs to attend.

During the first week of school, Mrs. Zwerneman, a friend of the Baxters from San Marino, California, organized a sightseeing trip to the Huntington Library near her home for Mrs. Young. A rather unusual collection of six people were selected to join the excursion. In addition to Mrs. Zwerneman and her mother, the group included Mrs. Young, who had stayed over a few days to get Norvel situated; Mrs. Baxter and one of her favorite students, Helen Mattox; and Norvel Young. *Ostensibly*, Norvel went along to drive Mrs. Zwerneman's car. And *ostensibly*, Helen was Mrs. Baxter's guest. But one has to wonder if there wasn't a little matchmaking going on, since Miss Middlebrooks was already working behind the scenes with Ruby Young to assist providence. Though it wasn't exactly a date, it was the first time Helen spent any real time with Norvel. He was 23, she was 20, and everyone else was middle-aged or older – the situation smacked of a set-up. To top it off, Miss Middlebrooks took Helen aside one day and told her what a "good catch" Norvel would be. (Incidentally, a few months later when Helen and Norvel were dating steadily, Miss Middlebrooks told Helen she was losing all her friends because she was spending too much time with Norvel!)

As the fall semester continued, Norvel sought and received permission from the college president to date Helen. (It was an unwritten rule that faculty did not date students.) She enjoyed Norvel's company very much. She found him fun to be with, but she also discovered him to be a serious person who loved to analyze and discuss theological issues and world affairs, a person who seemed to want especially to search for the truth on any subject. She loved to sit and listen to the intellectual discussions in which Norvel would engage with his friends and colleagues. However, since she was light-hearted and fun loving, as well as a spiritual person, she began to wonder if her companionship with him might hurt his work as professor and preacher. After all, she was just a college senior, while he was a world-traveled professor. She need not have worried. He was smitten with her.

Nearly 60 years later, Mildred Thatcher wrote to Norvel, "… Bobbie (Craig) Fry and I often talk about what fun it was to hear the dates from the palm trees being tossed at Helen's window to let her know that you were there. (We thought it was quite romantic.) We would then watch Helen go downstairs with a glow on her face to meet you." Eleanor Harper said to Norvel, "When you were dating Helen, I well remember how you would enter the lobby, start playing *Moonlight Sonata*, and we on the second floor of Marilyn Hall (over the lobby) would shout down the hall, 'Helen, Norvel's here!!'"

Helen and Norvel became nearly constant companions, and within three months or so they knew they were in love. In December 1938, Wanda Roberts and Batsell Barrett Baxter were married in Taft, Texas, and Norvel served as best man. When he left for the wedding, Helen felt truly alone for the first time. Needless to say, Norvel was anxious to get back to California, and Helen was more than ready to have him back. Nearly 60 years later, J. P. Sanders reminisced with Norvel about that December of '38, "We met at Christmas time in Fort Worth and you told me about Helen. I knew you were head-over-heels in love, and when I came to L.A. in April for the meeting at Vermont Avenue [Church of Christ] you introduced me to Helen and we went for a drive to the beach."

During the 1938-39 academic year, Norvel often was a guest preacher at the Van Nuys Church of Christ or the York Boulevard Church of Christ or another area church. Helen often accompanied him on those Sunday forays into the community. Occasionally, Norvel would talk to Helen of preaching full time. He loved the teaching he was doing, but he truly was concerned for people's spiritual welfare, and he longed to tell them about Jesus. He told Helen that his world tour had convinced him of the great spiritual needs around the globe. He expressed to her a feeling of being caught between the two desires – to teach at the college level and to preach Christ to the world. The Pepperdine opportunity had arisen and he knew he needed teaching experience and also more education. He admitted that he loved the Christian college environment, but he just did not know where he would eventually fit in, and didn't even know if he would stay in education. The call of the gospel of Jesus penetrated his heart and set it aflame.

By early 1939 Norvel Young was ready to move forward on a step of vital importance. He asked Helen to become his wife on March 3. He took her to dinner at Andre's restaurant in Los Angeles' Wilshire district. The proposal didn't really come as a total surprise to Helen. They knew their feelings for one another and they had been talking openly of marriage and the future for several weeks. Still, when the question finally came – "Helen, will you marry me?" – it came with unexpected force. Perhaps the shock was because she had not dared to let herself think about the possibility of realizing her dream of marrying a man who loved the Lord as she did. For her, Norvel Young was an answer to prayer. Of course, exactly the same thing was true for Norvel, as his letters to Helen's parents would soon reveal.

Both Norvel and Helen were nervous about the immediate future. Their parents were far away and it would be difficult to properly announce their engagement from such a distance. They knew that Mother Young, being the formal Southern lady she was, would want to announce the engagement at a gala party with all their friends from church and the Nashville community—it was the only proper thing to do. However, others, like Miss Middlebrooks, would be shocked because they believed that Helen and Norvel were "moving too fast," seeing too much of each other.

On that fateful evening of March 3, Helen told Norvel she would give him her answer in a week. In truth, she was about to burst with excitement and joy, but she thought it was appropriate to make him wait a few days. Inside, however, she already knew the answer, and she was silently shouting, "Yes! Yes!" She also thought she ought to write her parents and let them know of her plans. She knew they would be pleased—they liked Norvel and thought he would be good for Helen—and telling them of the engagement before others heard was the right thing to do. She ended up waiting about a week after she gave Norvel her answer before she wrote to the Mattoxes.

Norvel and Helen kept the news quiet as long as they could. When it finally began to get around, Helen's college friends thought it was a wonderful thing. They were excited that she would be marrying a young professor. After all, most of her friends had taken a history class from "Mr. Young." And now Helen Mattox was going to marry their professor! On the other hand, everyone knew the two were seeing one another and must have known, at some level, that there was a possibility that things could get serious.

About a month later, on April 4, Norvel sat down to write one of the most important letters of his life. It is a touching correspondence that is fascinating to read from the vantage point of the decades that have passed. Norvel wrote:

> Dear Brother and Sister Mattox,
>
> As it is impossible at this time for me to talk with you personally, I shall do my best to write to you on a very important subject clearly and in a straight-forward manner.
>
> On March the third I asked your daughter, Helen, to marry me, and a week later she made me inexpressibly happy by accepting. Now it is my earnest request that you honor that engagement with your blessing and give me her hand in marriage. I would feel presumptuous in making that request of the parents of any Christian girl, but especially do I feel so of the parents of one that I esteem so highly as I do Helen. I know that it is impossible for me to know just how much I am asking of you in such a request. I am aware however that I sincerely love her with all my heart and that such love makes me feel grateful beyond

words to her parents and family for all that they have contributed to her beauty of person and of soul. I do know from my own experience as a son that it means years of care and sacrifice. And so the very depth of my love that makes me ask her hand in marriage causes me to partially appreciate how much she means to you.

Frankly I do not have much to offer her in comparison with what she deserves. I have my love which I have tried, with His help, to keep pure for the one life-companion. For several years it had been my prayer that I might find a Christian girl whom I could love and assist and who would assist me in living the Christ Way. I firmly believe that Helen is that one, and I am sure that it is largely because of her Christian home and background. My own background has been plain but one of Christian parents and training. It is my intention to devote to Christian college teaching, as well as preaching, and writing with the aim of serving Christ in this life and reaching heaven in eternity. As you know this doesn't assure a great financial income although I believe that Helen and I shall not want for the necessities of life. At the present it is only fair to say that my income for the coming year will be about $200 per month including teaching and preaching. This is on a twelve month basis and during the summer the college intends for me to continue work on the doctor's degree.

As our plans are now, Helen and I want to get married August the 31st, her birthday. Naturally this may seem too hurried, but we feel that it is reasonable. During the whole school year we have enjoyed associating together part of three or four days nearly every week. Since Christmas we have been in love and have talked over our plans and ideas quite a bit.

Hence we feel that although our courtship has not been long that it has been under such conditions that we know each other well. To wait another year with Helen continuing her work would mean a sacrifice to both of us and the only reward would be some additional savings. We have a few hundred dollars now and believe that we could live on my present income. Of course if it were necessary to wait we would make the sacrifice, but we believe a few extra material conveniences would not be worth a year of separation.

Helen and I both regret that this has to come in the nature of a surprise, but being away from home it seems unavoidable. Helen has always wanted to work and be able to do nice things for you and from that standpoint alone regrets leaving at this time. But I hope that you will not feel that you are losing her, but rather that together we may be thoughtful children to both of you as well as the whole family. My prayer is that we may be able to make you happier because of our marriage and that we may be more acceptable in our lives to Him.

Sincerely and gratefully yours,
Norvel Young

If getting married was not enough to think about, Norvel also had to deal with the pressure that was being applied for him to prepare himself for additional university history courses. It was not an unreasonable expectation on the part of the Pepperdine administration; Norvel was, after all, teaching college history courses — with an M.A. in English. As June approached, he decided to cram in some summer classes in history.

He decided to study history right in the thick of things: New York City. Norvel was accepted at Columbia University for the summer term, and when it came time to travel to New York, a little ad hoc cadre headed for the Big Apple. Mother Young, always behind the scenes orchestrating better scenarios, decided that two of her nieces ought to go with Norvel to the City and she would accompany them. Annette Roberson and Emma Suddarth could also pick up some summer units at Columbia, was her reasoning … and decision.

The three cousins and Mrs. Young found an apartment and the scholars busied themselves with study. Only on rare occasions did they take the time to simply be tourists. Then, right in the middle of summer, and in the middle of his courses, Norvel became violently ill. The doctor determined that it was acute appendicitis. When Norvel heard what an appendectomy was going to cost, he poured out his "poor student" story and began to negotiate. The doctor finally agreed to do the operation for $150.

In those days, doctors insisted on a long recuperation after surgery. So while Norvel was in the hospital for about ten days, he convinced cousin Annette Roberson to go to his classes and take notes for him. He studied the notes in the hospital and when he was released, he somehow was able to pull the courses out of the fire and pass with flying colors. But needless to say, Norvel never forgot the events of the summer of '39 leading up to his wedding.

His lifelong friend, Batsell Barrett Baxter, wrote Norvel six days before the wedding. Baxter was in Los Angeles and Norvel was in Oklahoma City preparing for the great event. Baxter began the letter with some good-natured ribbing about bachelorhood and marriage, with a salutation that read, "For the last time, Dear Norvel (bachelor)." He quoted Sir Francis Bacon as saying, "He that hath wife and children hath given hostages to fortune; for they are impediments to great enterprises, either of virtue or mischief." Then he wrote, "Now, all of this, of course, came to my attention too late to prevent me from getting entangled in the quicksands of matrimony. But, fortunately, it is just in time to allow you to change your mind and escape with your bachelorhood."

About two-thirds through the letter, Baxter turned serious and wrote, "Norvel, I know you and Helen must be about the two happiest people in the world. And you both should be, for I don't know of a finer couple anywhere, and I don't know of a finer boy and girl anywhere. I'm so glad that you found each other. You just can't help but have a happy and useful life together."

Baxter closed with well wishes for Norvel's family and Helen's family, and with anticipation for their arrival back in California after the honeymoon. But he had one final jab: "It will be fun to see you under the intoxication of matrimony and to remind you of some of those apt observations which you made concerning a certain other young couple" — referring to Norvel's ribbing of Batsell Barrett and his new wife, Wanda, after they were married the previous December.

Helen graduated in the spring 1939, in Pepperdine's second graduating class. She was happy to finally be finished with college. And she was excitedly looking forward to announcing the engagement at home. Only a few people knew her and Norvel's plans at commencement time. When the traditional wedding invitation went out, it read:

Mr. and Mrs. Judge Perry Mattox
request the honour of your presence
at the marriage of their daughter
Helen Elizabeth
to
Mr. Matt Norvel Young, Jr.
on Thursday, the thirty-first of August
Nineteen hundred and thirty-nine
at eight o'clock in the evening
Drexel Boulevard Church of Christ
Oklahoma City, Oklahoma

This summer went by quickly, filled with plans and preparations. And soon the day was upon them.

AUGUST 31, 1939

How appropriate that Norvel and Helen were married on August 31— Helen's twenty-first birthday. And how appropriate that the wedding take place at the 12th and Drexel Church of Christ in Oklahoma City. This was Helen's home congregation— where she had grown up. The minister was her very own beloved brother, Billy Mattox. Amid palms and ferns and tall baskets of coral gladioli, and under candelabra that rose high above the floor, Helen and Norvel would take their vows.

Helen chose the same musical program that her sister, Kathryn, had used: Marie Quillin sang two songs, "Oh, Promise Me" and "I Love You Truly," while an acappella choir accompanied her; and the choir sang the Bridal Chorus from *Lohengrin* as Helen and her attendants entered the church. The final musical selection was one that had been sung at family weddings for generations, "Blessed Be the Tie That Binds."

Mrs. Kathryn Silvey, Helen's sister "Kate," was the matron of honor and wore a pale blue gown. And the bridesmaids, wearing coral pink gowns, were Annette Robertson and Billie Craig (Helen's roommate from Pepperdine), and Kathleen Langford and Alvalyn Baucum (friends from Harding). Betty Woodring was the candle lighter and wore a gown similar to the bridesmaids, while Patty Nell Mattox, Helen's niece, was the flower girl and wore a little blue Empire gown to match Kathryn's.

Helen was stunning as she walked down the aisle with her father. The gown was a beautiful white satin that had a fitted bodice buttoned with satin buttons. Her lovely veil with a coronet of orange blossoms had great sentimental value. It had been handed down from the wedding of Alexander Campbell's son, to a cousin of mother Mattox. Both Helen's mother and Kathryn had worn the veil for their weddings. Also, in Helen's hand, beneath a cascade of roses, was a white satin-covered Bible, which had been carried by her mother and her sister.

Waiting for her at the front of the church was her husband-to-be and his best man, brother Franklin Young. Other groomsmen were Norvel's good friend J. P. Sanders, Norvel's cousin James O. Baird, and Helen's brothers, Joe and Paul Mattox. What Helen didn't know was that Norvel had gotten to the church building a little late and he and Billy Mattox found that there was no outside entrance into the small room where the groomsmen were waiting at the front. They were faced with two choices: walk down the aisle in front of all the waiting guests, or climb through a window into the small room. They chose the latter. Both Norvel and Billy squeezed themselves through the window, with the help of the other young men and quickly got into position. As they walked smartly out of the door near the pulpit, no one knew about their acrobatics.

With Helen's brother, Billy, saying the ceremony and pronouncing them husband and wife, and with both sets of parents looking on approvingly, the moment could not have been more perfect. Except for one thing ...

Helen later remembered, "When I saw Norvel standing at the front of the church, he looked like a ghost. Poor thing, he was still feeling the effects of his appendectomy. What a summer he had: New York, Columbia University, an appendectomy, and a wedding!" It didn't help to crawl through a window, either.

The reception was held in the garden of the Mattox home at 3240 N.W. 11th Street, Oklahoma City. The long table was spread with a three-tiered wedding cake and punch and coffee. During the reception, Norvel walked by Billy Mattox and slipped him ten dollars. It was customary for the groom to give an expression of appreciation to the minister for performing the ceremony. Billy quickly returned the money to Norvel – for which the groom was relieved and thankful. Norvel really needed that and more for the honeymoon.

The next day, the local newspaper reported, "Dignity and beauty characterized the wedding of Miss Helen Elizabeth Mattox, daughter of Mr. and Mrs. J. P. Mattox, with M. Norvel Young, Jr., of Los Angeles, which was solemnized Thursday evening, at 8 o'clock, in the Church of Christ at 12th-St. and Drexel Boulevard."

Four weeks later on Wednesday, September 27, 1939, Pepperdine's student newspaper the *Graphic*, for which Helen had worked during her junior and senior years, ran photos of Norvel and Helen with copy that read:

> Norvel Young, popular young professor, and Helen Mattox, member of the graduating class of 1939, were married August 31 at Oklahoma City in a ceremony officiated by the bride's brother, Fred Mattox [actually, the ceremony was performed by brother F. W. "Billy" Mattox].
>
> Helen, secretary of the senior class of '39, was assisted by her sister, Mrs. Silvey, as maid of honor, and Billie Craig, another former Pepperdine student, among the bridesmaids.
>
> The best man was the groom's brother, Franklin, while J. P. Sanders ushered.
>
> The couple met on the Pepperdine campus last year and were constant companions throughout the school terms.
>
> They are residing at present in the home of Mr. and Mrs. B. B. Baxter, but soon expect to move into their own residence, probably on 81st Street.

THE NEWLYWEDS

After the wedding on the evening of August 31, the newlyweds drove north about 30 miles to Guthrie, Oklahoma, and spent the night "in the best hotel in town," Helen remembered. The next morning, September 1, was still vivid nearly 60 years later: they awakened in their happiness to the sound of newsboys yelling the headlines, "Hitler Invades Poland! Europe at War!" The two were very disturbed, especially Norvel. He ran out and bought a newspaper to read during breakfast. He fondly remembered Germany from his round-the-world trip just two years earlier. Even at that time, young Germans with extended arms would greet him and his cousin, James Baird, shouting "Heil Hitler!"

Norvel had been following the ominous events in Europe, but now that the die had been cast, he was shaken. His mind drifted back to the exciting days he spent in old Heidelberg, where he and James decided to ask their parents for additional money to go on through the Middle East and Asia. Norvel and Helen discussed the strong possibility that the United States might be drawn into the war soon. Still, they were determined not to let the bad news spoil their honeymoon.

From Guthrie, Oklahoma, they drove on north to Wichita, Kansas, to visit the Parrish family. Norvel had known Myrtle Parrish at Abilene Christian College, and he established an even closer relationship with the family during the summer he spent in Wichita and the surrounding area, selling Bibles and periodically preaching for the church there.

From Wichita the new couple pressed north, then west to Jackson Hole, Wyoming, heart of the majestic Grand Teton mountain range. Of all the breathtaking scenery they would see, this place seemed to capture their souls the most. They spent two or three days in a little log cabin next to a serene lake, with a backdrop of the beautiful sawtooth-like mountains. They woke up to scenes of elk wading into the lake for a morning draught of water. One night they ate elk steaks. It was a time before creeping commercialism had set in on many of the scenic spots in America. Helen said, "The Grand Tetons have always been a precious place for us. We had such wonderful memories that we always wanted to go back and visit. We never made it."

Norvel and Helen drove a little farther north to Yellowstone National Park. Again they stayed in a log cabin and watched as the proverbial Yellowstone bear ate their snacks and lumbered off. But though the famous National Park boasted of marvelous sights like the geysers and the waterfalls, the Youngs had left their hearts at the special place beneath the Grand Tetons.

On their first Sunday as Mr. and Mrs. Young, they were in

Denver, Colorado. They attended church and heard a well-known preacher with an unlikely name, Yater Tant. They had lunch with him after church and discussed spiritual matters. Later, Tant would become a major spokesman for a faction among Churches of Christ that opposed and was critical of cooperation between congregations. Though Norvel was the epitome of all that Tant opposed – campaigns that promoted joint efforts among churches for the purpose of accomplishing good works, such as benevolence, orphans' homes, mission efforts, and so on – still they remained on friendly terms throughout life.

From Denver they drove west to Northern California and winded their way to the splendor of Yosemite National Park. Half Dome, El Capitan, Yosemite Falls, Camp Curry – the accumulated beauty of this honeymoon trip was nearly overwhelming. But amid the wonder, they were beginning to worry about money. Norvel was shocked to find that they had gone through all the money he had saved – his first lesson about married life: money disappears quickly! He just couldn't imagine that they were almost broke. He thought for sure he had taken plenty of money for the trip, but now they were almost out of gas as well as cash – with several hundred miles to go. These were the days before credit cards and easy check cashing. He decided to head toward the San Francisco Bay area, because he knew Dr. William Green and his wife, Ruby, were in Berkeley, across the bay from San Francisco. If they could make it there (on fumes!) they could cash a check.

Norvel was eager to see the Greens because they had recently returned from a European trip. Only about three months earlier in May, while Norvel was still in Los Angeles, he had received a postcard from Dr. Green that said, "Dear Norvel: I think of you often as we wander about scenes many of which must be familiar to you. I don't remember your mention of Venice, but you surely cannot have missed the place on your 'grand tour.' We enjoy the Italian scenery, and disregard (as far as possible) the political atmosphere. We are regularly addressed in German as it is assumed that all tourists are from that country (and most are). But we find most of the people very agreeable. Your friend, William Green."

Norvel wanted to hear more about the European situation now that Hitler had invaded Poland. What would happen to the beautiful cities and nations he had enjoyed so much? He and Helen finally reached the Bay area with little gasoline to spare.

They were welcomed warmly by the Greens and also by Woodrow Whitten, who was going to school at the University of California where Dr. Green taught. The Greens' sons, William and Ralph, were just little boys at the time. The newlyweds were offered the guestroom, and they stayed for about three days. The 1939 World's Fair was taking place on Treasure Island in San Francisco Bay, and Norvel and Helen were excited to visit the special event, as well as tour the City by the Bay. Their stay took them over a Sunday, so the Berkeley Church of Christ, where Dr. Green was an elder, asked Norvel to preach for them.

Fortified with cash, the newlyweds headed for Los Angeles. Remembering the honeymoon trek across the West, Helen exuberantly concluded that the three weeks had been "a most wonderful time!"

Back in Los Angeles, the Youngs stayed with the Baxters, Batsell Barrett and Wanda, in their apartment while they hunted for a house to rent. It didn't take long to find one near the campus at 1110 West 81st Street. They settled in and prepared for the semester that was beginning at Pepperdine College.

Mr. and Mrs. Pepperdine were very kind to the newlyweds. They gave them gifts and provided parties for them. Since the new Mrs. Norvel Young was only 21 years old, Mrs. Pepperdine took her shopping, showing her where the good stores were and which ones had the best prices.

Before many months, Helen and Norvel had Mr. and Mrs. Pepperdine as guests for dinner. Helen had decided to make hot rolls, but she miscalculated on the amount of dough to use for each roll. As she removed the rolls from the oven, each one looked like a small loaf of bread! With embarrassment, she cut each one in half and served the still ample half-rolls for dinner.

Mrs. Pepperdine was an excellent cook. In fact, for many years she had the entire graduating class to the Pepperdine home for a luncheon, and she prepared all the food herself. But she was also quite frank. And Helen Young learned that the founder's wife would not hesitate to tell you when you were wrong.

Just a few days before Helen and Norvel's first anniversary, Norvel sat down and wrote a letter to Helen's mother, Irene Mattox. Many years later, Helen's sister, Kathryn, found the letter among their mother's things after her death and returned it to Helen. It is a priceless insight into a love that would survive and thrive for nearly 60 years. In part, the letter read:

> George Pepperdine College
> Los Angeles, California
> August 26, 1940
>
> My dear Mother Mattox,
>   This is a letter which I have been planning to write for many months, but I have hesitated until now. . . .
>   I hardly know where to start, but I am going to say that I love you more than you know or than I can well express. One of my family failings has been a strange timidity at expressing tender emotions. However, I have found that underneath they feel very deeply. Although you and I have not had many opportunities for intimate contact, I have steadily grown to love you and your family.
>   In spite of all that I may say or do I know I shall never be able to express my intense appreciation to you for the wonderful gift you gave so graciously to me. Every day I learn to love her more. As our first year together as husband and wife draws to a close, I am more conscious of how completely wrapped up

in her I am. My very life seems in her hands. Without her the future would suddenly become inane and futile. Only the great Cause that we fight for could make possible any real happiness apart from her. I am aware that time can bring many changes, but this is the way I feel now.

Mother Mattox, she is so lovely in person and in spirit. She knows only to love and be loved. To think a deceiving or treacherous thought seems beyond her comprehension. And contrary to so many, her goodness is not negative, she is always wanting to make others happy. She is genuinely sympathetic and unselfish. Her motives are always pure though she makes mistakes of judgment. Everyone learns to love her. In my work she has many responsibilities in meeting and adapting herself to strangers, but I am never for a moment afraid. She always creates confidence and love. I have never seen anyone that is like her . . .

And don't you see why I can't help loving you always more and more, for you gave her to me. As Ella Wheeler Wilcox expressed it, you were working and planning and caring for her when I was a little boy in rompers. You were nursing and bathing her, giving her medicine and care when she was sick, sewing her pretty little dresses, scolding her for some little misdemeanor, talking to her about the life before her, telling her of Jesus, sending her off to school, comforting her when she was afraid, watching her little soul grow and directing its tendencies. How many thousand things did you do for her while I knew nothing of her. Then sacrificing to send her to school, buying pretty dresses, and writing her motherly advice, setting her standards by your example and admonition, keeping her from the pitfalls of youth. And all the time I was doing nothing for her.

And now she comes forth in the bloom of young womanhood, beautiful, healthy, graceful, lovely in character, ready to deserve the finest of husbands, and you present her to me.

Of course I had dreamed of her, looked for her, and prayed for her, but I had had no part in creating her, and molding her very soul. I know every day how unworthy I am of this gift, but I resolve that, as with all of the good things which He has given me, I can only show my appreciation by devoting myself to caring for, and passing on in some measure this gift to others by service for Him.

Mother Mattox, you see how every day my love and appreciation of you grows with the joy and happiness of life with Helen. I shall always be most thankful, if I know my own heart.

All that I have said to you could be said to Brother Mattox with equal sincerity. May God bless and keep you both, and may Helen and I be able to make you happier in every possible way.

Your devoted son,
Norvel

YOUNG PROFESSOR YOUNG

At Pepperdine College, Norvel taught a number of history courses: Ancient History, History of the Middle Ages, History of the Reformation, Latin American History and History of the American Frontier. In addition, he preached regularly, first at the York Boulevard Church of Christ in Los Angeles, then at the Van Nuys Church of Christ. A little later he preached for the Long Beach 9th and Lime congregation and the Los Angeles Sawtelle Avenue congregation.

A year after Pepperdine College had been founded, the Vermont Avenue Church of Christ was established across Vermont Avenue from the campus. Helen was a charter member. It was

September 1938, and the college now had a church nearby for students, faculty and staff. Within months of the forming of the congregation, George Pepperdine donated a lot for a church building at the eastern edge of the college campus. In late 1938, the church bought a structure that had formerly been St. Michael's Catholic Church, located on West Manchester Avenue. The structure, for which they paid $800, was moved down Manchester, then north on Vermont to the location. It was completely remodeled and upgraded, including a redesigned steeple. The congregation held the first service in its new home on April 27, 1939, with a dedication service the next Sunday, April 30.

Dr. Hugh Tiner, the college's new president, was acting minister, and as they planned the building dedication schedule, he remembered hearing J. P. Sanders at the Hillsboro Church a year earlier. Norvel remembered that after Tiner returned from Nashville, he said, "I have just listened to one of the best preachers I ever heard. We ought to have him come conduct a meeting for the Vermont Avenue Church."

Sure enough, Sanders was invited to come to California and preach a series of sermons that coincided with the opening of the new Vermont Avenue Church building. Sanders later said, "In that meeting, I spoke in [the college's] chapel every day and then spoke to the church every night. During that period of time, I met Gloria." Events were swiftly falling into place, events that would have long-term implications for J. P. Sanders, Norvel Young and Pepperdine. Sanders renewed his friendship with Norvel during that preaching trip, and he also met Gloria Millay, a student at the college who would become his life-long mate.

From that point, Norvel began urging President Baxter and Dean Tiner to hire J. P. Sanders at Pepperdine. In addition to preaching for the Hillsboro Church, Sanders was teaching part time at David Lipscomb College in Nashville. He recalled that it was "actually, a full-time load on half-time contract." So when the invitation to become the chairman of the religion department came from Pepperdine College, 33-year-old J. P. Sanders seized the opportunity. He also was invited to become the regular minister for the Vermont Avenue Church next to the college.

"I had a lot to do with encouraging J. P. to come," Norvel later said. "You know me, I am promotional minded. I felt like they needed him. One reason why I felt this way was because I was concerned about some of the directions of the school. The school had a lot of money, and there was a tendency for it to be independent of the church. Mr. Pepperdine did not want to get contributions from the churches."

Norvel continued, "I believed that Pepperdine College, at that point, was in danger of leaving its connections with the church, and the school was under some criticism at the time. I thought J. P. would lend a lot of credibility." And indeed he did. Many West Coast church members knew of the scholarship and Christian dedication of Sanders.

There were several factors drawing J. P. to Pepperdine: There was the opportunity to become a department chairman, and as such to influence the development of young preachers, for whom he was concerned. There was the opportunity to work on a doctorate, and to share in the excitement of the halcyon days at a young school with his friend Norvel Young. And, perhaps more important than he would admit, there was a beautiful Pepperdine student named Gloria Millay.

When Sanders arrived, he needed a place to live, so the Youngs rented him a room in their newly acquired house on West 81st Street. The Youngs paid $60 a month rent and they and Sanders agreed on $20 a month rent for a room for J. P., which included breakfast. So Helen Mattox Young was now running her own "bed and breakfast!" To put the rent in perspective, Norvel later said, "We were only making $150 [monthly salary]."

J. P. lived with Helen and Norvel for the next two years. He also enrolled in a Ph.D. program in religion at the University of Southern California. "In the fall of that year," remembered Helen, "J. P. bought a bright maroon Oldsmobile, and this dashing young bachelor teacher became very popular with everyone."

With J. P. Sanders moving to California, it was necessary to move *Twentieth Century Christian* magazine, as well, since J. P. was still serving as editor. The magazine used Pepperdine College's address for a short while, but the publication continued to be printed in Nashville. Its circulation at the time was 2,000, or perhaps a little more, and it was enjoying a growing success. Mr. Pepperdine gave Norvel and Sanders $1,000 to send about 7,000 subscriptions to young people.

In the summer of 1940, the Yosemite Family Encampment began, and Pepperdine President Hugh Tiner was asked to be the speaker for the inaugural encampment. Helen and Norvel traveled north to the breathtaking valley they had visited on their honeymoon, riding in the car with Hugh and Lola Tiner and Jimmie and Vivian Lovell. Because the Youngs were newlyweds, they received some good-natured teasing from the others. It was a delightful, as well as historic, time for the young couple.

HELEN AND NORVEL IN NASHVILLE

In the spring of 1941 after the school term concluded, the Youngs headed for Nashville, Norvel having earlier tendered his resignation. He knew that whatever lay before him as a career, a doctorate would be very helpful. So he entered a doctoral program at Peabody College (now part of Vanderbilt University), studying under famed historian Freemont P. Worth.

The choice of Peabody had been a somewhat pragmatic one. They considered whether or not to go to Chicago where Norvel could study under William Warren Sweet, a renowned scholar who specialized in church history. In the end, finances won out. They chose Peabody because they could live with Norvel's parents and cut costs. The Young home was large and spacious with plenty of room for Norvel and Helen. Always the visionary, Norvel's mother, Ruby, encouraged her daughter-in-law to also go back to school. So Helen began work on a master's degree in sociology at Peabody as Norvel studied for his doctorate in history.

During the summer before school began, Norvel was asked to preach for the venerable old Belmont Church of Christ in Nashville. Obviously, his contact at the church was his father, who served as an elder for the congregation. But it was not merely narrow nepotism that was at work, and Matt Young was not simply promoting some young, inexperienced would-be preacher. His son was now a very mature 25-year-old who had traveled around the world, had taught three years at a California college, had preached regularly for churches during that time and had established himself as an excellent speaker since his days as an undergraduate at David Lipscomb College and Abilene Christian College.

Toward the end of the first semester at Peabody in 1941, Norvel was asked to speak at a worship service on the campus of David Lipscomb College, in the second-floor auditorium. What his subject was, he could not remember, but he could never forget the afternoon of that day. It was Sunday, December 7, the day, as President Franklin D. Roosevelt would say, that would "live in infamy." All afternoon the family huddled around the large console radio in the living room of the Young home, listening to the reports coming in of the Japanese attack on Pearl Harbor.

Norvel remembered that only four years earlier, he and James Baird had visited in Japan on their world tour. They had met and become friends with missionaries there: Barney Morehead, O. D. Bixler, Elbridge Linn, Sarah Andrews, Hettie Lee Ewing and Lillie Cypert. Now the terrible war that was ravaging much of the world had reached Hawaii, American soil. Where were his friends now? Were they in danger? Would the Japanese invade Hawaii with ground troops? The questions swirled in Norvel's head.

They were difficult days in early 1942 as America entered both the Pacific war and the war in Europe. But Helen and Norvel pressed on in their degree programs. Norvel was interested in church history, and his dissertation advisor suggested that a study of the history of colleges associated with Churches of

Christ had not been undertaken. The idea appealed to Norvel because he was looking toward the possibility of someday returning to a career in Christian education. In fact, when he left the faculty of George Pepperdine College, he received an advance of $500 to apply toward his doctoral studies. It was later discovered that Dean E. V. Pullias had recommended a $1,000 advance, but Mrs. Helen Pepperdine, who was on the board of trustees at the time, thought the graduate work could be done for $500.

At the conclusion of his dissertation, Norvel decided not to immediately return to George Pepperdine College. So the advance had to be repaid. It was not an easy task for a young couple during the war years to repay the substantial sum of $500.

Not only was money in short supply, but transportation was very difficult during the war. Tires and gasoline were rationed and could be obtained only with sufficient ration coupons. As with most Americans, this meant that Helen and Norvel were very limited in their travel. The United States' entry into the war caused Norvel to reflect back on the ominous signs he and James Baird had encountered in both Germany and Japan. As a 21-year-old, he had not thought too much about it at the time. Now in retrospect, all of the pieces seemed to fit together. And it was difficult and painful to think of the lovely places they had visited and the friendly people they had met now being destroyed by a horrible war.

M. NORVEL YOUNG, PH.D.

Norvel finished his class work, then in 1943 concluded and defended his dissertation and earned his Doctor of Philosophy degree in history. He wanted to publish his dissertation on Christian education, but did not have the money. Had it not been for John Allen Hudson, who agreed to publish it at his own expense, the scholarly work of M. Norvel Young probably would have been lost to us for all practical purposes.

With their educational preparation behind them, Norvel and Helen began praying about the future. They had already decided not to return to Los Angeles and Pepperdine College. Norvel had become disenchanted with the school's direction and didn't want to go back as a professor. He and his whole family were sad about the treatment of President Batsell Baxter, who was pressed into resigning. Obviously, it had hurt the president's son, Norvel's great friend, Batsell Barrett Baxter. The Youngs were now afraid that Pepperdine would lose all connections with the church and become a secular college. In the meantime, Norvel took courses in Vanderbilt's School of Religion.

Norvel was preaching at that time for the David Lipscomb College church and helping to raise money for a new church building. The structure would be completed in the mid-1940s shortly after Norvel and Helen left, and would be named the Granny White Pike Church of Christ. Although he enjoyed preaching occasionally, he really didn't desire a permanent career in ministry. One option was to stay in Nashville and work with his father. Ruby and Matt Young would have liked for them to remain there, with the hope that Norvel would someday become president of their beloved David Lipscomb College. But wisely, his parents never pressured Norvel and Helen to make Nashville their permanent home.

Looking back, Matt Young was a successful entrepreneur and had established a solidly successful business in Nashville. It is nearly certain that son Norvel could have followed in his father's footsteps and been even more successful. Norvel's formal training was in history and education, and he never had even one course in business. However, his father taught him how to get along with people, how to use common sense and how to think like a business person. As a result, balancing budgets and managing money came naturally to Norvel. In truth, Matt never wanted Norvel to follow him in business. The senior Young did not think making money was a very "high calling," as he put it. He used to say, "The lowest form of intelligence is the ability to make money." Many people who struggle over finances today would tend to disagree with him, as would those who have built successful enterprises!

But if Norvel and Helen did not stay in Nashville, they had to do something soon to make a living. So they pondered what their next move should be. The war seemed to put everything on hold and make every plan tentative.

About this time, Norvel received two invitations to become the preaching minister of local congregations. One invitation came from the Cleveland Avenue Church of Christ in Wichita, Kansas. The other was from the Broadway Church of Christ in Lubbock, Texas.

The Broadway Church in Lubbock had a couple of things in its favor. The previous preacher had been the great Grover Cleveland Brewer, a man who perhaps was ahead of his time, preaching grace and undenominationalism in a time noted for its reactionary legalism and sectarianism. Brewer had become well respected in the city. In addition, Liff Sanders, who was the first preacher from Churches of Christ to be established in Lubbock, was still with the Broadway Church, serving as an elder. His irenic spirit had influenced the church for many years. All in all, the Broadway Church was very much a part of the city of Lubbock and not isolated and withdrawn into its own fellowship, as some churches tended to be.

On the negative side, Lubbock, with its dry, flat prairie land, could not compare in Norvel's mind with the lush, verdant hills of his native Tennessee. Nor could it compare with George Pepperdine College's sun-washed, garden-like Southern California. But the will of God and the good of His people were always the most important things in the lives of Norvel and Helen Young.

They chose Lubbock.

THE TEXAS
PLAINS

*"As we look back," said Helen, "we feel
that Lubbock was our home. We were young
and the people there took us to their hearts
and nurtured us, helped us, loved us."*

A t some point, somewhere in the minds of Norvel and
Helen Young, a seed was planted. It was a seed that,
when fully grown, produced the spirit of a servant.
Though the two were separate individuals, the seed grew in them
as if they were one. It grew in their combined, shared heart. They
seemed to always know they were on Earth for the benefit of
others.

When Norvel was just 21 years old, he had founded a magazine that he thought might encourage young people in the
Christian life. The venture was not to gain riches. If he had
wanted riches, he would have stayed in Nashville and joined
his father in business. After six decades of being published, that
magazine is still a profit-losing rather than a profit-making enterprise. But hundreds of thousands of Christians and seekers
have been encouraged to press on in their faith as a result of the
little publication.

Likewise, Helen always wanted to serve and support. She
began life with her husband with two goals: to support him in
whatever form of service he chose, and to find ways that she

herself could serve people. Many years later, Norvel would say, "There are givers and there are takers. We've tried to live our lives as givers."

THE CALL OF BROADWAY

After founding the magazine and serving a short stint in Christian education in California, the first truly great chapter in the lives of Norvel and Helen came with the move to Lubbock in 1944. The process that brought them there began when G. C. Brewer's wife happened to be in Columbia, Tennessee, and heard Norvel preach at a local church. She was so taken with the young man that she returned to Lubbock and told her husband about him. To her, Norvel had the same global vision and non-sectarian message that her husband preached.

In his autobiography, G. C. Brewer wrote, "After laboring with this church [Broadway Church of Christ] about six and a half years, I again faced my old problem of going out and holding more meetings than the church thought it proper for me to do and I turned loose the work and again went out into the field." His evangelist's heart drove him to preach where "the fields were white unto harvest." He would leave the pastoring to others.

When Brewer decided to leave Lubbock, he remembered his wife's positive impression of Norvel. To assist the church leaders in their task of replacing him, Brewer sent Norvel a telegram. "Would you be interested in coming to the Broadway Church of Christ in Lubbock, Texas?" the telegram asked.

The terse communication certainly got Norvel's attention. Though he had met G. C. Brewer only briefly, the whole Brewer family was an institution in Nashville. In addition, Brewer had preached in Los Angeles and was one of those who had influenced George Pepperdine to begin his college. For these and other reasons, Norvel admired Brewer. But the telegram was unspecific, and Brewer did not mention that he was leaving Lubbock. Norvel did not know if he was being considered for a position as associate minister or some other ministry position.

He soon discovered that Brewer was resigning as the preaching minister of the Broadway Church and was interested in leaving the congregation in the hands of a positive, grace-oriented, forward-looking preacher. The least he could do, Norvel thought, was to talk with the church's elders about the opportunity. But when he traveled to Lubbock and interviewed with the leaders, he found that he generally had two strikes against him.

The first strike was his age. At just 28 years of age, he was a far cry from the stately older preachers to which the Broadway Church was accustomed. It was difficult for the leaders to envision this young man having the maturity to challenge the church and set the tone for advancement.

But the second strike, surprisingly, was his education. At that point in the 1940s, a doctor's degree was not so much an advantage as it was a disadvantage among Churches of Christ. Many of the members had heard stories of young ministers who had gone off to college to pursue a doctorate, only to lose their faith. Just as it has been in every age, this was a period of great struggle for the minds of people, and many college campuses sought converts to secularism and atheism as much as churches sought converts to Christ. To Norvel's knowledge, there was no full-time minister among Churches of Christ with a Ph.D. at that moment. In fact, even on the faculties of the Christian colleges, Ph.D.s were few.

So not only was Norvel a relatively young man, he was *Doctor* Norvel Young as well! In the end, however, the elders had one important question for him: Had his doctoral work helped or hurt his faith? Satisfied that his faith was rock solid, they asked him to follow the legendary G. C. Brewer as minister of the Broadway Church of Christ.

A DIFFERENT KIND OF PREACHER

Later, after Norvel had accepted the position and he and Helen had moved to Lubbock, Norvel found that the townspeople had no problem with his doctorate. In fact, they were rather impressed with his credentials. Even many of the members of the church, as it turned out, were proud to have a minister with a doctor's degree. The next 13 years would be filled with excitement and accomplishment for the Broadway Church and for Helen and Norvel Young.

However, the period would not be without its challenges. Very soon, the problem Norvel faced was not people's attitude toward his education, but rather, their attitude toward his vision ... and what the vision of the church ought to be.

The Youngs had been in Lubbock only about a year when the electrifying news came that Europe had been liberated. Peace in the Pacific followed soon after. Norvel began thinking of his journey through Europe in 1937, before the war. One of the most vivid memories from that world tour was of the beautiful, ancient German city of Heidelberg on the Neckar River. Now he saw photographs of Cologne and other cities of war-torn Germany in ruins. And as he thought of the suffering of the people, he knew he had to help. To encourage the compassionate work of rebuilding Germany, he began editing a newsletter called *Germany for Christ*. The newsletter also promoted the work of his friend, Otis Gatewood, who spearheaded a large team of mission workers into Germany. Norvel traveled and spoke to many churches and other groups on behalf of the work in Germany.

The controversy that grew concerning Norvel's work was over whether or not cooperation between Churches of Christ in intercongregational projects threatened their cherished congregational autonomy – whether or not such cooperation among independent churches was biblical. There were certain preachers of a more conservative position who opposed such projects, but much of the opposition came from small, mostly rural churches. One particular man in the region began editing a small journal that purported to set the record straight. When he took some verbal shots at Norvel, Norvel confronted the man and came to terms with him. "But I also made a friend," said Norvel later. It was another example of how Norvel could turn liabilities into assets. Largely through the leadership of Norvel, the Broadway Church, with the help of other churches, raised half a million dollars for postwar relief efforts in Germany – a very gracious gesture and an amazing amount of money for the 1940s.

"Norvel became a great preacher at Lubbock," said Helen many years later. It was not simply the biased opinion of a preacher's wife, but the evaluation of one who had become an excellent communicator in her own right. She continued concerning Norvel, "That was because he gave so much time to [his preaching]. He realized how important it was. He is not a person who likes to sit and study for long periods. He wants to be up and doing things. So it was a sacrifice for him to spend a lot of preparation time for sermons. But he became a very fine preacher in those years."

Norvel's models for preaching included Hall L. Calhoun, E. H. Ijams and J. P. Sanders. Calhoun had a "professional" style of preaching, although he certainly could "wax eloquent." The Christ-like spirit of Ijams also had a great deal of impact on Norvel. Sanders, on the other hand, was only ten years older than Norvel, but he was an experienced preacher, and he was a very inspirational speaker.

In the end, Norvel Young developed his own style of preaching. He tended to be more enthusiastic than the average preacher and always pressed for a practical application rather than simply making a theological point. He never thought of himself as primarily a preacher. Rather, he saw himself as a conversationalist, a teacher of the Bible who stressed the important things about Jesus. His messages were not "preachy" or rhetorical. He tended to "come alongside" his listener with a message of encouragement. And in the final analysis, he was faithful to the little plaque on the back of the pulpit of the Broadway Church at that time that reminded every speaker who approached the podium, "Sir, we would see Jesus."

The year after Norvel and Helen moved to Lubbock, a young Clois Fowler entered Texas Tech as a freshman. He and his roommate became members of the Broadway Church. Fifty years later, he wrote to Norvel and said, "... your preaching, your optimistic view of life in general and church life in particular, gave me a whole new vista for spirituality for Christianity in our restoration heritage. My enduring memories were of your enthusiastic presentation of the gospel message, your love for the lost and the respect you had for all of us, young and old."

Most of all, Norvel Young viewed himself as a promoter for the cause of Christ. He did not find as much satisfaction in preaching as he did in influencing people to change for the better.

Sometimes he found preaching a difficult chore. He remembered well one particular sermon – the one for the dedication of the new building – when the largest crowd ever recorded for the Broadway Church assembled. He spent many hours preparing and worrying about his message on the subject of dedicating ourselves before we dedicate our building. He wanted it to be just right. "I covered a lot of territory," he recalled, "but I didn't preach a great sermon. However, I did it with a great deal of enthusiasm!" Helen was quick to correct his statement by saying, "It was a *good* sermon!"

Looking back on the Lubbock years, Norvel smiled at Helen's affirmation that "he became a very fine preacher in those years." He replied, "Well, I've often said that, if Helen could have done the preaching, I could have done the promoting, and that church would have really taken off!"

But, as a matter of fact, the church really did "take off" under Norvel's ministry. The whole city of Lubbock knew of Dr. M. Norvel Young and the Broadway Church of Christ. For one thing, Norvel preached weekly on the radio, specifically on local stations KCBD and KSEC. And he started a "Know Your Bible" program on television, using a panel to answer Bible questions. Even more, he was known around town as a minister who was involved in the community, who was always working for the betterment of the city of Lubbock. Far from retreating within the walls of the church where he could pontificate to his flock, he was a very public figure who did his best to treat everyone in town, non-member as well as member, equally.

Not long after becoming the minister for the Broadway Church in Lubbock, the Youngs went back to Nashville for a visit. There, Norvel had the opportunity of baptizing a boy that they had known in Nashville. Helen had taught the boy in Bible class and, of course, Norvel had been the pulpit minister the boy heard week after week. Fifty years later, after the boy had grown up to become a popular singer and a celebrity (and later, chairman of Pepperdine's University Board), he sat down and penned Norvel a letter:

> As you well remember, you baptized me way back in 1945, when I was a 13 year old boy, seeking salvation, forgiveness of sin and relationship with a Living Lord. You spent some time questioning and counseling with me, as you always did as Minister of the David Lipscomb congregation, and judged that I was understanding and ready for this vital, all important step.
>
> You became, in that precious moment, my "John the Baptist," and my life was changed forever. I'll always be grateful, Norvel, for that and so much more."

The letter was signed, "Pat Boone."

THE YOUNG CHILDREN

One of the great events of the early years in Lubbock occurred not quite a year after the Youngs' arrival in the city. Their first child was born. They had waited to have children until they had finished their education. Now, as they entered their first great work together, their daughter, Emily, was born early Monday morning, February 26, 1945.

Helen's mother, "Mother Mattox," came to Lubbock for the birth. "She and Norvel were most congenial, discussing world affairs, politics and church affairs, as well as family," Helen said with pride. "Mother came to help us with each of the births of the children." In that day, women stayed in the hospital for about a week after childbirth.

Because Helen and Norvel were such public people, little Emily's birth was a major Lubbock event. Everyone would tell Norvel, "Be sure to take good care of Helen." The Broadway Church family especially was very excited. One woman in the church loaned Helen all the maternity clothes she needed.

Helen was ecstatic to have her baby girl when Emily was born. Naturally, the little girl got lots of attention, such as when she was six months old and Norvel took her (with a baby bottle in his pocket) to "show her off" at the Kiwanis Club. When she was four to six years old, many commented on how much she looked like the young Shirley Temple, with her curly, strawberry blond hair. And of course, she always had beautiful clothes, because of the gifts of church members. Years later, Helen glowed as she thought of the warmth and love of the church.

In the midst of the joy, a dark cloud slipped overhead. Helen developed a fever and had to go back into the hospital. The doctors couldn't determine the cause, but soon it went away on its own. And Helen could return to her new daughter.

The very next day after Emily was born, Frank Pack sat down and wrote a letter to Norvel and Helen. After bringing them up to date on his academic activities, Pack wrote, "I'm so thrilled over that new niece and we've had a lot of fun thinking about names and wondering how the father got along, etc." He continued, "Well, I'm almost as thrilled for you as if I were in your place. I feel like I'm kind of kin to it, and uncle Frank is really happy about her being in 'our' family. I hope that Helen is fine, and I pray for you every night that all may be well." He concluded, "Lots of love to our new girl and best wishes to you both."

Less than a month later, Norvel replied to Pack, "My, I wish you could see your little 'niece.' I too am relieved that she looks like her Mother." He jokingly added, "However, I have received almost too many notes to that effect."

Frank Pack had visited with the Youngs in Lubbock early in February, and Norvel had asked him to preach for the Broadway Church on Sunday. Pack told Norvel and Helen, "I would not take any amount of money for that visit in your home. It made me love you all the more and appreciate the wonderful work that you are doing ... I love you both for what you are, and I assure you that you stand high in the love and affection of all those Lubbock folks as well as so many out here [Los Angeles]."

On February 12, Pack left the Youngs and returned to California. Norvel sat down and wrote a letter to Frank's parents in Memphis, Tennessee. In part he wrote: "[Frank] consented to preach for me Sunday morning and the whole congregation was very pleased to hear him. There were a number of fine compliments. Of course, we have been talking a great deal since he has been here and I wanted to write and tell you again how very highly I regard him as a friend. I admire his serious sincerity and his ability and his humility. I believe he is going to accomplish great things for the Lord in our generation. You are to be highly complimented upon rearing such a fine son."

About two weeks after little Emily was born, Norvel received a very interesting letter from W. B. West, Jr., head of the Department of Religion at Pepperdine College. The letter began, "Congratulations on the arrival of Emily Mattox. I know that both of you must be very happy and very grateful for this precious bit of humanity which God has given unto you. Does she look like her father or her mother? Shall I send application blanks for her to enroll in George Pepperdine College?"

The next paragraph was a report on the undergraduate and graduate programs in religion at Pepperdine. But the letter was not yet half finished. Norvel knew that W. B. West must have something special in mind. The letter continued:

> In order for us to have a department of religion second to none in the country, we must have as strong a faculty as possible. You know the old saying, "As is the teacher so is the school." Brother [Ralph] Wilburn and Batsell Barrett have distinguished themselves in great service to the Department of Religion this year. We regret to lose Batsell Barrett, but share with him the feeling that his father needs him. Brother Wilburn is now in Chicago for two or three weeks during which time he will take his final examination for his doctorate, and he and we fully expect him to take his Ph.D. degree the last part of this month. We are now in quest for a splendidly trained, eminently capable, and thoroughly loyal to the truth man for the Historical Field with emphasis on Church History. President Tiner, Dean Pullias, and I are sure that *you are the man* for whom we are looking, and they have authorized me to write you asking if you would be interested, beginning September 1, 1945, coming to Pepperdine with the rank of Associate Professor of Church History with the same financial compensation as Brother Wilburn will receive.

West's letter continued with persuasive words, such as, "We know that you are doing a great work in Lubbock, but after all, it is only local whereas at Pepperdine you will be shaping the lives of many hundreds and thousands of students who will go to the various parts of the United States and the world and through these students you will live." West talked about the wonderful opportunities at Pepperdine and about how Norvel and Helen would be of great help in the college's work. He mentioned that Norvel most certainly would also be able to find a part-time preaching position should he desire one. For Dr. M. Norvel Young, not yet 30 years old, it was a real ego-booster.

But amazingly, J. Roy Vaughan, representing a committee appointed by the Board of Directors of Florida Christian College, was writing Batsell Baxter *at the same time,* requesting a recommendation from Baxter concerning Norvel Young. Baxter, who had been Pepperdine College's founding president, was now president of David Lipscomb College in Nashville. But Vaughan was not asking for Baxter's recommendation of Norvel for a faculty position – Florida Christian wanted Norvel for its *president!*

President Baxter's response to Vaughan included the following:

> His [Norvel's] mind is more mature than his age indicates. He is a splendid Christian man and an excellent business man. He has the combination of character and strength and good judgment and Christian zeal that would make an ideal college president. He is not afraid of hard work and he knows how to make sacrifices. He is an influence and power far beyond his years. He is now preaching for the Broadway church in Lubbock, Texas. This is the largest church in Texas. ...
>
> [Helen] Young is a splendid Christian woman, courteous, consecrated, makes friends easily, has excellent judgment, and would make an ideal President's wife. I can recommend them both without any reservation.

Baxter didn't mention that his own institution, David Lipscomb College, was also courting Norvel Young for a teaching position. On March 12, 1945, Norvel had written to President Baxter and said, "I also want to express appreciation for your continued interest in our coming back to Lipscomb. I am sure that you know that from a personal point of view it would please us no end to be associated with you and Batsell Barrett in the work there and of course to be near the home folks ... It is my earnest hope that we shall never disappoint you. ... We shall always be grateful to you for the opportunity which you gave us at George Pepperdine [College]."

But as flattering as were all the offers, Norvel and Helen had made a commitment to the members of the Broadway Church and to the people of Lubbock. And they had only begun to fulfill that commitment. The "largest church in Texas," as President Baxter had called it, would become the largest Church of Christ in the world during their tenure in a few years. Still, the thought of returning to Pepperdine and the thought of serving as a college president had struck responsive chords in Norvel's heart. Maybe someday the opportunities would return, he thought ...

Norvel and Helen received a letter from Horace Lipscomb, a church leader in Nashville who was a nephew of nineteenth-century church pioneer David Lipscomb, congratulating them on the birth of Emily. He suggested that in 1965 a 20-year-old Emily would be the May Queen at David Lipscomb College (named after his illustrious uncle). His "prophecy" was at least partially right: in 1965 a 20-year-old Emily was the May Queen – but at Lubbock Christian College, rather than at Lipscomb College.

A little more than two and a half years after the arrival of Emily, on October 19, 1947, Helen and Norvel had a son, Matt. The Youngs were no longer just a couple or even a little family. Now they were a *growing* family.

As mentioned earlier, Matt was born on the day Norvel's grandfather, the great S. F. Morrow, died. Little Matt was born on a Sunday. So Carl Spain, who was employed by the Broadway Church as director of Texas Tech Bible Chair, preached in place of Norvel. Norvel was at the hospital, rejoicing at the arrival of his new son but also grieving at the loss of his grandfather. And Spain used that very drama in his sermon to illustrate the fleeting nature of life. He spoke of the birth of Matt and the departure of S. F. – the span of a life, the brevity of life for all of us, the need to live significantly.

Again, Mother Mattox came to help her daughter after the birth. She and all the Youngs were thrilled to have a little boy. Emily loved the role of big sister, and as the years passed she became even more motherly with the younger children.

Matt brought a new feeling to the small brick house that sat on the property where the Broadway Church's new building would one day stand. He had medium brown hair, and he was a big and healthy boy. Soon the men of the church were spoiling him with cowboy hats and little boots. As he grew older, some member or the other would have him out to the ranch to ride ponies.

Matt was a typical little boy: he loved to play with trucks and toy six-shooters and hammers and other tools that tend to intrigue children. And he especially loved animals: he had a cocker spaniel dog named Taffy. He was fond of going to Daddy's office and pretending to work beside him. And he stood proudly beside his dad when the corner stone was laid for the new Broadway Church building. A woman who was a church member and who made children's clothes and sold them at the local baby stores made sure Matt was well dressed.

As he grew older Matt enjoyed sports, and Norvel would play baseball with him in the yard. He and Emily enjoyed riding their bikes to the neighborhood park. He was about nine when the family moved to Los Angeles. And all was not play: his dad put him to work painting the wrought-iron fence around the President's' home on the Pepperdine campus. As he entered high school he wanted to play football. But early on, an injury sidelined him – for which Helen was secretly thankful, because she didn't want him to be more seriously hurt. However, Matt did play on the high school basketball team.

A couple of years after Matt was born, Helen had a miscarriage. But then, nearly five years later, she gave birth to a healthy little girl on June 8, 1952. Helen and Norvel named her Marilyn

Morrow Young. While Emily had weighed just 7 pounds 6 ounces at birth, Marilyn weighed a little more than 10 pounds. She was a strikingly beautiful child with lots of dark hair.

Mrs. Tierce Lay in Lubbock, a member of the Broadway Church, was entirely taken with Marilyn. She supplied the little girl with lovely clothes. Helen especially remembered one satin coat with lace and dress to match that Mrs. Lay made and gave to Marilyn. The little girl looked like a princess.

As she grew, Marilyn loved to read and to play games. Mother Mattox, a very strong woman herself, was convinced that Marilyn was filled with self-confidence. She was an extremely bright little girl who easily excelled in academics. Her spiritual sensitivity, energy and humor were early indicators of the career she would later choose in life – that of a professional counselor.

In many ways, Marilyn was more like her father in her intensity and thoughtfulness. In later years, Marilyn would live through some difficult days that would, at times, parallel some of Norvel's struggles. And she was ultimately able to overcome many challenges because of the security of the love that she felt from her parents.

Just slightly more than 14 months after Marilyn was born, a little sister made her appearance, completing the family. Sara Helen was born on August 18, 1953. It was a somewhat awkward time for the Youngs. Norvel had promoted the idea of bringing John White to Lubbock to discuss the possibility of his coming as director of the new Children's Home of Lubbock. White was an official with the department of human welfare in Texas. Just as he got into town for the interview, Sara decided to arrive on the scene.

As a child, Sara was even more blonde than big sister Emily. According to Helen, "She was a very sweet child." Perhaps it was because she was the baby of the family or perhaps it was her disposition, but she charmed everyone. All her life she seemed to have a talent for getting along with people.

When asked for some "one-liners" on her children, Helen responded: "All four are intelligent, hard working, loyal and wonderful. Emily is lovable and nurturing, and while she is a leader, she is not aggressive. Matt is more serious, studious and assertive; though somewhat introverted, he is a caring physician and a devoted father. Marilyn is brilliant and beautiful, the more reserved of the two younger children, thoughtful and caring. Sara is charming, agreeable, quick and so winsome. They all have leadership qualities. The three girls are marvelous Bible teachers. I'm thankful that all four are in serving professions. We are a close family. The girls are best of friends and talk to each other every day no matter where they are. They meet regularly to pray together. Each of the children has a deep faith."

Helen and the children probably never knew the important roles they played for the people in Lubbock. Clois Fowler, mentioned earlier, had another enduring memory of his college years at Texas Tech and as a member of the Broadway Church in the late 1940s: "Helen had the children around her, holding one youngster on her hip, standing by [Norvel's] side, greeting us as we left the building. You will never know how much that one small, kind, continuing act of friendship and warmth impressed me. You both had all the time in the world for small-talk that made us feel whole and wanted."

Dr. James R. Wilburn came to Pepperdine in 1970 as part of a six-person task force to plan the Malibu campus and academic programs, and he went on to serve as a vice president and a dean of two different graduate schools at the university. Wilburn remembered that, as a struggling young parent many years earlier, he wondered from whom he might seek counseling on how to be a better parent.

He sat down and wrote a note to Helen and Norvel Young because they were the best parents of whom he knew. "Shortly, I received a seven or eight page letter from Helen," he said. "She recounted stories of her family, the Mattoxes, and stories of her own children. She was more candid than I would have expected. And I'll never forget her advice and wisdom."

BUILDING A GREAT CHURCH

Because of Norvel's solid expository preaching and the tireless efforts of both of them, the Broadway Church had become the largest Church of Christ in the world by the time the Youngs left. And it was a marvelous experience for Helen and Norvel. "As we look back," said Helen, "we feel that Lubbock was our home. We were young and the people there took us to their hearts and nurtured us, helped us, loved us."

Norvel reminisced, "We had a strong eldership and people who loved to serve. I'll never forget ... I taught a Bible class, and it was a large class – more than a hundred. It was held in an annex building next to the church. And Helen was such a help in that. Not long after we arrived, she learned all the names of the class members, and one morning she stood up with me and named everyone – all 100 or more of them. Helen has a special talent for remembering names. And that makes people feel important." That ability to memorize certainly can be traced to Helen's father insisting on her memorizing scripture in her early years.

Helen quickly added, "I do have a facility for being able to memorize names – which is a very low form of intelligence." To which many of us would probably respond, "How can we get more of that 'low form of intelligence'?"

Though Norvel and Helen both were talented, the progress in Lubbock did not come easily. They worked extremely hard. For example, they would attend an event such as the church's professional women's class, when so many husbands were away during the war. Or they would meet with young people's groups. Then they would go home, write down the names they had learned and memorize them. They poured hours and hours into meetings, visits, classes, and other church activities.

They also were prominent in the community. Norvel wrote a weekly column in the newspaper and he helped with election issues he felt strongly about. Helen was president of the Lubbock Women's Forum and on the City Library Board.

Though Norvel had been preaching for more than 10 years before he accepted the Broadway Church pulpit, he had never served as a full-time minister for a church. Many of the practical aspects of local ministry were new to him. He and Helen had the notion that they should visit every one of the people they met in the classes and in the church – and also try to get to know other people in town. They established a rigorous regimen of visitation. Even during the famous West Texas dust storms, they struggled against the stinging wind to do their work. What they did not know was that no one went outside in the dust storms. But many was the time when the Youngs plowed through the blinding dust to visit some church member or visitor.

When the Youngs arrived in Lubbock, the Broadway Church numbered about 500 members and met in a brick building on Broadway and Avenue N. By the time they left in 1957, 13 years later, the congregation had grown fourfold. And in 1950, with Norvel's promotion and leadership, the church completed a large new building on expansive property at Broadway and Avenue T. By the mid-1950s, they were having two services with a total of about 2,000 people in attendance. For a man who never intended to be a full-time preacher, M. Norvel Young was doing well indeed.

In keeping with Norvel's flare for doing things differently and "with style," the new Lubbock building became a pacesetter for Texas Churches of Christ. "We wanted to build in the Gothic style, but the Methodists had already done that," said Norvel with a smile. "We wanted a building that wouldn't look like all the other West Texas church buildings. Our architect and building committee traveled extensively to tour church buildings for ideas. We wanted a design that would be young when it was old. The style selected was Romanesque, pale beige brick with a tower that added beauty and a distinctive symbol of the church. The finished product was impressive."

But then he added, "Still, despite its architectural esthetics, the auditorium did not ideally suit our type of worship, I later realized. Although it seated 2,100, the ceiling was too high and not good for congregational singing. However, the classrooms, fellowship halls, nursery facilities and so on were excellent."

Other Texas Churches of Christ were influenced to construct new buildings in the architectural style of the Broadway Church. The College Church in Abilene, the Skillman Avenue Church in Dallas and the Tenth and Broad Church in Wichita Falls are examples of churches that echoed the new style.

During this period of great growth in Lubbock, there were very few large congregations among the Churches of Christ. Probably the largest was the College Church in Abilene, Texas, followed by the Broadway Church in Lubbock, then perhaps the Madison Church in Nashville, Tennessee. But there were two visionary men in particular, Norvel Young in Lubbock and Ira North at the Madison Church in Nashville, who believed that large churches were needed. Both of these leaders agreed that, if the autonomous Churches of Christ were not going to have a headquarters or ecclesiastical structure, they should at least have some "large churches in this big world," as Norvel would put it. They believed that the fellowship needed some large churches with strong enough bases that they could do more than simply care for their own. In other words, Norvel Young and Ira North maintained that a few large churches were needed to create big dreams and expansive plans – larger projects in benevolence, education, missions and home evangelism – to lift the vision of an entire religious movement.

By 1951 Norvel had been building the Broadway Church for seven years and had established himself as a dynamic leader in his fellowship. It was very appropriate, then, that he should be the keynote speaker for the Pepperdine Bible lectures in that year. Lectures director W. B. West, Jr. invited Norvel to come to Los Angeles and speak on the theme, "The Work of the Church."

It is difficult to imagine anyone who could have spoken with any more authority on the subject than M. Norvel Young, who was the initiator and encourager, and a sort of energy source, for a whole constellation of good works.

One of those good works would begin as a personal service to individual Christians in Lubbock. As teachers and other members needed Bibles, reference books, commentaries and other printed materials, Norvel agreed to order the items for them from Nashville. Soon he and two dear friends decided to blend their diverse individual talents into a business that would serve the churches. Jim Bill McInteer and Winston Moore joined Norvel in forming 20th Century Christian Bookstore and Publishing. It was an extension and expansion of the magazine publishing that had continued for a dozen years or so at that point. In addition to carrying a large variety of printed Bible School and other Christian materials, 20th Century Christian later began publishing religious books. McInteer and Moore carried much of the burden because the company was headquartered in Nashville, while Norvel was in Texas (and later California). One of the remarkable things about the three men, witnessed by friends and business associates through the years, was their willingness to set aside their personal opinions or agendas for the benefit of their relationship with each other and for the success of their service to the churches. They also formed 20th Century Christian Foundation to support the company and other good works. As with the magazine, the company and the foundation changed their names to 21st Century Christian as the millennium approached.

Another of Norvel's good works would get off the ground in 1952, when he and his great friend, Batsell Barrett Baxter, would together publish a special reference work. Called *Preachers of Today: A Book of Brief Biographical Sketches And Pictures of Living Gospel Preachers*, the book would be updated and reprinted between 1952 and 1982, for a total of five volumes. The first volume contained 1,360 biographical sketches of ministers from Churches of Christ, with nearly as many photographs to accompany the bios. It was published by the Christian Press of

Nashville. Interestingly, they did not dedicate the book to their mentors or favorite preachers. Instead, Baxter and Young dedicated the book on preachers to some very special people. The dedication read:

TO OUR MOTHERS
Fay Scott Baxter
and
Ruby Morrow Young
And to the Hundreds of Other Godly
Mothers Who Have Helped These Men
Stand Up to Preach

The two friends concluded their Preface to *Preachers of Today* with these words: "We pray that the kingdom may continue to grow and that tens of thousands of young men will decide to dedicate their lives to the preaching of the pure gospel of Christ. May these sketches inspire them to give themselves to the Cause. 'The harvest indeed is plenteous, but the laborers are few.'" And it was signed "The Editors."

In addition to those five volumes of *Preachers of Today*, Baxter and Young collaborated on another reference work, called *Churches of Today: A Book of Brief Sketches and Pictures of Twentieth Century Churches of Christ*. Two volumes were produced, in 1960 and in 1968. It was published by the Gospel Advocate Company of Nashville. The dedication for *Churches of Today* was a little more predictable:

TO TWO GREAT CHURCHES OF TODAY
WITH WHOM THE EDITORS HAVE LABORED
FOR MORE THAN A DECADE
BROADWAY CHURCH OF CHRIST
LUBBOCK, TEXAS
AND
HILLSBORO CHURCH OF CHRIST
NASHVILLE, TENNESSEE

At the conclusion of their preface to the 1960 *Churches of Today*, Baxter and Young wrote: "We also pray for the unity of all those who believe in Jesus Christ and who are seeking resolutely to obey His will. As the Kingdom spreads, we need to remember the motto of the Restoration Movement, "In matters of faith, unity; in matters of opinion, liberty; in all things, charity."

In the midst of all the wonderful ministry, the Young family was also blossoming – four children in a little more than eight Lubbock years. And Norvel and Helen's wonderful projects were also multiplying. With *20th Century Christian* magazine already a success and the Broadway Church quickly becoming the leader among Churches of Christ in the nation, they turned their attention toward other exciting opportunities: the rebuilding of postwar Germany, another Christian publication, a Christian children's home, a new Christian college, and more.

7

BUILDERS
WITH A VISION

He was the catalyst.
He was the symphonic conductor who
did not play an instrument and who could not be heard,
but without whom the music was impossible.

*E*ven in his early teen years, Norvel Young was a serious
and spiritual person. He wanted to express his faith
and share the good news about Jesus with others. He
knew the world would be a better place if there were more
committed Christians. So he wanted to preach. And, of course,
he served as an outstanding full-time minister for 13 years in
Lubbock, Texas, clearly demonstrating that he had the ability to
excel as a proclaimer of the gospel.

However, Norvel had other interests in addition to preaching.
He didn't really have aspirations of being a "great preacher,"
though he is sure to be remembered as one of the key leaders
and ministers of the Churches of Christ in his generation and
beyond. As he moved into his college years, he experienced a
desire to become involved in education, as well as ministry – or
education *as ministry* – that is, *Christian* education. So he moved
between the two career paths. Or were there only two? Were
there other careers, other missions, other ways to spend himself
in service? Though the career path was not set in stone, the gen-

eral direction was – Norvel Young would labor for the "great cause of Christ," no matter which careers he might follow.

He first thought of himself as a preacher, then as an educator, but finally settled on a third concept that captured his imagination. He began to conceive of himself as a builder and a promoter – a person who made things happen. It certainly seemed that God had given him that ability. He was always dreaming great dreams. But he differed markedly from the ordinary daydreamer, because he had the will and the ingenuity and the leadership skills to make his dreams come true.

That is why, even while serving the Broadway Church as its minister, he invariably was making new and exciting things happen. Interestingly, he was not always, or even usually, the one who led the effort or did the work in the trenches. And when the "exciting things" finally "happened," there were always plenty of people around to take the credit – and rightfully so. But any honest person involved in those projects would have to admit that, without Norvel Young, the exciting thing would not have happened. He was the catalyst. He was the symphonic conductor who did not play an instrument and who could not be heard, but without whom the music was impossible. He was the dreamer who made wonderful things happen.

GERMANY FOR CHRIST

One of those projects that Norvel promoted was the rebuilding and evangelization of Germany. From the time he was 21 and traveling across Europe, he had loved Germany. He remembered Heidelberg as the beautiful place where he and James Baird decided that they wanted to travel all the way around the world. The thought of the cities in ruin and the people in dire need hurt him.

Otis Gatewood was perhaps the key person in Germany after the war. Earlier, he had been supported solely by the Broadway Church in Lubbock to preach in Salt Lake City. At that time, Norvel recognized that Gatewood had a wonderful talent for selling a cause. But he knew, too, that Otis would have a tremendous problem pulling things together, organizing a great effort and making it happen.

Not long after the war, Norvel and Otis had promoted a meeting of church leaders from around the United States to discuss the opportunities of serving and preaching in postwar Germany. With his expansive vision, Norvel could see that the doors of opportunity in Germany were wide open for the next few years, but would eventually close. When the day of the meeting arrived, the Broadway Church building was filled with representatives from various congregations interested in the opportunity. And Otis Gatewood was there to promote his vision. It was the beginning of a new life for him. He would not only promote the great work, but he would also spend many of his years organizing European evangelism and Christian education — "making them happen."

Permission to work and serve in Germany was granted to the Churches of Christ by U.S. Army General Lucius Clay. The time was right. Though many Christians had suffered the loss of loved ones in the terrible war, they were ready to replace the killing with love. Paul Sherrod, for example, who was one of the Broadway Church elders, lost a son in the Philippines. The young man's body was brought back to Lubbock and Norvel was there to bury him. Even with that recent memory before him, Sharrod's life was transformed by the compassionate vision of taking the good news of Christ – and life-sustaining food – to America's former enemy.

While Norvel Young edited and sent his newsletter, *Germany for Christ*, to thousands of people, Gatewood hit the road to tell congregations about the needs and the opportunities in Germany. He also recruited individuals to personally go to Germany and help in the work. Among those individuals who were convinced were J. C. and Dorothy Moore of Nashville. Later Helen would say, "J. C. and Dot had not intended to go to Germany. But Otis was very persuasive. And eventually they were glad he was."

J.C. Moore was an astute businessman, and a few years later, he would join Norvel Young at Pepperdine College in Los Angeles, there becoming the business manager for the school. And the two men would one day return to a place in Germany that they both had come to dearly love, Heidelberg, and establish Pepperdine's first international study-abroad campus.

A VISIONARY JOURNEY

One of Norvel Young's closest friends through the years was Batsell Barrett Baxter. They attended college together, worked together during the summers, taught together at Pepperdine in the early days, and even studied for their doctorates at the same time.

They were very supportive of one another, and there was never a feeling of competition between them. For one thing, "Batsell was destined to be a preacher," said Norvel. Though the best of friends, Norvel and Baxter had very different personalities. Actually, Norvel had more similarities with his dear friend, Ira North, who was also a dynamic motivator. However, one difference between Norvel and Ira was that Ira's accomplishments were mostly in the Nashville area or in Tennessee, whereas Norvel Young's accomplishments were more varied and even international.

So although they shared several characteristics, Batsell Barrett Baxter and Norvel were essentially two dissimilar men whose *complementary* natures were in part the reason for their long, close friendship. Norvel, always the adventurer, had unsuccessfully tried to convince Batsell Barrett to accompany him and James Baird on their around-the-world trek of 1937. Now, a dozen years later, as Norvel and Helen prepared to go to Europe, Norvel again tried to persuade Batsell Barrett to join them.

Batsell Barrett and his wife, Wanda, had been married for about 10 years, and during that time they had not been blessed with children. In the summer of '49, they were trying to adopt a child and thought they should stay home. But the Youngs begged them to join the upcoming trip to Europe before the child came and obligated them to curtail any travel. Not only did the Baxters finally go along on the trip, but they also remained with the tour for the entire three months. And Wanda gave birth to a baby boy the following spring.

It had been 12 years since Norvel had seen Europe, during which time the continent had been ravaged by war. So he was anxious to see the changes that had taken place. He was also excited to share his warm impressions and experiences of Europe with those he loved. But the primary reason for the trip was to preach in evangelistic meetings, to establish churches, and above all, to deliver food and clothing to war-ravished people in Frankfurt, Germany.

The Youngs deposited their two children, Emily, age 4, and Matt, age 18 months, in Arkansas with Helen's brother, Billy Mattox, and his wife, Mildred. Their party of six people flew to New York, then set out for Europe. In addition to Helen and Norvel Young and Batsell Barrett and Wanda Baxter, there was Ruby Young, Norvel's mother, and Mrs. A. M. Burton of Nashville.

First stop was a few days in England. On June 22, 1949, a tired but elated Helen Young wrote to her father-in-law, Matt Young, in Nashville:

> Dearest Dad,
>
> I wish you could be with us tonight. We do miss you in all of these travels, but I'm afraid you would tire of seeing so many castles and cathedrals. Mommie [his wife, Ruby, who had accompanied the Youngs and the Baxters] said yesterday she has two sons with overly developed curiosities. Norvel wants to see every stone in every castle in England, but the rest of us are quite as interested so we get along wonderfully. Really it has been so far a perfect trip, or as the English say, "holiday." Mommie seems to be feeling fine, but a little tired just now. We will be in Paris next

week and she can have four days to see, shop and relax. It is driving some distance every day and changing hotels every night that tires her and Sister Burton. But really they are wonderful travelers and are having the time of their lives.

Tonight Wanda, Batsell Barrett and Norvel and I rented a boat and rowed up the Cam River here in Cambridge to view the beautiful college buildings on its banks. It was thrilling. In the morning we go to Harwich to board the boat for Holland at 9:30 a.m. Here I am almost through with my paper and I want to tell you how thrilled I am with this wonderful ballpoint pen. It is grand. I've written much every day and it is giving excellent service. Thank you so much.

Give Matt Norvel and Emily a big hug for us when you see them. We miss them so but are happy in the knowledge that they are well cared for.

We love you, Dad, so much and realize that you have in large measure made this trip possible by helping us in so many ways through the years. God bless and keep you.

> Devotedly,
> Your loving daughter
> (signed) Helen

From the British Isles, they traveled on to the Continent. When they arrived in Germany, the older women (both in their sixties at the time) worked hard with the missionaries during the day and also did some sight-seeing. They would then go to bed about nine o'clock, after which the two young couples would go out and do more sightseeing.

However, it was not simply a vacation. The days were busy and tiring, filled with long sessions of preaching, lecturing and serving people. Norvel and Batsell lectured at the university, and classes and lectures were attended by prominent as well as ordinary people. "Those were very hard times in Germany," Helen remembered. "There was still much suffering, and even mayors were going hungry."

When the Youngs, the Baxters, Mrs. Young and Mrs. Burton arrived in Frankfurt, Otis Gatewood and J. C. Moore, who were already working in the city, met them. They had leased a large, stately, brick mansion, and the place had been filled with food and clothing from America. Hundreds of Germans would come to the house every day in order to have supplies for survival. The visitors were also met by a cadre of American missionaries who had congregated in Germany in the midst of the need, all of them diligently working together. The group included Roy Palmer and his wife, as well as other missionary couples, along with single women like Irene Johnson and Kathrine Patton. Daily they would distribute food, then go out and conduct Bible studies and try to establish churches.

The group took time for some sightseeing, traveling by automobile throughout Europe. Then, after a trip through Italy, they went to Egypt and the new nation of Israel.

Many years later, Helen recalled the three-month European mission and Mediterranean tour in 1949:

> We had a wonderful experience. Mrs. Burton had a daughter-in-law who was there. She had been influenced by Otis Gatewood to go to Germany and serve as a missionary nurse. In the process of moving to Europe, she had taken with her a Chrysler automobile – one of those big, long ones that we don't have anymore. And so we had the use of that car, with a German driver, who was a devout Christian. When the work was finished, the six of us piled into the Chrysler and drove all over Europe. We drove on down to Italy, and from there we took a ship to Greece, Egypt and Israel. We returned by way of the British Isles.

A NEW HOME FOR BROADWAY

In many ways, the trip was the climax of the nearly four years (from 1945 to 1949) of hard work promoting the German relief and evangelism effort. But when Helen and Norvel arrived back in Lubbock, it was not to relax and recount their successes. It was fall 1949, and the Broadway Church was entering its massive building program. Norvel had been advised not to try to build a building at Lubbock. One older minister from Abilene had told him, "Whatever you do, don't try to build a bigger building. The Broadway Church has all it needs; it is one of the wonderful buildings in West Texas. You'll make a serious mistake if you do." And there were a significant number of others who felt the same way. But Norvel thought differently. He could not endure the status quo.

The project went forward, and the Broadway Church proved itself to be ahead of its time. On Sunday, October 15, 1950, the church opened its new $600,000 building. That price tag was significant for that time; remember, an automobile could be purchased for a couple of thousand dollars then. The structure included a 2,200-seat auditorium, Sunday School facilities for 2,000, a chapel with 300 seats and a well-equipped nursery. That Sunday there was an overflow crowd of 2,600 to hear the first sermon preached in the new building. Dr. M. Norvel Young's message was titled, "We Dedicate Ourselves," and he described the building as an "instrument to help us in our worship" rather than "a monument to be worshiped." It was a memorable day for all Texas Churches of Christ.

The newness of the beautiful building had hardly worn off when, two years later, the church had an evangelistic meeting with Norvel's dear friend, Batsell Barrett Baxter, as the speaker. Baxter recalled the great event in his autobiography, *Every Life a Plan of God*:

> One of the most inspiring meetings I ever had a
> part in was the one conducted for the Broadway

church in Lubbock, Texas, in 1952. Norvel Young was the preacher and Alan Bryan, the educational director, was in charge of publicizing the meeting. Both had done their work exceedingly well, as had the congregation in general. The meetings were in the relatively new Broadway building which seated 2,200. On the second Sunday morning the service began at 10:30 and continued until 1:30. The reason for the length was that sixty-two people responded to the invitation, with thirty-eight of them being baptized at that morning service. It was remarkable the way the brethren were able to get clothing from other congregations in the area and that the baptisms were able to proceed without delay, one after another. So thrilled were all of us with the response on that Sunday morning, that we decided to extend the meeting two more nights. The attendance was excellent on the two remaining nights and the total responses for the week were sixty-eight baptized with sixty restored, for a total of 128 responses.

The effort was so successful at the Broadway Church that area churches decided to have a joint meeting four years later, once more using Batsell Barrett Baxter as the speaker. Again in his autobiography, Baxter recalled:

Three times during these years I have had the opportunity to hold a city-wide or area-wide meeting. First, in 1956, there was the Lubbock, Texas, Bible Forum, held in the city auditorium which seats about 3,500 people. Norvel Young was minister of the Broadway church at the time and took the lead in planning this city-wide effort. The congregations in Lubbock and surrounding areas supported the meeting enthusiastically so that it was well-attended, with overflow audiences at most of the services. The meeting began on a Sunday evening and closed the following Sunday evening with fifty-two being baptized and fifty-two being restored for a total of 104 responses.

The flourishing Broadway Church, the exciting architecture of its new building and the tremendously successful evangelistic campaigns in Lubbock seemed to burst on the scene in the first half of the decade of the '50s. But visions of those things had been brewing in the mind of Norvel Young years before that. It is fascinating to recall that Norvel had introduced a special feature among Churches of Christ about three and a half years *before* that triumphal Sunday in 1950 when he preached the first sermon in the new Broadway Church building. At the 1947 Abilene Christian College Lectureship, he taught a session on the purpose and design of church buildings, an unusual topic for his fellowship at that time.

In the session he stressed that low price should not be the major criterion for the location of the building. Rather, the building should be situated for the highest visibility. In addition, buildings should be designed with growth in mind, he said, and be expandable. He believed that the exterior should look like a church rather than like a bank or some other kind of building. (Some Churches of Christ at the time avoided anything that might appear too ecclesiastical or too "churchy.") And while there shouldn't be unnecessary or ostentatious ornamentation, a church building certainly should be an example of fine architecture. In 1949-50, Norvel was able to influence the building program at the Broadway Church and implement the vision he had called for earlier at Abilene.

Part of his vision for a growing church was the relatively new emphasis on the church's Bible education program. Robert Hooper, in his book *A Distinct People*, wrote: "The Broadway church in Lubbock provided leadership in developing educational programs for the local church. For many years, Norvel

Young had been encouraging churches to do more in Bible school work. Broadway led among churches of Christ in placing its Bible school program under a specialized director, Alan Bryan." Norvel also tried to generate interest in another innovation. Hooper recorded:

> The most active proponents of the new vacation Bible school movement among churches of Christ were Norvel Young, Alan Bryan, and Ira North. As early as 1951, Young encouraged churches to consider a special school during the summer months for the teaching of the Bible. Having just completed such a session at Broadway, Young urged: "May I appeal to the elders and teachers of churches who are missing this opportunity to teach the Bible to plan for at least one week, if not two, of vacation Bible school training this year!"

When the Youngs accepted the ministry work at the Broadway Church in 1944, they had privately agreed together that they would stay two or three years and then move on to the next phase of their life's work, whatever that might be. But the war ended and the challenge of postwar Germany presented itself. In fact, while many people live their lives never seeing a single opportunity, somehow the Youngs had the vision to see opportunity after opportunity. Even as they were heavily engaged in building the membership of the church and promoting the work in Germany, they were moving on another important front.

ENCOURAGERS OF CHRISTIAN EDUCATION

Norvel Young adopted a dream that the Broadway Church had been considering for perhaps a decade or so: the idea of developing a campus ministry at the large Texas Technological University campus in Lubbock. They agreed that Christian students and non-Christian students alike needed a place to seek God, a place where they could study the Bible, take religion courses for college credit, and have wholesome fellowship with other students.

At that time, Bible Chairs or campus ministries were quite rare among Churches of Christ. Reflecting back, Norvel thought that the Bible Chair at Texas A & M in College Station preceded the one at Texas Tech in Lubbock. He remembered meeting with R. B. Sweet, who preached in College Station and was the first minister, as far as Norvel knew, who taught Bible for academic credit at a state university through an off-campus ministry program. Later, Sweet would write a series of Bible school lessons and establish a Christian publishing company that still bears his name.

Whether it was the first campus ministry or not, the program at Texas Tech certainly was *one of the first* in the nation. And as such, it was a forerunner and model. Carl Spain was selected to be the first campus minister. The Youngs later commented, "Carl was an outstanding man. We loved working with him." The campus ministry was up and running and Spain would put it on solid footing, staying for four years.

Later, Mont Whitson wrote concerning the Bible Chair:

> The first definite steps in the beginning of the Bible Chair at Texas Tech were in the fall of 1946, at which time the expenditures for such a work were included in the budget of the Broadway Church of Christ. Long before this time, however, Broadway had been thinking seriously of doing something for the Tech students. Back in the 1930s, G. C. Brewer, then minister, had discussed the possibility of a Bible Chair. Interest in this project grew rapidly after M. Norvel Young came to Broadway and began to campaign actively for the establishment of such a work.

Once again, Norvel was the catalyst and the energy behind a good work. Brewer suggested the project. The church talked about it for a decade or so. But it took the enthusiasm, encouragement and leadership of Norvel Young to get the project off dead center. Many people were involved in the success of the Bible Chair: the Broadway Church elders, Carl Spain, Mont Whitson and many others. But without Norvel's indispensable "campaign" it might have remained only an empty dream.

Others who worked with the Youngs during the Broadway years in addition to Mont Whitson and Carl Spain were Alan Bryan, who served as associate minister working especially with the Bible School; Furman Cauther, who also served as associate minister; and Horace Coffman, who directed the visitation program and the congregational singing.

A PLACE FOR HOMELESS CHILDREN

In the early 1950s, another important work was begun. The Youngs were instrumental in beginning the Children's Home of Lubbock. Norvel presented his case for the needy children, pleading with the elders to establish the institution. He convinced them to put $25,000 in the church budget — money that would be raised above and beyond the regular contributions. Norvel said he would do his best to promote the children's home, but if people did not support the idea, he would not complain.

The church members apparently liked the idea of a children's home, because the money was indeed raised. A widow named Ida Collins gave her farm to the church for a place on which to build the home. The idea for requesting the gift came from an elder for a church on the east side of Lubbock, Oscar Paden, the father of Cline and Harold Paden, well-known Bible teachers and missionaries. Though Norvel was uncomfortable with the timing, Oscar Paden talked to Mrs. Collins about making the gift as they were on the way to the cemetery to bury her husband. She agreed, and the Collins farm on the edge of the city, 20 minutes from downtown, turned out to be a perfect location for the children's home. Though the timing of the request may seem to us to be insensitive, it probably was a great blessing for Mrs. Collins to turn her attention toward the living and toward the great good that could come from the gift. It may have been the very best way she could honor her late husband.

Norvel persuaded John White, a trained counselor in the Texas social welfare system, to be the first director of the children's home. Individual houses, each equipped for 14 children plus house parents, were built, and soon the home was in operation. It became the first home among Churches of Christ to handle adoptions. The next year, Norvel was able to convince Inez Baucum to leave Oklahoma and join the home as its first licensed adoption director. The home has been answering the biblical call to "visit the fatherless" for more than four decades.

PAGES OF POWER

In 1955, the Youngs traveled to Nashville for an evangelistic meeting. While there, they participated in a meeting, which including Jim Bill McInteer, Batsell Barrett Baxter and others, in an upper room at the David Lipscomb College library. It was an inspirational gathering in which the group asked themselves, "What can we do to promote devotional living?" From that meeting came the concept for the quarterly devotional guide, *Power for Today*, a publication that has blessed many thousands of lives for more than four decades. Batsell Barrett Baxter suggested the name for the publication.

For the next 20 years, Norvel and Helen Young edited the encouraging little booklet, which has a page for each day – an inspirational message, a scripture reading and a suggested song. In 1975, Steven and Emily Young Lemley became associate editors and soon took over complete responsibility for the publication. They have now edited *Power for Today* for more than 20 years. From the beginning, *Power* was received enthusiastically because of its positive and practical orientation. Today, even without large sums of money for promotion, the devotional guide maintains a circulation of nearly 50,000. The stories of those whose lives have been profoundly changed are legion.

With all his other interests, Norvel was also asked to be on the board of trustees of Abilene Christian College. He accepted and became the first minister to be seated on the board. When the large Bible building was constructed in 1952, Norvel, Reuel Lemmons and John Banister were the major fund-raisers. They spent countless days traveling through Texas together, urging Christians to invest in training ministers for the future. During this same time period, Norvel was asked to be the editor of the influential Christian weekly journal, *Firm Foundation*, published in Texas. Though it was a great honor and a position of considerable influence at that time, being editor just did not fit into Norvel's vision of his future. When he declined, Reuel Lemmons agreed to take the editorial position for which he will always be remembered. Norvel did serve as associate editor for several years.

CREATING A COLLEGE

Another reason Norvel could not seriously consider taking the editorship was that he was overloaded with the many projects in progress beyond his preaching assignments at the Broadway Church. Perhaps the most ambitious project of all was the dream of a Christian college in Lubbock.

With well-established Abilene Christian College less than two hundred miles away, the idea of a Christian college in Lubbock may seem unusual from today's perspective. As it was being considered, people understood that it might pose some competition to Abilene Christian. And garnering support in a region known for its faithful support of ACC would be difficult. But in the late 1950s it appeared that there would be an almost unlimited supply of students. The question was not one of having too many colleges, but of where the nation would find room for all the Baby Boomers. This was a period of rapid growth in community colleges, as more and more schools were being built.

The growth of the city of Lubbock on the Southern Plain of Texas was striking. For years, its population was about 30,000. But in the 1950s it grew to about 150,000. And projections were that the city would reach 300,000 by 1970. There was a dramatic rise in agriculture in the area and the economy was booming.

At the time, Abilene Christian seemed to have more students than they could handle. In addition, Texas Tech, a major state university, was in Lubbock. And it was thought that a cooperative agreement could be reached that would allow students to attend a Christian college and have the resources of a large research university nearby, including transferable courses. The civic leaders endorsed the idea of a Christian college, and donors even beyond the Churches of Christ seemed ready to support the effort.

In 1953, Norvel Young and others had started Lubbock Christian School, beginning with preschool and planning to add a grade each year. It was so successful that they were able to add grades much faster. The board of the school included Dr. J. B. McCorkle, Paul Sherrod, J. C. Rigney, Dr. W. T. Rogers, J. Don Baldridge and O. T. Shipp, Jr. Norvel always refrained from being on the boards, believing it might make it more difficult to get others involved if the project was perceived to be purely a Broadway Church program. The cooperation of all the churches was necessary.

By 1956, the school had added grades much faster than expected and enrollment was much larger than expected. After many congregational meetings, an area-wide meeting was held in January to discuss the possibility of not only a high school, but also a Christian junior college in Lubbock. President Don H. Morris of Abilene Christian College addressed an audience of more than 700 interested people, and his topic was "The Need for a Christian Junior College in the South Plains Area." This was a magnanimous gesture from Norvel's good friend, and Morris' support was very important.

But even before that great meeting, Norvel and Helen began

having regular prayer breakfasts in 1955, laying the matter before God to see if it seemed that He wanted a Christian college in Lubbock. When the college finally became a reality about two years later, they believed it was an answer to those early prayers.

At the encouragement of Norvel, the Board of Trustees of the newly formed college selected Dr. F. W. ("Billy") Mattox, Helen's brother, to be the first president. Dr. Mattox was dean of students at Harding College at the time. Though he enjoyed preaching, Billy had continued his education at Norvel's urging, eventually earning a Ph.D. from Peabody College, Norvel's doctoral alma mater.

Norvel believed the college should be deeply spiritual, but not legalistic, and he thought Billy Mattox could lead the school in that direction. Mattox had been close to people whom Norvel admired as spiritual and positive Christians, such as J. N. Armstrong and K. C. Moser. Some of those older, heroic Christians eventually taught at Lubbock Christian College.

Norvel Young did not have a specific model or paradigm in mind for the proposed college – except that his dream was that it would be better than any Christian institution of learning he might set as a model. With Abilene Christian College so close, Lubbock Christian College naturally would take on some similarities.

When the college was finally opened in 1957, there were many people who deserved credit for the accomplishment. But there was one person without whom the college would not be a reality: M. Norvel Young.

Norvel's impact as a minister of the gospel was profound. He was a preacher in a West Texas town, not a major media market, not a world-class city on a coast facing Europe or Asia … and yet his influence was felt across the nation in Churches of Christ nearly everywhere. Joe R. Barnett would be one of those ministers who would follow Norvel in the pulpit of the great Broadway Church. On Norvel's 80th birthday, Barnett wrote:

My first personal contact with you was in 1956. I was a young preacher in the little church in Anton, Texas. I was scared to death when I called and asked the Broadway secretary for an appointment with you. Within a half hour she called back, said she had talked with you and you were looking forward to meeting with me. You gave me good advice and great encouragement that day.

Through many years I looked to you for counsel, and was not only received warmly, but as an equal. You were probably the major contributor to my development, and I will be forever grateful.

Norvel, I doubt that you'll ever know how many preachers you have inspired to reach for the seemingly unreachable. I'm sure there isn't any person among us who has so positively impacted this fellowship. Your positive spirit and unbending faith continue to inspire.

I loved you the first day I met you, and I still do.

S. F. Morrow family, Norvel's maternal grandparents, front of their home near Clarksville in Montgomery unty, Tennessee, in 1891.

The S. F. Morrow family in Nashville, Tennessee, in 1901. The oldest child, 17-year-old Ruby (Norvel's mother), is in the left center next to her father.

tt and Ruby Young's first home was located at 1905 ington in Nashville, Tennessee.

Norvel's parents, Matt Young and Ruby Morrow, on their wedding day in Nashville, Tennessee, April 25, 1906. Their wedding was performed by T. B. Larimore.

e S. F. Morrow family around 1921. Norvel, with legs ssed, is on the left seated in front of his mother and other. His father is third from the left in the back row.

Norvel as a small child

The Youngs moved into their new residence at 1904 Blakemore in Nashville around 1927. The *20th Century Christian* was begun in this home in 1938.

Matt and Ruby Young and their two sons, Stephen Franklin and Matt Norvel (center)

Norvel at age 6 in 1921

Franklin and Norvel (right) around 1918.

Helen's maternal grandparents, Fount Livingston Young and Mattie Higgins.

Helen's parents, Judge Perry Mattox and Irene Young, on their wedding day in Greenville, Texas, September 21, 1904. Their wedding was performed by her father, F. L. Young.

Irene Mattox and her children around 1926. Back row (l to r) Kathryn, Marguerite, F. W. (Billy), Frank, and Helen. Front row (l to r) Paul and Joe.

Helen (left) on her 3rd birthday with her sister, Kathryn

Helen (right) with her brother Frank around 1924

Helen's mother, Irene Mattox, on her honeymoon in Chicago in 1904.

Norvel, age 13, is third from the right in the front row. This 9th grade photo was taken on April 25. 1929.

Norvel as a young boy

Norvel's High School graduation photo in 1932. He enrolled in David Lipscomb College in September 1932.

Norvel riding his bike on the David Lipscomb College campus.

Norvel as a student at Abilene Christian College in 1935

Norvel on an outing with some David Lipscomb college classmates around 1933. He is third from the right in the second row.

Helen as a young girl

Helen as a High School senior in September 1934

One of Helen's yearbook photos at Classen High School in Oklahoma City

In the spring of 1938, Helen (second from the right in the front row) was a member of Alpha Gamma, the women's honor organization at George Pepperdine College.

Pepperdine student 1938

Helen graduated from George Pepperdine College in the class of 1939.

Norvel and Batsell Barrett Baxter spent the summer of 1935 selling Bibles in Wichita, Kansas. In the photo at right they are seen with Otis Gatewood (seated), their classmate from Abilene Christian College, who was the director of their team of Bible salesmen.

19 year-old Norvel (left) and 18 year-old Batsell Barrett Baxter, with their display kits, selling Bibles in the summer of 1935.

Norvel made an around the world tour with his cousin, James Baird, from June 1937 to January 1938. They bicycled through Scotland and England, witnessed an eruption of Mt. Vesuvius in Italy, prowled through ancient ruins in Greece, and waded in the Jordan River.

Norvel with his parents and brother before departing for his wedding in August 1939.

Norvel and Helen were engaged to be married when this photo was taken on the front porch of Batsell Barrett and Wanda Baxter's home in 1939.

Helen on her wedding day, August 31, 1939.

The newleyweds in Colorado

Norvel and Helen on their honeymoon in Yellowstone National Park

Norvel as a professor at George Pepperdine College in 1938-39

Norvel and his mother around 1939

Norvel and Helen with her parents and Max and Kathryn Silve and Lena Mattox, and Joe Mattox around 1941.

Helen on horseback at a relative's ranch in Granbury, Texas, in the summer of 1942.

Norvel was working on his Ph.D. dissertation when this photo was taken in Nashville in the spring of 1943.

Norvel was just 28 years old when he became the minister for the Broadway Church of Christ in Lubbock in 1944.

Helen in front of their first home in Lubbock in 1944..

Norvel and Helen's first home in Lubbock, Texas, was located at 2217 31st Street.

Helen and Emily in 1945.

A proud new father shows off his first child in 1945.

Helen in the early Lubbock years

The Young family in 1945

Christmas 1947 brought 3 generations together. Matt and Ruby Young (seated) with their new grandson, Matt, and (standing l to r) Judge Mattox, Emily, Norvel, Helen, and Irene Mattox.

The Young family in 1948

The Young family in 1951

Emily and Matt welcomed Marilyn to the family in the summer of 1952.

The Young family was complete with the arrival of Sara in the summer of 1953. This family photo of a Bible study was taken at Christmas 1956.

Reading stories was an evening ritual in the Young home.

The last family home in Lubbock was located at 3210 27th Street.

The year of 1957 proved to be historic when the Youngs left Lubbock and returned to Pepperdine College in Los Angeles.

Gathering around the family piano in the president's home on the Los Angeles campus in 1960

J.P. Sanders was minister of the Hillsboro Church in Nashville when the building was completed in 1931. Norvel preached here often through the years.

The Broadway Church of Christ in Lubbock was meeting in this building at Broadway and Avenue N when the Youngs arrived in 1944.

On June 8, 1949, the Youngs and the Baxters along with Mrs. Ruby Young and Mrs. A. M. Burton boarded a flight to London for a three-month tour of Europe.

In July, 1949, they visited the pyramids in Egypt. Seated on camels are (l to r) Norvel, Helen, Mrs. Young, Mrs. Burton, and Batsell Barrett Baxter. Wanda Baxter is standing on the right.

The Church of Christ in Washington, D. C. invited Norvel to preach in a gospel meeting in May, 1950. Standing next to Norvel (l to r) are ministers Elvis Huffard, Hugo McCord, and C. E. McGaughey.

The monthly *20th Century Christian* began in October 1938. The name was changed to the *21st Century Christian* beginning with the January, 1990 issue. By the 1950s, this magazine had increased its circulation to more than 50,000 subscribers.

Norvel rejoiced in the beginning of the Children's Home of Lubbock in April 1954. He shared the moment with Ida Collins, donor of the property, and John B. White, the first director of the Home.

In January 1955, Norvel (with hat on far right) shared the platform with President Don Morris (at the microphone) and others at the groundbreaking ceremonies for the Bible Building at Abilene Christian College.

Broadway Church of Christ in Lubbock dedicated its new building on October 15, 1950. More than 2,600 heard Norvel Young preach on "We Dedicate Ourselves."

The new Broadway church building included a 2,200 seat auditorium, a chapel with seating for 300, a well-equipped nursery, and Sunday School facilities for 2,000.

Norvel and Helen Young launched the quarterly *Power for Today* magazine in January 1955. Throughout its history this popular devotional guide has maintained an average circulation of around 50,000 copies per issue.

At the 1955 ACC Bible Lectures, Norvel met with (l to r) James Walter Nichols, speaker for the nationally televised "Herald of Truth" program, B. C. Goodpasture, editor of the *Gospel Advocate*, and Reuel Lemmons, editor of the *Firm Foundation*.

The elders of the Broadway Church of Christ designated July 28, 1957, as a special Homecoming Sunday. After a 13-year ministry, Norvel and Helen Young were saying good-bye and moving to California. Hundreds of visitors were in town for the three worship services and the Bible classes in the morning, and large crowds attended a church dinner at Pioneer Park and remained for a special farewell program in the afternoon. *Time* magazine featured this event in its August 5, 1957, issue.

At the age of 41, Dr. M. Norvel Young returned to Los Angeles to become the third president of Pepperdine College.

Donald Miller, Chairman of the Board of Regents, administered the oath of office.

Although he began serving as president of Pepperdine College in the fall of 1957, Norvel's inauguration was delayed until November 21, 1958. On that festive occasion he conferred with the founder of the college, George Pepperdine, who had personally recruited him to take up the leadership of the school.

Helen Young (left) and Helen Pepperdine flanked the new president in the receiving line after the inauguration.

At the strong insistence of Norvel Young, Dr. J. P. Sanders (left) returned to Pepperdine to serve as dean of the College.

Norvel took his place with other Christian college administrators at a conference hosted by David Lipscomb College in February 1958. (l to r) Jack Bates, Athens Clay Pullias, Don Morris, James Cope, Rex Turner Sr., H. A Dixon, Claude Guild, James O. Baird, and M. Norvel Young.

Norvel Young and George Pepperdine

The president meets with his administrative team. (l to r) George Hill, Loyd Frashier, J. C. Moore, Norvel Young, J. P. Sanders, Jennings Davis, and Howard White.

The first family of Pepperdine in 1964. (l to r) Emily, Norvel, Sara, Matt, Marilyn, and Helen.

Norvel and Helen in front of the president's home on the Los Angeles campus in 1964

At graduation ceremonies in 1960, President Young (left) and Dean Sanders (right) posed with platform guests Jamie H. Smith, J. Harold Thomas, Otis Gatewood, and S. H. Hall.

On May 13, 1961, George Pepperdine was honored as "this year's outstanding citizen of Los Angeles" and presented a gold medallion by County Supervisor (and Pepperdine alum) Kenneth Hahn. (l to r) Kenny and Ramona Hahn, George and Helen Pepperdine, Helen and Norvel Young.

Opening night of the Bible Lectures, March 22, 1962. Ira North was keynote lecturer and George Pepperdine (on gurney at right) made his last public appearance before a crowd of more than 10,000.

The Youngs visited with Ira North (left) and Frank Pack at the Bible Lectures.

Nine years into the Young presidency. This family portrait, one of the last before Emily was married, was taken in 1966.

Three generations assembled for Emily's engagement party in 1967. (l to r) Marilyn, Helen, Emily, Sara, and Grandmother Mattox. Emily married Steven Lemley on April 28, 1967.

When Pepperdine College was honored by the Freedoms Foundation at Valley Forge in 1961, President Young was on hand to accept the award.

At the World Congress on Evangelism in West Berlin in 1966, representatives from Churches of Christ included (l to r) Norvel Young, Otis Gatewood and Ed Rockey. In this photo they are standing with one of the featured lecturers from India.

The president's home on the Los Angeles campus.

Going over busy calendars at the president's home in 1966

The Board of Supervisors for the County of Los Angeles welcomed Norvel back to the city in 1958. Supervisor Kenneth Hahn, who was once a student in one of Norvel's history classes at Pepperdine, presented the commendation on November 12, 1958.

Norvel near the close of his presidency. This photo was taken on February 19, 1970.

Steven Lemley (left) and Emily Young were married on April 28, 1967. Norvel performed the ceremony at the Vermont Avenue Church of Christ. This family portrait was taken a short time later.

Norvel meets with Morris Pendleton in the spring of 1968.

Norvel meets with prominent Pepperdine supporters (l to r) George Elkins, Bryant Essick, and Don Darnell at the California Club around 1969.

Norvel meets with (l to r) Walter Knott and Edward Di Loreto

Norvel and Helen stood and sang the alma mater after the Waves defeated Loyola at the Homecoming baskeball game in February 1969.

Norvel and Helen explored the ruins of Persepolis, the pride of ancient Persia, on their visit to Iran in 1977.

Enjoying the culture in Seoul, Korea in August, 1983

Standing on "The Bridge Over the River Kwai" in 1985

Experiencing the joys of shopping in Taipei, Taiwan.

With grandsons (l to r) Chris Young and David Lemley, Norvel and Helen stand in front of the advertising billboard outside the hall where they were both lecturing in St. Petersburg, Russia, in August, 1993.

Helen on tour in Chaing Mai, Thailand, in 1983.

The 20th Century Christian team meets at the ACU Bible Lectures in 1982. (l to r) Mark McInteer, Norvel and Helen, Winston and Martha Moore, and Jim Bill McInteer.

Forty-six years of Pepperdine history were represented at the inauguration of Howard A. White (right) on September 13, 1978. Standing with him are former presidents (l to r) Hugh Tiner, M. Norvel Young, and William S. Banowsky.

April 1985 witnessed a smooth transition at Pepperdine as David Davenport (left) and Charles Runnels succeeded Howard White and Norvel Young in the offices of president and chancellor. After serving 14 years as president and 14 years as chancellor, Norvel served 13 more years as chancellor emeritus.

At a Homecoming Sunday celebration with the Broadway Church of Christ in Lubbock, Texas, in February 1973, the current minister, Joe Barnett (right), welcomed back his three predecessors (l to r) Norvel Young, George Stephenson, and William S. Banowsky.

Two of Norvel's longtime co-workers at Pepperdine, Bill Teague (left) and Charles Runnels, met with him in 1981.

At the Pepperdine Bible Lectures in April 1989, seven former presidents of senior Christian Colleges affiliated with the Churches of Christ assembled for a photo. Seated (l to r) James O. Baird, Clifton Ganus Jr., Howard A. White. Standing (l to r) Willard Collins, John Stevens, J. P. Sanders, and M. Norvel Young.

Norvel Young welcomes the guest speaker, actor Charlton Heston, to a Pepperdine graduation on December 12, 1981.

In the summer of 1984 Pepperdine was one of the sites for the Olympic Games. Norvel Young and Howard White welcomed (l to r) Flora Laney Thornton, Margaret Brock, and Mr. & Mrs. Peter Ueberroth to the campus. Peter Ueberroth was president of the Olympic Organizing Committee.

The guest speaker for the Pepperdine Associates Dinner in 1997 Was Tommy LaSorda, longtime manager of the Los Angeles Dodgers. He was welcomed by Norvel Young.

Norvel Young and Art Linkletter were friends for many years. They served together on the Pepperdine Board of Regents for more than 13 years.

Norvel visits with Roy Rogers and Dale Evans at a dinner in Los Angeles. Norvel was thanking Dale for writing the foreword in Helen's book, *Children Won't Wait*.

Plans for the Malibu campus were unveiled at the historic "Birth of a College" dinner on February 9, 1970. (l to r) Architect William Pereira and Governor Ronald Reagan share the moment with Norvel Young and Bill Banowsky.

Norvel (right) visits with (l to r) U. S. Senator George Murphy, William S. Banowsky, and David Lawrence, editor of *U. S. News & World Report*, at the inauguration of Banowsky as chancellor of the Malibu campus, on May 23, 1970.

Groundbreaking for the Thornton Administrative Center took place in September 1984. Donning hard hats for the occasion were four Pepperdine presidents (l to r) Bill Banowsky, Howard White, Norvel Young, and David Davenport. With them are benefactors Flora Thornton and George Page.

Norvel welcomed Norman and Ellen Cousins to campus in 1984. They were accompanied by their adopted daughter (a survivor of Hiroshima) and grandson, who was a student at Pepperdine.

Norman Vincent Peale, nationally-known minister and editor of *Guideposts* magazine, along with his wife, Ruth, visited with Norvel and Helen at the Brock House in the early 1980s.

Norvel Young and Margaret Brock visited with British author and journalist, Malcolm Muggeridge, and his wife, Kitty, at a Pepperdine Great Issues Dinner in February 1978.

Norvel Young in the early 1960's

Helen Young in the early 1960's

At home in the Malibu Beach House in 1971, and enjoying the models of the Malibu campus sent over by architect, William Pereria.

The Youngs celebrated their Golden Wedding Anniversary on August 31, 1989. Their friends and family honored them with receptions in Nashville, Lubbock and Malibu. Helen wore her wedding gown at each of the three receptions.

President Howard White hosted a celebration at Brock House for the Youngs 40th Wedding Anniversary on August 31, 1979.

When the Chief Justice of the United States Supreme Court, Earl Warren (center in judicial robe), visited Los Angeles in the early 1960s, Pepperdine President Norvel Young was among those who greeted him.

When Hubert Humphrey, the Vice President of the United States, visited the Pepperdine campus on September 25, 1968, President Young presented him with a special award for public service.

Norvel Young joined Los Angeles Mayor Tom Bradley at the centennial celebration for the Union Rescue Mission in downtown Los Angeles in 1991. Dr. Young served on the board of directors for the Union Rescue Mission for more than 10 years, and he was vice-chairman of the board from 1990 to 1998.

Clarence Thomas(center), Associate Justice of the United States Supreme Court, was the featured speaker at the annual Pepperdine School of Law Dinner on February 4, 1995. He was welcomed to Pepperdine by Ron Phillips, Dean of the School of Law, and Norvel Young.

Norvel visits with Republican political leader Jack Kemp on August 6, 1994. The occasion was Kemp's speech for the 25th anniversary dinner for Pepperdine's School of Business and Management.

When Harry Blackmun (left), United States Supreme Court Justice, spoke at Pepperdine's School of Law in January 1980, he was given an oral history of the school by Norvel Young and Charles Runnels.

On behalf of Pepperdine University, William S. Banowsky and M. Norvel Young presented an honorary doctor of laws degree to the Shah of Iran in ceremonies at the Golestan Palace in Teheran in 1977.

On a return visit to Teheran in 1978, the Youngs were the honored guests at an academic reception hosted by the wife of the Shah of Iran (right).

Norvel greets the King of Thailand on a visit to Bangkok in 1980.

On a visit to Beijing, China, Dr. Young was introduced to many high-ranking officials in the communist government.

Norvel enjoyed visiting with Yitzhak Shamir, the Prime Minister of Israel.

Dr. Young presented a Diploma of Honor to Prime Minister Dsai of India in ceremonies in New Delhi, India, in 1983.

A Pepperdine delegation led by Norvel Young, William Banowsky and Richard Seaver visited with Jimmy Carter in the Oval Office in 1977.

Richard Nixon, former President of the United States, enjoys a conversation with Norvel Young and Howard White outside the Brock House in 1981.

Norvel Young talks with Gerald Ford, former President of the United States, during a Pepperdine reception in Palm Springs, California. At the time, the two men were serving together on the Pepperdine Board of Regents.

Norvel and Helen with Margaret Thatcher, former Prime Minister of Great Britain, and Ronald and Nancy Reagan, at the former President's 80th birthday celebration on February 6, 1991. The photo was made in the Oval Office replica at the Reagan Library.

When Norvel Young visited Ronald Reagan at his Century City office in 1990, he presented the former American President with a copy of a pictorial history of Pepperdine University.

First Lady Barbara Bush was commencement speaker at Pepperdine on April 16, 1992. Prior to her address, she swapped stories with Helen and Norvel Young about living in West Texas. The Bushes lived in Midland while the Youngs were living in Lubbock.

The Youngs have always cherished their friendship with George and Reva Graziadio. They first became acquainted in the 1960s. In 1997, George and Reva became the benefactors of Pepperdine's Graziadio School of Business and Management.

George and Andrea Eltinge congratulate the Youngs on having a Chair of Family Life at Pepperdine's Graduate School of Education and Psychology named in their honor. The announcement was made on November 7, 1991.

Norvel helped Blanche Seaver celebrate her 99th birthday on September 16, 1990.

Dr. Jim Wilburn (left), Dean of the Business School, and Dr. M. Norvel Young, Chancellor Emeritus, share a moment with former Ambassador Leonard Firestone, donor of Firestone Fieldhouse, and Blanche Seaver, benefactor of Seaver College.

Norvel Young and Richard Scaife became friends in the early 1960's. In the photo above they enjoy an ocean view from the "Richard M. Scaife Bridge and Terrace" on the Seaver College campus.

Norvel Young always referred to George Evans (left) as "the unsung hero of the Malibu miracle" for his role in helping Pepperdine obtain the original gift of 138 acres in Malibu. In this 1997 photo, Norvel presents Evans with a token of appreciation for his generous spirit.

When the Union Rescue Mission in Los Angeles moved into new facilities in 1991, Norvel rode in the parade that was arranged to publicize the event.

The Young family assembled on Pepperdine's front lawn for a group portrait during Christmas 1996.

In the aftermath of the Ethiopian famine in 1985, Norvel accompanied a World Vision team who went over to help. In this photo, Norvel is seen working at the Ibnet Feeding Station.

During basketball season, Norvel often sat in the student section in Firestone Fieldhouse to cheer on the Pepperdine Waves.

When Pepperdine's Volunteer Center advertised a "Step Forward" day, Norvel answered the call and collected litter in Malibu.

More than 1500 attended the memorial service for Norvel in Firestone Fieldhouse on Friday, February 20, 1998.

President David Davenport welcomed everyone to the fieldhouse and then gave an eloquent tribute to his predecessor and friend.

All four of Norvel's children (l to r) Marilyn, Emily, Matt, and Sara, shared memories of the man they called "daddy."

George Graziadio spoke movingly of his love and admiration for Norvel.

Norvel's grave marker at Forest Lawn reminds visitors that "The Future is as Bright as the Promises of God."

In May 1998, Helen (second from left) accompanied three other former presidents of AWP on a "Literary and Hymn Pilgrimage to England and Scotland." (l to r) Patty Atkisson, Helen Young, Anna Pearl Adrian Miller, and Joan Biggers, are standing in front of London's famous Tower Bridge.

Helen's daughters (l to r), Sara, Marilyn, and Emily, hosted an 80th birthday celebration for their mother at her Malibu residence on August 31, 1998.

Helen enjoyed her visit to Stratford-Upon-Avon.

Christmas 1998 was Helen's first one without Norvel in 60 years.

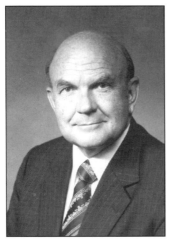

M.Norvel Young

Helen M.Young

Helen and Norvel posed for an offical "50th anniversary portrait" in August 1989.

The Youngs returned to Broadway Church in Lubbock for a Golden Wedding Anniversary reception in 1989.

The Youngs were close friends with Oly and Allie Tegner for many years. They congratulated the Tegners when GSEP named a chair in his honor.

The Youngs were traveling partners for nearly 60 years.

ANSWERING A
NEW CALL

*The daughters vividly recalled
the trauma of leaving Lubbock. "Everyone
was crying. And we cried for days as
we headed for California."*

It was early in 1957. M. Norvel Young was 41 years old and perhaps the most influential man in his particular religious movement. Beside him was Helen Mattox Young, fast becoming one of the most respected women among Churches of Christ in America. Together, they had led in the building of the largest congregation among Churches of Christ in the world. Norvel had initiated and led an effort that successfully raised half a million dollars for postwar relief in Germany. And he had been the key to establishing a new Christian children's home. They had been the driving force behind the founding of a new Christian college. And they had created two important Christian publications. The Youngs stood at the pinnacle of a mountain of accomplishments and could have retired at a relatively young age, confident of their place in the history of their religious movement.

But age 41 can often be a time to reflect, to take stock of where one has been and look forward to where one is going. For many, it is a time when they experience a "mid-life crisis" and some serious soul-searching.

Norvel Young never really thought of amassing a fortune or running for office or building a giant corporation. He had for a number of years thought of himself as a person who planted things. His mother loved to plant and grow flowers and green things of various kinds. He himself especially like to plant trees, probably because of their potential for strength and permanence.

Most of all, Norvel Young set his heart on being a planter of ideas and a grower of institutions. He wanted to be a builder of people and good works, all within a Christian context. That was who he was, and he could not retire from who he was. He was on the brink of the second half of his life. So at age 41 he, along with Helen, was ready for a new field in which to do some planting. What and where that field would be, they did not know. In the meantime, they had plenty of work to do in Lubbock, Texas.

CALIFORNIA ON THE LINE

The telephone call came out of the blue. It was January 1957, a time when long distance calls were still uncommon enough to send a ripple of excitement through the household. The man on the other end of the long distance line was from Los Angeles, California. And though he was very familiar to Norvel, he could not be called a close friend at that point in time. It was the voice of George Pepperdine.

Mr. Pepperdine got straight to the point. The college he had founded 20 years earlier was floundering. First of all, the school was in financial trouble. Mr. Pepperdine had established an endowment for the college, but that was being depleted. As his own financial condition had soured, he was no longer able to support the day-to-day operations of the school. The administrators had used endowment money to make ends meet, but obviously that was a dead-end strategy.

And there was more. Mr. Pepperdine told Norvel that he also was worried about the spiritual direction of the school. He feared that, if the present course were continued, the school would lose its Christian foundation or identity and become one more secular college. That is, if it survived its financial woes. Of course, there was honest disagreement on that dismal assessment. The president, dean and a number of faculty believed that the school was on the right course. Their vision was different from the founder's, and it was their opinion that Mr. Pepperdine would ruin the school academically if he and the Board of Trustees made the wrong choices.

George Pepperdine concluded his conversion with Norvel by saying that the board had agreed that Dr. Young was the only person they knew who could save the school.

Norvel listened carefully. But after considering the offer – or rather, the urgent plea – he declined. It was true that he was itching for a new field to plant. In fact, his first thought when Mr. Pepperdine put the situation before him was, "Lord, I've been preparing for this all my life." He was obviously right: he had spoken to the faculty of Pepperdine in its first year, taught in its second year, earned a Ph.D. in education, and spent more than ten years learning how to promote a good cause. He was ready.

He later said, "At one time, I would have jumped at the chance. But after two or three years of planning, I had just pulled everything together and launched Lubbock Christian College a year earlier. I had promised the founding president (who was also my brother-in-law), Billy Mattox, that I would be there to help get the school on its feet." In addition, Lubbock Children's Home was still a fledgling institution; it needed to be strengthened. And there was other unfinished business at the Broadway Church. He had to say "no" to the opportunity.

However, Norvel promised a surprised George Pepperdine that he would help him and the board find a new president for the college. Mr. Pepperdine was disappointed, but he was far from defeated. It was time to rally the troops.

Norvel soon received a call from Donald V. Miller, chairman of the college's board. Don was a dear friend who had been the business manager for *Twentieth Century Christian* magazine from the beginning. He added his own significant urgings to those of Mr. Pepperdine. In rapid succession, Bob Jones and other board members contacted Norvel. All had the same message: "We do not simply need a new president. We need M. Norvel Young."

The calls seemed constant. The Pepperdine people would not take "no" for an answer. Key college alumni – including Olaf Tegner, who would later become founding dean of Pepperdine's School of Education and one of Norvel's dearest friends – also began calling to encourage a positive response from Norvel.

In February, Mr. and Mrs. George Pepperdine and Mr. and Mrs. Don Miller decided to attend the ACC Bible lectureship. It was something they had done before, but this year they had an ulterior motive. They were really there to hunt down Norvel Young and once again plead their case. They truly believed that he was the only one who could combine exciting promotional and fund-raising skills with solid business sense – and anoint it all with a mature, positive spirituality.

The Pepperdines and Millers corralled the Youngs at an Abilene coffee shop for breakfast. And they put it to Norvel bluntly: "We need you. If you don't come, we will lose the school." Mr. Pepperdine also met with Reuel Lemmons at the Bible lectureship and secured his help in recruiting both Norvel and J. P. Sanders. By this time, as Norvel weakened in his resistance, he was saying that he would not and could not do the job alone; it would take both him and J. P. Sanders to succeed. Lemmons would later fly with Norvel to Nashville to continue talks with Sanders about the Pepperdine challenge.

Encouragement in the other direction for Norvel came, of course, from people in Texas. They believed that Pepperdine College had moved far beyond its affiliation with Churches of Christ and no longer had the support of church members in California or across the nation. Norvel would make a huge mistake in aligning himself with that "worldly college," they said.

An important consideration for Norvel was the way in which he would be perceived by his church brotherhood. In Texas, he was widely viewed as a progressive, always on the cutting edge of ministry, always ready to promote a new program that promised good. In fact, there were some extremely conservative church journals that seemed to delight in exposing Norvel Young as a "liberal." If he accepted the position at Pepperdine, he might still be identified as a liberal by some because of his affiliation with a college that was, in their view, teetering on the brink of secularism. And, on top of that, it was located in California, a place known for its corrupting influence on faith! However, *at Pepperdine* Norvel would be viewed as the old conservative, trying to corral the maverick school that had dashed off into the academic and spiritual wilds. The latter would be a new and somewhat awkward role for the optimistic and dynamic Dr. Young. To be cast in the role of "reactionary" by his foes at the college would be a bitter pill to swallow.

THE WATERSHED DECISION

Obviously, Norvel and Helen decided they needed to accept the challenge, a decision Norvel later admitted was "reckless." Why did they leave a thriving ministry that promised even more good works, in favor of a headache in California? For several reasons, perhaps the greatest of which was that *it was indeed* a challenge. "They appealed to our consciences and sense of mission," said Norvel. Reflecting back, he added, "We also felt we were moving into a bigger arena, and whether we succeeded or failed, we would be glad we tried."

Certainly, Los Angeles, California, was a "bigger arena" than Lubbock, Texas. But just how big their own personal arena would become, the Youngs probably never dreamed.

Many years later, in 1981, Norvel remarked, "In 1957 it was a professional challenge for me to return as president to the college of my teaching roots. President Robert Hutchins of the University of Chicago once commented that to secure a college president you must find one capable of handling the position but foolish enough to accept it. I certainly had the second qualification. The challenge was before me. George Pepperdine met serious financial reverses and was no longer able to make any gifts to balance the budget."

When their decision to leave was finally announced, Norvel helped in the selection of the minister who would replace him. George Stevenson was a good preacher and he was proposed as one who would carry on Norvel's positive direction in the pulpit. Stevenson was eventually called to the Broadway Church, and his five-year ministry continued the advancement of that great congregation. When Stevenson finally accepted another work, Norvel's former pulpit was filled by a young, dynamic preacher by the name of William S. Banowsky – whose name would prominently reappear before too many years in M. Norvel Young's future.

Daughter Emily was 12 when the Youngs left Lubbock. She described the Lubbock years as "so happy." She added, "Mother was always doing things for others. And Daddy even had time to play the piano. I remember that he would play a march, and the kids would march all around the house. We had time for family picnics and always had six birthday parties a year."

Another fond memory that Emily recalled was the opportunity to travel with her father as he preached in small towns around West Texas. She felt very grown up to get to go with him. She recalled the way the people in those churches were so excited to have her daddy come and be with them. In particular, she remembered one part of the services. "Whenever Daddy would offer the invitation at the end of the service," Emily said, "he would walk down the middle of the aisle with his arms extended wide and his hands wide open. He would invite the people to come to Jesus. I still remember his welcoming hands and how he extended them as he reached out to others." They were beautiful memories.

The Youngs did a lot of entertaining in conjunction with their church work, and Emily would slip into the living room to listen in on the conversation of the adults. They would always be discussing church-related subjects and issues, and Emily loved to drink it all in. Her deep spiritual interests continued into her adult years, and she became a popular speaker on religious programs.

Inviting people into their home was just a part of life for the Youngs. "Mother and Daddy's attitude," she said, "was 'Whatever is ours, belongs to the Lord.'" They really would never lose that attitude.

Emily especially remembered and loved the last house in which they lived in Lubbock. The Youngs lived in four or five different houses, all owned by the Broadway Church of Christ. As the family grew, the church would buy increasingly larger houses for them. The last and "favorite" house was located on 27th Street. The outside was covered with what local people called "Austin Stone," a whitish stone surface. The house had four bedrooms, which seemed very large to the children, since they were used to smaller houses. The home also boasted a guest cottage in the back, used for visiting preachers or relatives. Norvel always saw that Helen had some household help and at times a full-time helper lived in the guest house.

Daughter Marilyn, who was only five years old when the Youngs left Lubbock, remembered the house despite her young age. She and her younger sister roomed together. She also remembered the tornado warnings when she would have to take cover in the closet, since the house had no basement.

Norvel wrote a regular column called "What Does The Bible Say?" for the Lubbock newspaper. His last column was titled, "A Farewell Message." He began his farewell, "This column concludes our messages to you through this medium. We want to express to every reader our sincere gratitude for your studying the Bible with us. Thank you for all your letters and your personal comments."

Near the end of the message, he wrote, "Someday we hope that we shall all meet in that wonderful city of light where God wipes away all tears. There will be no death there, no parting, no sadness. We would like to receive a letter or card from those of you who have found this column helpful. You can write to us c/o Pepperdine College, 1121 W. 79th, Los Angeles, California... May God bless each one who reads these lines and guide us all into doing His will in our lives."

The Youngs were the front-page feature of the "Broadway Bulletin" church newsletter dated July 25, 1957. A note at the top left of the publication stated, "This edition of the Broadway Bulletin is dedicated to M. Norvel and Helen M. Young who have faithfully served with this congregation for the past 13 years." The headline announced, "Plans Complete For Homecoming Sunday: Farewell Program 3 o'Clock." Harvie M. Pruitt, educational minister for the church, wrote the feature article, which recapped the ministry of the Youngs in a succinct but somewhat restrained way:

> M. Norvel Young, minister of this congregation for the past 13 years, preaches his last sermons Sunday before moving to Los Angeles to assume duties as president of Pepperdine College.
>
> The elders have designated Sunday as Homecoming. Hundreds of visitors are expected at the three worship services and in Bible classes Sunday morning. Dinner on the grounds will be served at Pioneer Park, 7th Street and Avenue T at noon Sunday and a special farewell program for the Youngs will be held in the church auditorium Sunday afternoon.
>
> During the time Brother Young has been with this congregation, the Lord's cause at Broadway has grown tremendously. There have been approximately 4,000 responses to the invitation since 1944: 1,094 baptisms, 866 restorations and 2,011 to place membership. Also during this 13 years there have been six new congregations started in Lubbock: Eastside, College, Vandelia, Sunset, Northside and Parkway.

The Bible school enrollment has tripled for the enrollment in 1944 was a little over 500 and at present is 1,550. The budget in 1944 was $36,000 and at present is $228,000.

Brother Young, who worked several months as the only minister here at Broadway, was soon joined by Brother Coffman. Later a director for the Tech Bible Chair was added, then an educational director and personal work leader and then in January of this year a director of the Junior-Senior Bible chair. Six ministers now work together under the direction of the 17 elders and 37 deacons.

Probably one of the chief reasons that the work at Broadway has grown and prospered is because of the work done for others. The work in Germany was started and the Broadway elders have had the oversight of the Frankfurt work from the beginning. Through their leadership eight church buildings have been erected in Germany. The church here has supported the Henry Seidmeyers who leave for Germany in September.

Broadway during the past 13 years has supported the work in Lincoln, Nebraska, which is now self-supporting. The Tech Bible Chair and the Junior-Senior Bible Chair have been added to the work. The Children's Home of Lubbock, currently caring for 72 children at the home and scores of others through foster care, has become a very important part of the work of this congregation. Broadway has helped in starting the [predominately African American] Sieber Heights and the Latin American work in Lubbock.

The church has added Bible classes and teachers until presently there are 65 classes Sunday mornings, taught by 120 teachers and assistants. The annual Training for Service School has helped in teacher training and other phases of service through the past 11 years. The Vacation Bible School has grown: total enrollment this year was 976. The South Plains Bible School, sponsored by the Tech Bible Chair, has helped each fall for the past several years. At present Christians in Lubbock and on the South Plains are working enthusiastically to launch Lubbock Christian College, a new Christian junior college, on its first year of work.

With all of the increase in numbers and in work it was necessary for the Broadway congregation to build a larger building and move from the congested downtown area. The present building, completed in 1950 was completely paid for in five years. At present the educational facilities are not adequate and classes are being held in five buildings other than the church building. Plans are under way to increase the class room space by adding 12 additional classrooms in the fellowship hall.

The church has grown during the past 13 years. The church was growing in the previous 40 years. But never in the history of this church, has there been more reason for the church to go forward. A concentrated three-months' Campaign for Christ is at present underway to increase the numbers and spirituality of the congregation.

In retrospect, a remarkable thing about the article is that it well outlined the accomplishments of the Broadway Church during the period 1944 to 1957, but it seemed hesitant to give the Youngs too much credit. Norvel and Helen would have been the first to say that it was the leaders and the people who diligently worked and it was God who gave the growth. But as in the days of Nehemiah, God's great leader in Israel during the fifth century BC, there would not have been growth without someone to call the people to the cause and lead the way. Nehemiah had shouted,

"You see the trouble we are in: Jerusalem lies in ruins, and its gates have been burned with fire. Come, let us rebuild the wall of Jerusalem, and we will no longer be in disgrace!" And the people replied, "Let us start rebuilding!" M. Norvel Young, on the other hand, repeated the old adage, "It's amazing how much you can get done if you don't care who gets the credit." And he, too, called the people to a great work. It remained for future members and historians to consider the full extent of the impact of Norvel and Helen Young on the Broadway Church.

The daughters vividly recalled the trauma of leaving Lubbock. "Everyone was crying. And we cried for days as we headed for California."

Helen reminisced, "The Broadway Church gave us a farewell party in July 1957 on a Sunday afternoon. The mayor, the editor of the *Avalanche Journal*, city councilmen and others were there. The next morning we left. The people at Broadway had given us a new Buick station wagon. It was air-conditioned and spacious. It was parked out in front of the church after the ceremony. J. P. and Gloria [Sanders] came in either that night or the next morning, and we started out for California with three cars. They had three boys, and we had four children, all ranging from 3 to 12 years old. We traveled together. It was an exciting trip, but it was so terribly hot. We would exchange children – part would ride in the cool car and part in the other cars. In the second car, we had a pan full of ice and wash cloths to try to keep cool." The caravan arrived in Los Angeles on August 1, 1957.

The move was difficult for the Sanders children as it was for the Young children. Son Michael Sanders said, "I remember when we moved to Los Angeles. I don't think we kids wanted to do that, but we had the idea that this was something important for Dad. We had the sense that this was a mission that was beginning." Michael believed that it was perhaps most traumatic for his brother, Joel, because he was the oldest and had to begin again to make friends.

While everything was new for the Young and Sanders children, Norvel and Helen and J. P. and Gloria were very familiar with Los Angeles and its culture. The mothers quickly began settling the children in and establishing homes, while Norvel and J. P. began assessing the situation at the college.

REALITY SETS IN

But before even the little hills of success were in sight, Norvel and Helen had to endure the deep valleys of discouragement. "It was quite a shock to leave the cocoon of a small city and a church where we were loved and treated so kindly," remembered Helen. With a chuckle she added, "We weren't paid very much. But the doctor delivered our babies without charge. The cleaners would do our clothes without charge. Eggs and hams and produce of every kind were given to us. We always felt loved." Not only the church, but also the whole city of Lubbock appreciated and respected the Young family.

She continued to reflect, "When we came to Los Angeles, the church people were happy to see us; and Reuel Lemmons wrote some kind things in the *Firm Foundation* about our move to Pepperdine. But we also felt very unloved for the first time in our lives. I would sit in the Vermont Avenue Church and cry every Sunday because I felt many of the faculty resented our coming. But that was just part of it. We had to take that, and we still had to get out and raise money. The most disappointing thing to Norvel was that, though the churches were wonderful to welcome us, they really didn't have the means to support the school. Most members were first generation college people and not well off."

"We did have the feeling of discouragement after we arrived," confessed Norvel, "but we didn't feel we wanted to go back to Lubbock." Helen was busy settling into the stately president's home on campus and helping the children to adjust, but she remembered occasions when she simply sat down and wept. She missed the sense of community and family they had enjoyed in Lubbock. They had left a small city where they were loved, both by church members and by other citizens in town – and had come to a megalopolis where no one seemed to care and where, on campus, many openly resented them. "But still, we had a sense of calling," said Norvel. And that calling drove them forward, despite the tears.

Convinced that the board had made a major blunder in selecting Norvel Young as president, many faculty members, including the scholarly and popular Dean E. V. Pullias, had resigned in the summer and accepted a teaching position at USC. On April 16, 1958, the *Los Angeles Mirror & Daily News* ran stories with headlines that read, "Mass Exodus of Faculty Impends at Pepperdine" and "Teachers Quit at Pepperdine." One story read, in part:

> Pepperdine College, which got a new president in July, will have to replace 25% of its faculty in September.
>
> At least 15 of 60 full-time professors are leaving at the end of this semester as a result of the shake-up in which M. Norvel Young replaced Dr. Hugh Tiner as president.
>
> Dean of Students R. C. Cannon, who will exit with the 15, said the faculty feels a "lack of appreciation" was shown for Tiner and Dr. E. V. Pullias and their part in the development of the college. Pullias, who was dean of the college, resigned reluctantly when Young took over.
>
> Cannon said also that many faculty members feel that Pepperdine, which was a nonsectarian Christian school under Tiner, will come under the control of the Church of Christ. ...
>
> The new president comes from Lubbock, Tex., where he was a Church of Christ minister.

Cannon said that after teaching in a school free
of church control, the faculty felt they couldn't stay
on ...

Cannon predicted that church "pressure" will be
greater than in the past.

But Young promised it wouldn't. "We will continue
to guard academic freedom," he concluded.

The story had a number of inaccuracies. But it was accurate in
describing the large percentage of professors who chose to
follow the dean. The faculty resignations were obviously meant
to torpedo Mr. Pepperdine's choice of leadership for the
college. And to make matters worse, the resignations were timed
to hurt the college the most, taking effect in about a month at
the end of the school year, which meant that the new administration had only the summer months to quickly look for replace-
ments for the disgruntled faculty.

All this made the new chief executive's job much more difficult. It was a time for damage control in every area, including
public relations. Huge personnel problems were now heaped
on top of mountainous fiscal problems. But Norvel and J. P.
Sanders had no choice but to forge ahead.

Dr. Fred L. Casmir was a faculty member when the new
leaders arrived, and he remembered that when he took his stand
with the new administration, he felt a chilling ostracism from
many of the other professors. Still, Don Miller remembered, "It
was amazing how much Norvel and J. P. were able to do in that
first year. Their patient and consistent work enabled them to
assuage most of the tremendous negative reactions to their coming by the end of the first year. A great tribute to J. P. is that he
came in to a faculty that was torn – just shattered – down the
middle. More than one-third of the faculty resigned as a result
of the board's actions. J. P. was able to heal the wounds and
build a fine faculty." Norvel's choice for dean was vindicated.

THE NEW DEAN

To replace the popular Dr. Pullias, Young turned to an old friend. One day as he talked with his father on the telephone before moving to Pepperdine, Norvel said, "I'm thinking of asking J. P. Sanders to come to Pepperdine as the next dean. What do you think?"

It was not an easy question. Sanders was serving as dean of David Lipscomb College at the time, and he also was preaching for the Hillsboro Church of Christ in Nashville. As dean of Lipscomb, Sanders had been instrumental in bringing about accreditation for the school. Since Norvel's father was both a member of the Lipscomb College Board of Trustees and a leader in the church in Nashville, the proposition advanced by Norvel was one of keen interest to him and affected him very directly. Matt Young advised his son that the idea, though a tough prospect for Nashville and Lipscomb to face, would be a good prospect for Pepperdine.

But even before he discussed Sanders with his father, Norvel had really settled on his choice for dean. Don Miller remembered, "In trying to induce Norvel to come, his condition was that he have Dr. J. P. Sanders, who was at that time serving as dean of the faculty of David Lipscomb College in Nashville."

Norvel told the board, in as many words, "I won't come without J. P." Whether that really would have been true if Sanders had declined, we will never know. But based upon the way they lived their lives, one suspects that Norvel and Helen would have come to Pepperdine by themselves if that were necessary, though it would have been tremendously more difficult.

Miller also remembered, "I made the first official contact with J. P. He was much less easily moved than Norvel. Norvel was quite challenged, but J. P. was very content and very happy in the situation at Lipscomb. I think I spent a month and 200 to 300 dollars in telephone calls to J. P. at all hours of the day and night trying to induce him to join Norvel."

It took about three months for Sanders to finally agree to make the move to Pepperdine. Norvel himself reflected, "J. P. did show a great deal of courage in coming. He gave up a lot. I gave up a lot. We both had security. I had security at Lubbock because we were making a good budget. We had a million-dollar building, and we were starting a college. J. P. had security with a good college that had become a four-year accredited college. J. P. didn't make any money in the move. I suspect that he took a financial loss. I think I did too, especially in terms of fringe benefits. But I think this was one of the biggest, most courageous things that J. P. ever did. He risked his career by taking on Pepperdine. Many, many people thought he had made a terrible mistake." Indeed, a number of friends tried to dissuade him. And some at Lipscomb never seemed to forgive him.

Sanders recalled that his decision to accept the position came because he knew the situation at Pepperdine. "I knew that Norvel needed somebody who understood it to help him out," he said. "I came out with a sense of feeling a responsibility to bring about the changes that Norvel and I wanted to make."

Looking back, Helen Young attributed a large part of J. P. Sanders' final positive response to his wife, Gloria. Helen said, "Gloria was a woman of courage. She loved California from the time she came to Pepperdine as a student and eventually met and fell in love with J. P. And she also knew Pepperdine needed J. P."

Dr. J. P. Sanders was a brilliant choice for dean. He was a highly regarded academic. He had been a successful administrator, leading Lipscomb through the accreditation process. He was a respected churchman and beloved preacher. And to top it off, he was Norvel's old friend and mentor. When the Youngs and the Sanders arrived in Los Angeles together, their strength was doubled and the difficult task of replacing faculty was made easier.

Though the embers of hope were never extinguished inside Norvel Young, there were others who were convinced that the dream known as George Pepperdine College was over. That was especially true after Norvel's first year when it was found that the school was still in the red. Board of Trustees members George Evans and Bob Jones both were convinced the cause was lost. After all, the college could no longer borrow money, and Mr. Pepperdine had a number of notes floating around. Only some "creative projects" could keep the ship from sinking. The school had to pay cash for every single purchase, so Mr. Pepperdine kept money in an old safe at his home on West Adams Avenue in Los Angeles. The picture was grim. Only a few knew just how grim.

Don Miller said, "The tragedy of the whole issue was that neither the board, Norvel nor J. P. was aware of the crucial financial state the school was actually in. With the Pepperdine Foundation having gone bankrupt, the annual operating deficit was between a half million and a million dollars a year."

If it survived, it appeared that Pepperdine College would be a starving little school that would be unsuccessful in attracting either students or donors. Even Norvel Young thought they might have to pare back and become a small Bible college. But he quickly pushed that thought out of his fertile mind.

TIME FOR ATTENTION

If some people in Southern California were not thrilled with the arrival of Dr. Norvel Young as president of Pepperdine, there were others who noticed with great interest. The Youngs and the Sanderses were barely in Los Angeles when the current issue of TIME magazine hit the newsstands. The issue was dated August 5, 1957. On page 58, the "Religion" page, was a photograph of a smiling Norvel Young in the first column. In the second column was a picture of the Bishop of London with the Queen Mother. The article, titled "The Nondenomination," read as follows:

Three services were held at the Broadway Church of Christ in Lubbock, Texas last Sunday (two in the morning and one at night); there was a giant picnic for 2,000 church members at noon, and at 3 p.m. there was a going-away party with an air-conditioned Buick as the main gift. Object of all the attention: Broadway Church's personable pastor – Matt Norvel Young, 41, an expansive man in an expanding church.

Reasoning Approach. When Norvel Young went to Lubbock 13 years ago, there were five Churches of Christ in the city (pop. 139,000) with a total membership of about 1,300. Today there are 14 churches with 7,000 members (children under twelve not counted). And the biggest of these – the biggest Church of Christ in the world – is 1,800-member Broadway. Part of the credit for this growth goes to Lubbock, but much of it goes to Norvel Young's friendly, reasoning approach.

The Churches of Christ, as Norvel Young likes to point out, are not a denomination at all. Their essence "is that we want to restore worship to the simple worship as set forth in the New Testament. We teach from the Bible, not from printed interpretations of it. Each individual interprets the Bible for himself. Anybody can start a church, in his home or wherever; he has to get permission from no one. We believe in just being Christians."

The Churches of Christ are the result of a split from the Disciples of Christ in 1906 over questions of how literally the New Testament picture of the church should be followed. Says Young: "Each generation must interpret the Bible for itself. We believe that in this way each generation can remain nearer pure Christianity. If our generation were to write down its interpretation of the Bible, in another 100 years we would be just another denomination." Young's flock calls him Brother rather than the "Doctor" to which he is entitled (he has an M.A. from Vanderbilt University and a Ph.D. from George Peabody College), because the Churches of Christ play down the difference between clergy and laymen. "Each individual is a priest," Young explains. "We encourage them to influence their friends and acquaintances."

Binding Force. Today the Churches of Christ number some 1,200,000 baptized members in 15,000 fully autonomous churches. Brother Young is the nearest thing to a binding force among them; he edits *Twentieth Century Christian*, a monthly magazine promoting Churches of Christ beliefs, writes and edits (with his wife Helen) a bimonthly of daily devotional reading called *Power for Today,* and a weekly column for the Lubbock *Avalanche Journal*. Next week he leaves Lubbock for Los Angeles, where he will head George Pepperdine College, one of four senior colleges run on Churches of Christ principles and supported by private donations. There Young hopes to double the 1,200 enrollment in ten years, eventually make the faculty 100% members of the faith (present proportion: 60%).

"Hold fast to the faith, once and for all delivered to the saints," Young told his congregation in his farewell speech. "Don't let the world make you conform to its pattern."

SEARCH
AND RESCUE

President Norvel Young began building a team.
He told the administration and faculty, "Pepperdine
will not be just another college. It will grow to
become a great university.

George and Helen Pepperdine traveled to Wenatchee, Washington, where Hugh Tiner was preaching in an evangelistic meeting. Mr. Pepperdine told Tiner that it was time for him to resign and that the board had already selected M. Norvel Young to replace him as president. Tiner agreed, realizing he had reached the limit of his ability to advance the school. Indeed, earlier in the year, he had offered his resignation and was asked to withhold it for a time. Years later, Dr. Hugh Tiner would spend the last productive chapter of his life as the beloved minister of the Uptown Church of Christ in Long Beach, California.

As mentioned earlier, Dr. E. V. Pullias resigned as dean, convinced that the board had made a major blunder in selecting Norvel Young as president. And soon, many professors and department heads followed Pullias in tendering their resignations. It was a devastating blow. But Dean Sanders and President Young filled the vacancies with a number of professors who would become the mainstay of Pepperdine for years to come.

Donald V. Miller, chairman of the Board of Trustees during those days, remembered:

> The balance sheet showed assets of $6 million, all donated by Mr. Pepperdine and his Foundation. He had placed the bulk of his personal assets, which he counted as granted him by the grace of God, into the George Pepperdine Foundation. It was his intent that the earnings of these assets would fund the operation of his little college and other deserving Christian works. He intended to be the sole source of funds for the college.
>
> [The year] 1957 was a crucial year for the school. The college had to find and appoint a new president. The health of Mr. Pepperdine took a turn for the worse. The Pepperdine Foundation, because of unwise investments, became insolvent and went into bankruptcy. Mr. Pepperdine resigned as chairman of the Board of Trustees, though he remained a member, and a successor, [myself], was named.
>
> Into this turmoil, the Board, after strong persuasion, induced Dr. M. Norvel Young to resign as minister of the Broadway Church in Lubbock, in the midst of a successful ministry, to become the third president of George Pepperdine College. This would be his first venture into the field of college administration, though for this he had been academically trained, and the Board knew this fact.
>
> For the previous two years, the school had operated in an unfunded deficit because of the Foundation failure. Dr. Young and the new dean, J. P. Sanders, faced the challenge of securing new faculty to replace the one-third who had resigned. In addition, [they had] the great task of meeting operating deficits to assure the continuity of the institution and

to restore calm and balance to the young college. What a task the Board had asked the new administration to tackle. The new administrators approached the challenge with zest, and by the end of their first year, things were amazingly well, and normal activity prevailed.

In the succeeding years, Dr. Young and his talented mate, Helen Mattox Young, working in concert, began the acquaintance and cultivation of a host of friends of the young college whom Mr. Pepperdine and Dr. Tiner, former president, had cultivated as interested friends, though none had been approached as possible donors. The Youngs were highly successful and earned the respect of that group, together with an ever widening number of outstanding business and professional people who liked the concept upon which the college was built.

REBUILDING THE FACULTY

It seemed reasonable to the board to allow Norvel to select his own management team. Through Dr. Lloyd Nelson of USC, who later served as chairman of Pepperdine's Board of Trustees, Dean Pullias was offered a position at USC. He accepted the job, and a vacancy was created in the deanship. Pullias served with distinction at USC and also served as an elder for the Vermont Avenue Church of Christ for the rest of his life.

Norvel's first thought was to replace Pullias with his longtime friend and college classmate Batsell Barrett Baxter. But in a conversation with Norvel, Baxter asked that he not be considered. He simply did not want to leave his native Tennessee. As with so many other things in the lives of Norvel and Helen Young, Baxter's decision to not be considered for the position proved providential – because Norvel turned to his friend of many years, and his mentor in many ways, J. P. Sanders. Sanders, a decade older than Norvel, was an experienced college administrator and a fine academician. And like Norvel, Sanders could be tempted with a noble challenge. He had led David Lipscomb College through the accreditation process as its dean. Who better to assist in snatching Pepperdine College from the jaws of financial disaster? Who better to help recruit qualified faculty to fill the vacancies of those who balked at the leadership of Norvel Young? And who better to help re-establish the school as a thoroughly Christian college than this consummate preacher and respected spiritual leader?

Some people were expecting Pepperdine College to retrench and become a two-year, junior college. But that was never in Norvel Young's mind. It did occur to him that they might have to reduce the curriculum from a complete offering of liberal arts courses to that of a Bible college. Would he have stayed on as president if that had become necessary? "Well, we really didn't have that many invitations to go elsewhere," Norvel said with a smile. "People expected us to succeed. And that kept us going."

President Norvel Young began building a team. He told the administration and faculty, "Pepperdine will not be just another college. It will grow to become a great university. California is ripe for that. But Pepperdine will be something different than our sister schools." He added that it was time to do something for young people that would influence them for generations to come, something that could be accomplished only with the help of God.

Norvel did not follow the management style that Sanders was used to at David Lipscomb College. There, the president was always at the forefront, making announcements and appointing faculty. As dean, Sanders was always in the "back seat." But President Young intentionally promoted Sanders as dean in the fullest sense. The two would discuss at length proposed faculty appointments, but the final choice belonged to Sanders. And after the selections were final, it was Sanders who made the academic announcements. It is illustrative of the management style Norvel would continue to employ, a participative approach that was, in many ways, ahead of its time.

With the resignations and departures of the first year behind them, Dean Sanders and President Young began filling faculty vacancies in the second academic year. They recruited a number of professors who would become the mainstay of Pepperdine for years to come: Thomas Campbell, Loyd Frashier, Lewis Fulks, Walter Glass, Harold Holland, Warren S. Jones, G. C. Morlan, Paul Randolph, Jack Reynolds, and Howard A. White. James C. Moore, Jr., came as comptroller. They were key appointments.

Some of the new faculty were from other Church of Christ-related schools, while some were just finishing master's or doctor's degree programs. Loyd Frashier was teaching at Georgia Tech and the Youngs were very thankful that he agreed to come to Pepperdine. He left the large, well-equipped laboratories of Georgia Tech for the meager facilities of Pepperdine, and though Norvel tried more than once to raise money for a science building on the Los Angeles campus, it wasn't until the Malibu campus was completed that Frashier and the other natural science faculty had adequate labs and equipment.

Howard White was teaching at Lipscomb when the call came from Pepperdine. When Dean Sanders contacted him, he politely declined. Norvel persisted and encouraged White to come for an interview even if he thought chances were slim that he would be interested. But then Sanders and Young had another problem: they had no money to fly White and his wife, Maxine, to Los Angeles.

Norvel called an old friend, Howard Youree, in Nashville. Youree was the successful owner of a trucking firm and operated a large fleet of trucks in the Nashville area. He also was an elder at the church on the campus of David Lipscomb College, which later became the Granny White Pike Church of Christ. Even though Youree knew Howard White and would prefer him staying at Lipscomb, he agreed to donate the round-trip airfare for the Whites.

Howard and Maxine White flew to Los Angeles and stayed in the president's home on campus for three or four days. They met with J. P. Sanders and faculty members, and, of course, with Norvel and Helen. Years later, Dr. White commented, "There were so many people coming and going in that president's home that, when you left your bedroom for the bathroom, you never knew who you would meet in the hall!"

As far as Helen Young knew, it was the Whites' first trip to California, and they apparently were impressed enough to succumb to Norvel's enthusiasm and vision. Helen also remembered that Maxine seemed more adventuresome than Howard, and she certainly was an important influence in their moving to California. In fact, she noted, the same was true with Gloria and J. P. Sanders and Della and Frank Pack. With all these couples, it was the wives who seemed immediately to see the attraction of the college and the area. And without their positive feelings toward the work at Pepperdine, things might have been different.

By the time the Whites flew back to Nashville, Helen and Norvel thought they had a pretty good chance of getting them to come to Pepperdine. Dr. White did accept the challenge, and it was a very providential move, to say the least. He would go on to serve not only as a professor, but in several administrative posts, culminating in his tenure as executive vice president under President William S. Banowsky, and finally as the fifth president of Pepperdine University.

Of course, building a solid faculty is not something administrators can do once and move on. It is an ongoing process. Dean Sanders continued to add faithful and scholarly faculty members as the years passed. And each professor who was added had to count the cost. Salaries were not really adequate, and the cost of living was usually higher in Los Angeles than in the college towns from which the new professors came. But J. P. Sanders and Norvel Young could issue a powerful challenge and lay out an exciting dream because they themselves had accepted the risks because of the vision before them.

RECOVERING THE MISSION

There were some bright spots among the stormy clouds of that first year at Pepperdine College in 1957-58. Reuel Lemmons, editor of the religious journal *Firm Foundation,* wrote editorials urging the church constituency to "give the school a chance." And President Don Morris at Abilene Christian College encouraged the effort by selecting Norvel Young as ACC's Alumnus of the Year. That helped by putting Abilene's stamp of approval on what the Youngs were trying to do in California. Many southern and midwestern churches had written off Pepperdine as a lost cause in regard to Christianity, but now there seemed to be some stirrings of hope.

Norvel and Helen remembered, "We sought a lot of advice and prayer. Prayer was a big part. Still, there were times when we wondered if we had done the right thing. We did have feelings of discouragement, but we didn't feel that we wanted to go back. We felt sure that we were moving into a bigger arena, and whether we succeeded or failed, we believed we would be glad we came to California. There really was a sense of calling."

A few days after they arrived, the Young and Sanders families were honored at a reception at the president's home on the Pepperdine College campus. Organizing the affair was Kenneth Hahn, Walter King, Ken Davidson, Don Miller and others. They had invited people from all the Churches of Christ in the area – those most prominent in attendance were members from the churches in Santa Ana, Long Beach Ninth and Lime, Central Los Angeles, Inglewood, and Bakersfield. The lines of well-wishers were long and enthusiastic. Needless to say, the new leaders were encouraged.

The Youngs settled into the large president's home on campus, and the Sanders family stayed with them until they could find a home. It turned out that the school owned a house on 78th Street, just a short walk from the campus, and J. P. and Gloria and the children soon moved there. The homes were opened to church and community people alike. It was a new administration with a new attitude and approach. And that approach was reflected on campus as a directive returned the students to the previous policy of required attendance at chapel services every weekday. An increased Christian emphasis was also evident in the aggressive recruitment of Christian students and students who wanted to prepare for the ministry.

In Pepperdine's pictorial history, *Crest of a Golden Wave*, published on the university's 50th anniversary, Patricia Yomantas wrote profiles on each of the school presidents to that point. In Norvel Young's profile she reported:

> In the early years of his presidency, Young would spend Monday through Friday as Pepperdine's president and chief executive officer, raising money, reforming the school's budget, and reaffirming to faculty and students the worthiness of the Pepperdine mission. He would spend the weekends as a traveling salesman, on the road to places like Bakersfield and Riverside, Fresno and Redlands, hopeful of recruiting students and supporters; hoping to raise more than the modest $25,000 coming to the University each year through fund-raising efforts. He would speak at churches, at community meetings, before civic groups, preaching the word of Christ and promoting Pepperdine. Any sleep he was able to get came in brief moments in the back of the yellow Buick station wagon he and his wife, Helen, received from the Lubbock church. While Norvel slept, Helen would drive to the next destination, their children keeping her company in the front seat. Like a barnstorming politician, Young would spread his word to all who would listen, sometimes to several groups in a day, revived only by a quick nap in the back of the Buick and an unwavering belief in the mission of

Pepperdine College. It was 1957 and, as he had done so many times before, M. Norvel Young was working for the future.

In the same profile, Yomantas described M. Norvel Young with the following words:

> He is a trailblazing optimist – a man who likes his verbs to end with *s*. He believes in people, he believes in the future, he believes in the inherent spirit of both. Mostly, he believes in God. "I stand on tiptoe looking forward to what God will do in my life in the years ahead," he says. "How can you be pessimistic when the future is as bright as the promises of God?"

The annual Pepperdine Bible Lectures, a gathering of members of the Churches of Christ on the campus to hear outstanding preachers and teachers, had steadily declined in attendance and by the early '50s, it was a very small gathering. Begun in 1943 in the depths of World War II, the lectures provided a vital service to the churches and to others, and were a statement of hope in troubled times. They were finally discontinued in spring 1957 as the internal administrative problems mounted. No one was in a mood to assemble and listen to spiritual messages with so much trouble brewing.

One of the ways Norvel reached out to the church constituency in the first few years was through those annual lectures. In his first year, 1957-58, he reinstituted the lectures, and even more, he revitalized them. By 1960, the campus auditorium was filled to capacity and overflowing. It was decided to move the main lectures off campus, and Norvel so promoted the March 1961 series that a crowd of more than 6,000 people overflowed the Shrine Auditorium in Los Angeles.

The next year, the lectures were moved to an even larger off-campus location: the Sports Arena near the L.A. Coliseum, ten minutes north of the Pepperdine campus. Ira North, who had pledged his support of Norvel's efforts to revive Pepperdine spiritually as well as financially, spoke at the Sports Arena on March 22, 1962. The audience numbered more than 10,000. George Pepperdine was so ill at that point that he had to be brought to the arena by ambulance. A microphone was brought to him and he addressed the assembly briefly from his gurney. It was his last time with his spiritual brothers and sisters.

Ira North also appeared in advertisements for Pepperdine in *20th Century Christian* and other magazines. It was a courageous thing for North to do, since his church in Nashville was in the heart of much of the cynicism and criticism that surrounded Pepperdine. During the early 1950s, North and Norvel Young had been friendly rivals. The Madison Church of Christ, where Ira North preached, was a fast-growing church. It was challenging the Broadway Church of Christ, where Norvel preached, as the largest Church of Christ in the world. The "rivalry" was indeed amiable, because they both subscripted to the old adage, "There is no competition between lighthouses." So, when President Young turr :d to Ira North for support, North fearlessly did all he could to promote Pepperdine.

Not only did Norvel call on his old friends for moral support, but he also won new friends at the college. Phil Pennington remembered when he entered his senior year at Pepperdine in fall 1957. It was the same time that Norvel Young was entering his first year as president. Nearly 40 years later, Pennington wrote to Norvel Young:

> You'll recall becoming President of Pepperdine College as I became editor of the student newspaper. And while the newspaper wasn't your most critical concern, it did get your attention because you recognized it could affect student opinion – important to any new college chief executive ... particularly when the editor, like all college editors, felt himself some-

thing of a firebrand, a crusader and a personal defender of the First Amendment.

I wondered about this young administrator, a preacher, from Lubbock. Would I be told what to write? Edited? Reviewed before publication? Or, horrors of all, censured!

Complicating the situation was the fact that the longtime faculty advisor to the GRAPHIC, Robert O. Young, had just resigned and the publications were put under the guidance of the chairman of the English Department, Dr. Wade Ruby, a friend of both yours and mine. (He had officiated at my dad's funeral service nine years earlier.)

But Dr. Ruby didn't feel at ease "guiding" a journalism endeavor. He wanted to dedicate his time and wisdom to teaching Shakespeare and Wordsworth, which he did better than any English professor in the country, and with more passion.

So he told me, "Run the paper."

And it was then that my tenure with Pepperdine could have gone sour, or soared to the respect, trust and love that continues to this day:

"Hello, Dr. Young, I'm Phil Pennington and I'm editor of the school newspaper (that's pretty important!) and I'd like to meet with you if you're available … "

"How about tomorrow at 10 a.m., and then let's make it weekly," you responded into the phone.

In the months that followed, you not only didn't have me "edited," but as a true teacher you encouraged me and recognized a student editor and his staff need to learn by doing.

More than once, probably even more often than I know, the GRAPHIC tilted windmills and raised eyebrows which must have at least, caused you to clinch your fist and grit your teeth!

Still, you were always supportive. When we missed our weekly meetings, you gave me a letter of possible items of interest to the student body ...

Our friendship has continued after my graduation ... and it will continue well into the future.

FROM RED TO BLACK

By 1957 when Norvel and Helen arrived, the enrollment boom at Pepperdine, provided by the post-war G.I. Bill, was over. The number of students applying for college admission had generally diminished, and that added to Pepperdine's problems. To make matters worse, some students were upset about the hiring of Norvel Young as president – even though none of them even knew him. They obviously had been influenced by disgruntled faculty and administrators. A number of these students threatened to transfer to other colleges, and a few followed through. Norvel was justifiably concerned.

President Young struggled through the fall term with a chilly reception from some faculty members. Then in February 1958, he and Helen went to the Abilene Christian College Lectureship. They were visiting with Ike Summerlin, an oil executive from Houston, whose wife had just been honored at the lectures as Woman of the Year at the 20th Century Christian luncheon. Norvel called his assistant on campus in Los Angeles, and that is when he heard the news: eight heads of departments, along with 20 other faculty members, had announced their resignations. Those 28 professors represented nearly half of the faculty at that time. Most of them agreed to stay through the end of the term, but the news of their imminent departure had to be made public in February. The announcement put a pall over the campus. Which is exactly what the professors had hoped for. It was a time for damage control in every area, including public relations. Personnel problems were now heaped on top of fiscal problems. But Norvel and J. P. had no choice but to forge ahead.

The embarrassment was palpable. The next four months were pure agony for Norvel and Helen Young. However, as they looked back later, they realized that what appeared to be a tragedy of tremendous proportions was really a blessing in disguise. The next term brought a crop of new professors who would faithfully serve Pepperdine for the next three decades or more, and who would create a new spirit for the school.

In retrospect, and in all graciousness, the Youngs understood that those faculty members who announced their resignations were very emotional at the time. Not really knowing Norvel, they prejudged him as the narrowest kind of fundamentalist, which they perceived as incompatible with enlightened college leadership. They decided that they would rather see the school die a decent death than prostitute itself by pleading for money from Churches of Christ. They probably thought that the churches would try to control or manipulate the college and the new president if their money saved the school. The faculty resignations in January 1958 were probably calculated to scare Norvel off, get him to quit, shake up the board, and bring everyone to their senses or their knees. The news caught Norvel completely off guard, showing how unprepared he was for such negative attitudes toward himself. He never considered them his enemies. He could not understand why they viewed him as their enemy.

It seems quite fortuitous that the Youngs were in Abilene when they received the shocking news. They took the sad development as a major disaster, but they did not think of resignation. They were surrounded by people who loved them and who pledged their support toward what the Youngs were trying to do. Reuel Lemmons, Don Morris and others encouraged them. Ira North in Nashville, a widely respected figure among Churches of Christ, promised to help the Youngs and Pepperdine College.

There were some positives among those early negative times. Norvel remembered, "The board was united and George

Pepperdine and Don Miller, the chairman, were supportive. Bryant Essick, the chairman of the President's Board, an advisory board that Hugh Tiner had established, was encouraging. The first year we failed to balance the budget by $30,000. The second year we were in the black, and this year [1981] we celebrated our 25th consecutive year with a balanced budget."

Board Chairman Don Miller put it, "The world has many dreamers, but rare is the dreamer who has the ability to then plan, and organize, and by skillful execution, bring his dream into reality! Dr. M. Norvel Young is such a dream builder ... By the second year, the college budget was balanced, and has been so ever since that time. Under Dr. Young's dream building, graduate schools were developed, and the college became a university."

But there were many lean years. Money was so tight that Helen remembers that she and Gloria Sanders would entertain guests on campus using their own family food budget. Of course, faculty and staff salaries were bare minimum. There was a great deal of sacrifice on the part of many people – faculty, staff, administrators – in turning the college around financially.

One bright spot was the formal inauguration of Norvel Young as the third president of Pepperdine. The event was delayed until Friday morning, November 21, 1958, the first semester of his second academic year. By that time, the faculty situation had settled down and the financial picture was looking better. The Board of Trustees at that time included Kenneth Davidson, Leland P. Derrick, Robert P. Jones, James L. Lovell, Orbin V. Melton, George Pepperdine, Helen L. Pepperdine and Clarence Shattuck, with Donald V. Miller as chairman.

The ceremony began at 10:30 a.m. with a gala organ processional, as representatives from about 150 colleges and universities from across the nation marched in academic cap and gown. As is customary, the institutions were listed in the program by founding date, beginning with Harvard in 1636 and William and Mary in 1693, ending with Lubbock Christian College in 1957 and Magic Valley Christian College in 1958.

Dr. Paul S. Smith, president of Whittier College, was the featured speaker at the event, which was held in the auditorium on campus. Smith, whose topic was "The Place of Education in Education," was a good man and had been very encouraging to Norvel.

Then it was time for the central event. The *Los Angeles Mirror and Daily News* reported, "The audience of more than 1000 persons rose to its feet as the former Church of Christ minister was inducted by Donald V. Miller, chairman of the Board of trustees."

In his inaugural address after the induction, President Young promised to work diligently for both academic excellence and Christian values. With perhaps an eye toward those critics who may have underestimated his academic commitment, he pledged to support a strong, qualified and dedicated faculty. He also mentioned the need for expanding the campus and constructing major buildings that were pressing.

President Young said, "Pepperdine is a college with a purpose: It is the development of a wise, spiritually centered character, of vocational skills and of attitudes necessary to effective citizenship in a democracy." To fulfill this purpose, he said, "We pledge our administration to maintain and improve the quality of our academic program as a liberal arts college and to cultivate Christian values in living."

According to the *Los Angeles Examiner*:

> Dr. Young declared, "The challenge is tremendous in these days when so much demand is placed upon the private Christian college. We boldly ask college and community support because we firmly believe in the intrinsic value of the distinctive training offered by Christian colleges." Praising the college's contribution since its founding in 1937, Dr. Young promised the audience: "With the help of God we shall add to this record of scholastic excellence and sound Christian training."

Among the other goals that he articulated, were the raising of admission standards, greatly enlarging the endowment fund and promoting understanding among the various constituent groups of the college. Dr. Howard A. White would later call Norvel's administrative style "inclusivist." He claimed that President Young "sought to maintain the best possible relations with all the institution's constituents ... sought to strengthen the ties with the Church of Christ with which Pepperdine is affiliated."

Following his presidential address, the third president of Pepperdine College, M. Norvel Young, then presided over the induction of Dean Joel Pilant Sanders. George and Helen Pepperdine were beaming at the new prospects of the school.

After the inaugural ceremony, there was a luncheon in the gymnasium for all the dignitaries and a reception at the president's home on campus. There were the usual well-wishes and polite conversations, but there was more. The inauguration of M. Norvel Young was a signal that most people were beginning to be optimistic about the future of Pepperdine College. A month earlier, a local newspaper reported, "Pepperdine Faculty Adds 4 Teachers." It listed Dr. Edna West as the new director of Teacher Training at the elementary level and Dr. Jack Reynolds as director of the secondary level. Dr. Rex Johnston had become director of the Extension Division. And head of the Audio-visual Department was Dr. G. C. Morlan. The article mentioned that Washington High School principal Dr. Paul H. Fisher would also be Visiting Professor of Education. The rough road of 1957 was slowly being repaired by 1958.

In that same year of 1958, one of the many things that energized Pepperdine was a project conceived and produced by alumni. Dick Meltvedt and Joe Orlando hit upon the idea of making a film that would depict Pepperdine College in its most favorable light. It could be used for student recruitment and public relations. The pair did indeed complete the project, producing an excellent film on a shoestring budget. Since the year was 1958, the movie was called *Twenty-one Years*, corresponding to the age of the school, and the implication was that Pepperdine had "come of age."

The new president was all for it, thinking it might help rejuvenate the school. Quickly, other alumni rallied to the cause. Kenny and Gordon Hahn helped organized a fund-raiser for the film at the Hilton Hotel. And labor was donated. For example, famed composer Les Baxter, a Pepperdine alumnus, wrote the musical score and performed it with his orchestra. Ken Ross wrote the script, and of course Meltvedt and Orlando produced and directed the effort. The film was professionally shot throughout Southern California, in addition to the on-location filming at the Pepperdine Los Angeles campus. There was even a staged scene of two young men who were supposed to be driving down Pacific Coast Highway in Malibu on their way to the Los Angeles campus. One of those young men was student John Katch, who later became a successful Los Angeles executive and a Pepperdine University Regent. The scene had the two students stopping at a gasoline station and asking how far it is to Los Angeles. In the film, the answer by the station attendant as he pointed down the coast highway was, "Sixty-one miles." Ironically, if one were to stop at that same spot on the coast today and ask how far it is to Pepperdine, the answer would be, "About a mile or two." When the film was completed, it was "premiered" at the auditorium on campus, with a packed house, complete with Hollywood-style searchlights out front scanning the L.A. night skies and drawing in the crowds.

One of the key people in Norvel's first years as president, indeed thoughout most of Pepperdine's history, was Olaf H. Tegner. Oly had been a student under rookie history professor Norvel Young in 1939 when Norvel taught at Pepperdine. Oly became friends with his professor and with his classmate, Helen Mattox, who, of course, was soon to become Mrs. Norvel Young. Oly also met his lifelong mate, wife Allie, at Pepperdine.

Aside from a stint in the Navy, Oly Tegner would give his entire life to the school. He founded the alumni association and served in a number of roles at Pepperdine, including managing athletics. After earning his Ph.D. and spending several years teaching, he would become the founding dean of the Pepperdine School of Education (later to become the Graduate School of Education and Psychology). When Norvel arrived in 1957, Oly, the "man of many hats," was teaching and also serving as publications director and director of the alumni association.

A few disgruntled alumni wanted a copy of the alumni mailing list so they could contact everyone and ask them to withhold support from the school because of the hiring of Norvel Young. Oly Tegner, who maintained the mailing list, refused. In fact, as the years passed, he became a bridge between the new administration and the old, between the alumni and the new president. Even though he loved and respected Dean Pullias and those faculty members who opposed Norvel, Oly had confidence that Norvel could save the school. He knew a change was needed and supported Norvel through thick and thin. He earned everyone's deep respect.

"President Tiner was a wonderful man," remembered Oly, "and great in public relations. But he just couldn't seem to raise money to solve the college's financial problems. Norvel, on the other hand, had good business sense. And he quickly began making contacts for financial support."

Through the years that followed, the Tegners and the Youngs would remain steadfast friends. And Oly would serve as perhaps the key peacemaker and the glue that would hold the college together. As the decades slipped by, Oly Tegner made contact with estranged alumni and wooed them back to Pepperdine, one by one. His role was indispensable.

In the mid-1950s, Pepperdine President Hugh Tiner became acquainted with two dynamic young men, George Graziadio and George Eltinge. The "Two Georges," as they were often affectionately called, had established themselves as the Eltinge and Graziadio Development Company and had an impressive list of large projects to their credit. They built and owned more than 100 shopping centers in 21 states, many of the centers housing K-Mart stores.

Norvel Young met the two Georges when he came to Pepperdine in 1957, just a few years before the turning point for the Eltinge-Graziadio partnership. In 1962, the small bank the partners had been doing business with was taken over by a major bank. "Suddenly the players changed," said Graziadio, "and we found that we were not as welcome as we had been." The two Georges, like their innovative friends at Pepperdine, "dreamed a large dream," in Graziadio's words. With minimal capital, they started their own business-oriented bank. And by the late 1990s, Imperial Bank had 15 regional offices in California and business banking offices in Arizona, Texas and Massachusetts, as well as other subsidiary businesses. But that first modest location for Imperial Bank was not far from Pepperdine's Los Angeles campus.

As the years went by George Eltinge and George Graziadio and their wives became dear friends of Norvel and Helen Young. The two Georges became staunch supporters and benefactors of the school. Then sadly in August 1994, at the height of their success, George Eltinge died.

But the Youngs didn't even dream that nearly four decades after meeting them, George and Reva Graziadio would announce in March 1996 that they were endowing Peppedine's School of Business and Management. The school would forever become known as The George L. Graziadio School of Business and Management.

VINDICATION OF THE FOUNDER

Norvel Young could never satisfy himself with one or two or ten projects at a time. He was not only involved in re-establishing Pepperdine College's financial and spiritual health, but he also was traveling and trying to build up the church as a whole. Dr. Abraham J. Malherbe was the Buckingham Professor of New Testament Criticism and Interpretation at Yale University for many years, and in 1995 he recalled an incident that illustrates Norvel's presence and impact on people. Malherbe wrote:

In the early 1960s, when Abilene Christian College was planning to begin its three year graduate program in ministry, it used consultants to assess the college's resources and design of the program. One of those consultants was Douglas Horton, recently retired as Dean of the Harvard Divinity School. Those of us who knew Douglas were confident that he would understand us and provide us with a judicious assessment of our prospects. The dates for his visit to Abilene were set, and then the college's administration was faced with what appeared to them a quandary – what to do with Dean Horton on the Wednesday evening that he would be in town. A canvass of churches in Abilene did not yield one with a program that particular evening that the administration thought appropriate for a Dean from Harvard. I suggested that we take him to Highland [Church of Christ], where Norvel was holding a [preaching] meeting, for that was the only occasion on which Dean Horton would hear someone actually doing what we were educating people for, preaching the gospel. With some misgiving, the suggestion was accepted, and J. W. Roberts and I took Horton to Highland to hear Norvel preach.

J. W. had agreed to my suggestion with some misgiving, and he was a bit nervous. He settled down a bit when Horton sang most of the songs without looking at the hymnal. But he fidgeted quite a bit as he noted the intensity with which Horton followed Norvel's sermon. And when, after the invitation [some call it an "altar call"], Horton rushed down the aisle toward Norvel, J. W. did not know quite what to think or do. We watched him shaking Norvel's hand and having a brief, animated conversation with him. He returned to us with his face beaming. "Splendid!" he said, "It never hurts to have one thought follow another logically!" We were thankful for Norvel.

The meeting, according to the usual criteria, was a resounding success. But to us, it was, in addition, an instance of unintended consequences. His reasoned sermon became a paradigm in a fuller discussion with the Dean about our understanding of what preaching should be.

In 1957 when George Pepperdine and others first contacted Norvel and Helen about working with the college, the Youngs initially thought that they might simply help with the rebuilding of the college, much as Ira North, Reuel Lemmons and many others eventually helped Pepperdine. But as time passed, it became apparent that Mr. Pepperdine had only one candidate for president in mind. If he had a back-up plan, no one knew it. He apparently believed that Norvel Young was the one and only person who could rescue the college in the way he envisioned. He probably reasoned that Norvel was the only person who could also save the George Pepperdine legacy and rescue this major Pepperdine contribution to society and to history.

Within months of Norvel and Helen's arrival, it became obvious that Mr. Pepperdine's judgment was vindicated: the college would indeed survive. And eventually, even Mr. Pepperdine's grand vision of building a Christian college that would serve society and would withstand the winds of time seemed to have been vindicated by the work of Norvel and Helen Young.

George Pepperdine was very proud of the Youngs and their work. A birthday party was held at the president's home for Mr. Pepperdine about a year before he died. And during the party, he and Norvel moved out to the porch for some fresh air and conversation. As they stood on the steps of the gracious president's home, Mr. Pepperdine looked out over the green lawns, the pale blue buildings and the palm-tree lined Promenade drive. He turned to Norvel and said, "If I died today, I would die a happy man." Norvel was very touched and gratified by the statement. By that time in the early 1960s, he, with the help of many others, had brought the college a long way. They had not yet dared to dream of where it might go someday.

Mr. Pepperdine's statement about dying as a happy man was based on his insight that young people need training in how to make a living, but they also need help in setting a course and in building a life. And as his own life inched toward his final breath, he was satisfied that Norvel Young had led the way in searching for the soul of the college and in rescuing it for that original purpose. Though there were mountainous challenges and desperate tragedies to come, the school had turned the corner. Mr. Pepperdine had no way of knowing that his founding statement would become a polar star, would be read annually at the University's Founder's Day Convocation and, like a gravitational force, would draw the institution back to his vision again and again.

George Pepperdine's seemingly irrational insistence that Dr. M. Norvel Young become the third president of the college was indeed vindicated.

10

L.A. CRISIS

*Norvel and Helen could envision
a college campus with a spiritual mission
situated on the slopes of the Santa Monica Mountains,
overlooking the vast Pacific Ocean
like a silent sentinel.*

Norvel Young was not the only leader at work to turn Pepperdine around in the late '50s. Less than a year after arriving in Los Angeles, Helen Young was the primary creative force in establishing a new organization that would promote the college for decades to come. Working with Mrs. Pepperdine and others, Helen became the founding president of the Associated Women for Pepperdine in June 1958. Through dues and a variety of fund-raising activities, AWP has provided scholarship aid to thousands of Pepperdine students in the intervening years.

Helen Young's self-confidence was given a boost in the Lubbock years. As the wife of perhaps the most influential preacher among Churches of Christ at that time, she was called upon to serve as unofficial hostess on many church and civic occasions. Now she became the *official* hostess of Pepperdine College. And as the early difficult days gave way to happier times, she began to prove what an outstanding ambassador of goodwill she was. Her "people skills" became obvious, as did her speaking and administrative abilities. She was acknowledged by those close to the Youngs as Norvel's "not-so-secret weapon" for success.

From an enrollment of 1,084 in 1957, Norvel had led the college to about 1,500 students by the mid-1960s. In his second year as president, he began a modest extension classes schedule, which gradually grew into a military extension program that reached across the nation and even overseas. It was part of a multi-faceted entrepreneurial approach that Norvel hoped would pull Pepperdine out of the red. All of his efforts paid off. President Young's second academic year, 1958-59, and every year thereafter, was to conclude with a balanced budget.

Obviously, part of solving the financial problems of the school involved increasing tuition. As Norvel began his second year with the college, yearly tuition, room and board were $1,238. Over the next decade, those charges would double. Even by 1961 rising costs were apparent, and Pepperdine worked hard to provide financial aid. Dean J. P. Sanders assured students in May of that year that Comptroller J. C. Moore would develop "a tailor-made program for every student with financial difficulties." Indeed, Moore spent many hours with students, arranging grants, loans and employment to make a college education possible for nearly anyone.

Also in 1961, the college purchased two buildings and four lots at the corner of Vermont Avenue and 81st Street. New dormitories had already been built and the cafeteria enlarged. Now many administrative functions were moved from the campus to the new Vermont buildings, a half block away, to create classroom and other academic space on the campus proper. Other buildings were purchased along Vermont to house academic and business operations.

In addition to strategic planning and management, Norvel Young was also skillfully handling people problems. To illustrate the kind of manager Norvel was, Terry Giboney, who served as student body president in 1959-60, reminded Norvel:

As I reflect on our friendship over the years, one particular incident on the old Pepperdine campus stands out in my mind. I was the student body president and one night something came up that a couple of friends and I thought only the President would be able to resolve. We went to your home fairly late at night and Helen answered the door. You had already gone to bed, but she told you we were there and you came out in your robe and slippers. You listened with respect and compassion and we left feeling very 'heard,' even though we realized afterwards that we had been a bit impulsive and should not have bothered you so late at night. In any case, a lesser person would have probably told us to come back tomorrow or might have berated us for not going through proper 'channels.' Your accessibility and willingness to patiently listen to a bunch of impulsive students on a quest will never be forgotten.

In the midst of putting the college on solid footing, Norvel somehow found time to indulge his passion for travel, and mixed in some faith and adventure at the same time. His good friend, Los Angeles County Supervisor Kenneth Hahn, remembered, "When you returned to be president of the college, we enjoyed visiting the world together with Bill Stivers and Oly Tegner. Your courage in taking a letter and Bibles into Moscow in 1963 was outstanding. I thought at any moment the KGB would arrest you and put you in jail. I was glad when the plane took off and we were on our way home." It wouldn't be the last risky chore Norvel would undertake. Walter and Anna King, who were students at Pepperdine College in the early days, wrote, "We were deeply impressed when you and a group of our friends first took Bibles into Russia. Your interest and concern for those people continues today." Norvel would not only smuggle Bibles behind the Iron Curtain, he would convince others to participate in the conspiracy. He seemed fearless.

Also in 1963, the *Firm Foundation* journal ran a "Special Pepperdine Issue" on February 5. The cover article was by M. Norvel Young and titled, "Beginning A Second Quarter Century of Christian Education." The journal issue came at a unique time: George Pepperdine died on July 31, 1962, just two months short of the College's 25th anniversary. Mr. Pepperdine had lived to see his school well established – President Young had been there for five years and finances were back in the black. More importantly, the mission seemed intact and there was a sense that things were on the move. Now the school was entering its second 25 years.

President Young was philosophic as he scanned the decade of the 1960s that lay ahead. Though he had no way of knowing just how turbulent the years would be, he seemed to understand that there was an ominous tone echoing back from the future – it seemed fraught with danger. He wrote:

> At the dawn of its second quarter century of service, Pepperdine College, along with other independent Christian colleges, holds a unique position in the history of higher education. It is a position which portends both imminent dangers and unparalleled opportunities. There is the danger that we will be dwarfed in the fierce competition with tax supported institutions. The danger that we may be ill-prepared or lose confidence as we leap into the space age with its explosion of new scientific information. The danger that we may falter and fail to develop to the fullest the individual potential of each student. The danger that we may become fascinated by cliches and traditions and succumb to the soft siren of security at the price of intellectual and spiritual conformity. But most dangerous and deadly of all is the threat of losing sight of our distinctive purpose – of forfeiting our special mission in the field of higher education.

The dangers of the next quarter century are so many that some observers regard the course we steer as a futile one. An army of "educational experts" gloomily predict that the next twenty-five years will witness the demise of the private liberal arts colleges of America. The plague of economic malnutrition, they prophesy, will eliminate all educational institutions which are not nourished by tax support or government subsidy. And we must soberly remember that the shortage of funds is constantly accompanied by the temptation to be satisfied with a level of academic mediocrity. On the other hand, however, is the danger that in search of the much needed financial support, we will sell our birthright for a mess of pottage. That is, we might trade our independence and our unique Christian personality for adequate funds from Washington or from any special interest group which bargains to exchange our distinctiveness for gold.

President M. Norvel Young concluded the article with a crescendo and a commitment:

Pepperdine will be no less dedicated to these purposes now that its founder has been called to his eternal reward. In every dollar that is invested in our future, in every parent that extends to us his trust, in every student that seeks at our feet his guidance, and yes, even in the passing of our founder, our obligation to the unique and distinctive purposes of Pepperdine College is redoubled. We are dealing with the most precious natural resources – brain power, character, personality, idealisms – the human soul. May our performance during the perilous quarter century ahead be worthy of our aim and purpose.

We will need the encouragement of our brethren and the blessings of God.

A HOME IN HEIDELBERG

Of the many crucial decisions Norvel Young made during those first half dozen years, one of the most significant regarding the future personality of Pepperdine was his decision to begin a "Year-in-Europe" program. He realized how formative his own traveling experiences had been in his early years. Now he wanted to expand the education of Pepperdine undergraduates to include that same kind of international experience. And for Norvel, there was only one place where that experience should be centered: his beloved Heidelberg!

The story of Pepperdine's Heidelberg campus and program has its preface in the late 1940s. During the days when Otis Gatewood was traipsing the country with a vision of preaching the gospel to post-war Europe, he visited Nashville. His challenging words touched J. C. and Dorothy Moore, and Dorothy said, "J. C., let's do this. Let's go to Europe for the Lord." And they did. They spent four years, from 1948 until 1952, in and around Frankfurt, Germany. Of course, there was a strong connection with Norvel Young, because the Moores were sent to Germany by the Broadway Church in Lubbock. So, when the Youngs and the Baxters and their group visited Europe in 1949, they were anxious to see their old friends, the Moores.

But J. C. Moore did more than proclaim the gospel from a pulpit. He built buildings. He was an excellent business manager, and the Broadway Church leadership put him in charge of financing and constructing about seven new church buildings. In fact, the Church of Christ building in Frankfurt, constructed in 1948, was the first new structure to go up in that city after the war. All other construction to that point had been repairs and restorations. Among the buildings J. C constructed was the church building in Heidelberg.

In 1961 President Norvel Young decided to move ahead on his dream for a Pepperdine presence abroad. Naturally, he had been encouraged in the project by J. C. Moore, who was now the comp-troller at Pepperdine College. When Norvel presented the idea to the Board of Trustees, they reminded him of what he already knew: there was no money for such a program in the tight bud-get. However, they said, if he could find a way to break even on the program, he could proceed. He, Dean Sanders, J. C. Moore and others began researching the idea from all angles in an effort to keep expenses to a minimum. If they were careful, they thought they could keep costs down to the amount students would pay for tuition and living expenses on the Los Angeles campus. Students could purchase special rail passes in Europe, where tourism was still being encouraged with lower prices. J. C. Moore's experiences doing business in Germany were invaluable.

It was announced in November 1962 that Germany had been selected as the sight for the program. And those who knew him were not surprised that Norvel had chosen Heidelberg as the site. At least a few knew that he had fallen in love with the city in 1937, just before the war began in Europe, and he and Moore had both been deeply involved in post-war relief efforts in the Heidelberg area.

When Norvel let it be known to the faculty that he was look-ing for someone to direct the inaugural program in September 1963, Howard A. White, who was then dean of graduate studies, jumped at the opportunity. He and his wife, Maxine, and J. C. and Dorothy Moore and their families traveled to Heidelberg with the first 36 Pepperdine students to study un-der the new program. Other faculty members who helped with the program during the first year were Dr. and Mrs. Frank Pack, Dr. Erika Weigand, Richard Walker, Robert Morris and Glenn Boyd. Students lived in the Golden Rose Hotel just off the Hauptstrasse, the narrow main street of old town that had been closed to vehicle traffic to enhance pedestrian shopping. Classes were held in Amerikahaus, not far away. Not only were German instructors used, but also American missionaries from across Europe traveled to teach in their specialties. They were, of course, glad to get a little extra salary for their efforts.

Only a month and a half after arriving, the Pepperdine group was shocked by the news that, back home, President John F. Kennedy had been assassinated. They found that the German people shared their own grief over the national loss. But despite the troubling news from America, the students finished the year giving the program glowing reviews, and it was clear to all but the staunchest cynics that the program was on its way to becoming a Pepperdine tradition.

Two years later, Norvel and J. C. Moore traveled to Heidelberg to put the finishing touches on a home for the Year-in-Europe program. There was still no money in the college budget for a European campus, but an interesting situation had developed. It turned out that the Frankfurt church building that Moore had built in the 1940s was adjacent to the University of Frankfurt. The university now wanted to expand and needed that property. So the church, which consisted of a German congregation and a mostly American (military) congregation, decided they could merge with another church located in a Frankfurt suburb. They then sold the property and donated the proceeds to Pepperdine College, with the provision that Pepperdine should make it possible for German young people to train for Christian ministry at a new "Bibleschule," which the college would establish in Heidelberg. Pepperdine was more than willing to make the arrangements, including tuition-free classes using local missionaries as teachers, and offer a certificate in Bible for the German Christian students. And in return, they had their money to buy a Heidelberg campus.

When President Young and Comptroller Moore got to Heidelberg in early 1965, they went to a real estate agent who said, "I've got just the property for you." He took them up the hill overlooking the city and the Neckar River, not far from the old castle. The gracious mansion had once been the residence of a professor at the University of Heidelberg. Immediately after the war, it was used by the U. S. Army military police, and later by the local Heidelberg police. It seemed perfect. Norvel and J. C. looked out toward Philosophers Way, across the river, and said, "We'll take it!" A few years hence, the beautiful facility would be named in honor of the one whose fingerprints were everywhere in the transaction. Generations of students live and study in "Moorehaus," a tribute to James C. and Dorothy Moore, not only for arranging the purchase of the building, but also for their many years of service to Christian education and to a tattered, war-torn Germany in the late '40s.

H. Glenn Boyd, who with his wife, Shirley, had been missionaries in Germany when the Year-in-Europe program was founded, said to Norvel many years later:

> "We well remember the day in 1965, that you and J. C. Moore visited us for lunch in Karlsruhe, Germany, along with Emily, to invite us to move to Heidelberg and live in the newly purchased villa. We had been in Karlsruhe for eight years and did not anticipate leaving that work any time soon. When we said that we could not leave the work, your reply was simply, 'We are not asking you to leave this work, rather, we want you to move to Heidelberg and continue your work here.' We argued that that would be a 35 miles drive, to which you answered, 'Nearly every one of us drives that far in Los Angeles. That is no problem.' We moved to Heidelberg in 1966, and are still grateful to you for your expression of confidence and support, which has continued, as is typical of you, throughout these years.

Once again, Norvel had orchestrated a symphony out of a tavern song. He had his program in Heidelberg. Pepperdine students would be enthralled with the beautiful Europe he knew. He and Moore had found a large and gracious old home for the program, and now he had found a Christian family to manage the headquarters. And while he was at it, he had encouraged a mission work. It was a good trip.

Pepperdine College was surviving financially, the academic programs were being strengthened and a new campus was being opened in the lovely old city of Heidelberg. As it headed into the mid-1960s under the presidency of M. Norvel Young, the college was on the move.

THE WATTS RIOTS

In the summer of 1965, President Young traveled to Washington, D.C., to extend his fund-raising efforts from there. From his hotel room he called home to check in with Helen, and she told him that people were rioting in the Watts area of Los Angeles, just to the south of the campus. But she advised Norvel not to come home and cut his Washington trip short. It would be over soon, she assured him. She was wrong.

Unaware of how extensive the riots would become, Norvel notified Vice President William Teague to handle the situation. As the hours dragged into days and the violence escalated, Teague decided to close the school and send the students to off-campus locations, away from the danger. From the nation's capital, Norvel watched the events swirling near his college with feelings of helplessness and frustration. When the National Guard was called in because of the prolonged disturbance, they used the campus as a staging area and headquarters.

A worried President Young quickly made arrangements and flew home as the riots continued into a second and a third day. "Flew *home*" is not quite correct. At the urging of William Teague, Helen and the children had evacuated the president's home on campus and were staying with Pepperdine professor William Stivers and his wife, Frances, and their family in Inglewood.

But as bad as the situation seemed, Norvel was not ready to panic. Always the optimist, he did not believe the riots would destroy the school. However, as a pragmatist, he also believed that it would become increasingly difficult to recruit students and raise financial support, especially in places like Dallas, Nashville and other southern and midwestern cities where many people were always suspicious and ready to believe the worst about California. In fact, one board member who lived in Dallas resigned soon after the Watts Riots.

Still, Norvel was hopeful that the ugly situation would wane and finally disappear. After all, the late '50s and early '60s had seen much growth and expansion of facilities at Pepperdine College. It seemed out of the question to think about moving to another location. "We were a little slow in joining with those who advocated finding new property," said Norvel. "I kept thinking, 'This will go away.'"

During the days of violence, the Pepperdine campus was a haven that experienced no damage or even real threat of harm. Local community leaders were very encouraging, assuring the president and others that it was unlikely that the campus would ever be attacked in any way. They promised their personal support to protect the school.

But as the months went by, the noticeable tension in the aftermath of the civil disturbance exerted a pressure on the board to consider finding another location for undergraduate students. There was no thought of selling the original Los Angeles campus. Rather, the idea was to find additional space in view of the expanding programs. Since the recent violence tended to primarily discourage undergraduate recruitment, the proposal was to continue adult programs on the original campus while finding property more conducive to residential, undergraduate students.

Looking back, Don Miller wrote:

> The decade of the sixties brought new challenges for the growing [college]. Demographic changes and social unrest erupting in the Watts riots near the campus sealed the fate of an expanding [college] in that location. Dr. Young and the Board grappled with

the task of moving to a location that would provide for the expansion. Dr. Young once compared the feat of relocating a college campus to moving a "cemetery" in complexity. It would involve seeking a suitable site, inducing those owners to make a land gift, and the massive job of raising millions of dollars for land development and building the necessary buildings, a super-human task.

Quite a number of the faculty were not sold on finding a new undergraduate campus. Norvel and Helen remembered that Dean J. P. Sanders was not really in favor of a new campus. Nor was Dean of Graduate Studies Howard A. White, who would later become the fifth president of Pepperdine. And Chairman of the Bible Department Frank Pack believed that the College should just build a taller fence and stay put.

Pressure from the violence alone may not have been enough to make additional property acquisition possible. But, evidenced by new programs, increased enrollment and acquired adjacent properties, the growing success of Pepperdine College also added pressure to finding a larger campus. Pepperdine was "on a roll." As serious as the grievances of the inner city people may have been, it was no time for Pepperdine to be sidetracked from what many perceived as its destiny.

In 1966 President Young appointed a committee to investigate various prospective sites for an additional campus. Donald Darnell was named chairman of the group that was composed of members from the President's Board.

In 1970 Norvel looked back to that time and recounted:

> Pepperdine's faculty, administration, and boards embarked upon a self-study, designed to prepare the College to enter the 21st Century – with its vast and unpredictable changes – as a viable, independent, Christian college providing education for the whole

man. During this period, it became evident that we needed to apply the most modern management principles to college education. We wanted Pepperdine to maintain its personal emphasis on good teaching, but the demand for our services continued to increase. We wanted to grow to serve the increasing number of young people who chose Pepperdine for a Christian education.

A past study had indicated that our Los Angeles campus was admirably suited to education for life in the city, but that we did not have adequate space for additional residential programs that we wished to inaugurate. We decided to take the college to the people rather than attempt to bring all the people we wished to serve to one central location.

Executive Vice President William Teague made it public in January 1967 that Pepperdine was looking for additional space. The college, he announced, was moving toward a "multi-campus concept." There was already a thriving European program housed in Heidelberg, West Germany. And the Los Angeles campus, he emphasized, would not be sold, but would be used for the growing number of graduate studies programs.

Three months later, in April 1967, Norvel Young was in Canyon, Texas, delivering the 20th Willson Lecture Series at West Texas State University. The student newspaper, *The Prairie*, ran a feature about the series on April 7, with a photograph of Dr. Young. In part, the article read:

Dr. M. Norvel Young opened the current Willson Lecture series at West Texas State University Tuesday, by asking if Jesus Christ, and the ideals he taught, are relevant for the college student in meeting the problems he faces in the world today. ...

Dr. Young spoke of several revolutions occurring in the world today. He said that the teachings of Jesus were revolutionary in his time. He said they were different from the common meaning attached to the word revolution, in that they were constructive rather than destructive teachings.

Young said that Christian religions are also in the midst of revolution, commonly called the ecumenical movement. He said changing attitudes in the various denominations are marked by attempts to define common beliefs of each and to establish closer relations among the various groups. Also, he said that opposition of people holding other ideals and philosophies is becoming open and pronounced today.

Young has traveled and lectured in several countries, including Far East and Iron Curtain countries. He attended the World Congress of Evangelism in Berlin in 1966.

In a smaller article, Norvel's final lecture was announced elsewhere in the newspaper. It said, "Dr. M. Norvel Young, president of Pepperdine College, Los Angeles, California, will present his final lecture this morning in the annual Willson Series. ... Topic for today's speech, to be given at 10 a.m. in the Administration Building auditorium, will be 'Love or Perish.'" It is interesting that a state school asked Norvel to come and lecture about spiritual topics. Certainly, those things were on the minds of many people in the revolutionary days of the '60s.

Perhaps the most profound thing that happened in 1967, in its long-term effect on both Norvel Young and Pepperdine, was when a corporation called Tenneco agreed to give a leave of absence to one of its young lawyers named Charles B. Runnels. Tenneco had assigned Dr. Runnels to research oil project sites in the Southwest and California. When they heard that Pepperdine was in need of good people to assist in their search for a new campus location, they agreed that Runnels was the person.

That man who was on loan from Tenneco stayed on and became an indispensable part of Pepperdine, first as assistant to the president, next as vice president for Business Relations, then as vice chancellor and finally as chancellor. Almost 30 years later, Charles Runnels wrote:

> Norvel, I can well remember when Tenneco announced they were sending me to Los Angeles on a special project. The elders at our congregation were afraid for us because they had heard all of the unpleasant stories about Los Angeles. However, they did encourage me to look up Norvel Young as soon as I arrived because you were recommended as the only one who could advise us and keep us faithful in the church. I did just that, and I recall the first time you and I met, you offered me a job. What a compliment to a person you had never met before. Now we realize that you have always had excellent judgment and an eye for attracting good people so our University could prosper and reach for higher goals.

Indeed, Charlie Runnels and his wife, Amy Jo, became the same kind of dynamic team that Norvel and Helen were. Like the Youngs, their sacrificial lives were filled with friends.

MALIBU DREAMING

More than 40 fine locations were studied, some as far away as Temecula and San Diego. The more promising ones were in places like Palos Verdes, Calabasas and Westlake Village. Each of the sites had favorable aspects, but each also had some problems. The Palos Verdes property, for example, was too small and confining. And the Westlake Village property, near the 101 freeway and Lindero Canyon, straddled the Ventura-Los Angeles county line, which could potentially prove to be problematic.

But the only prospective campus site that really stirred Norvel Young's imagination was the one in Malibu. When asked to speculate on where he thought the college would have been built if Malibu had ultimately been rejected, Norvel said, "Probably in Westlake Village." But from this present perspective – in other words, in hindsight – it is difficult to imagine a "Pepperdine University in Westlake Village" generating excitement among people across the country and around the world.

On the other hand, Norvel and Helen could envision a college campus with a spiritual mission situated on the slopes of the Santa Monica Mountains, overlooking the vast Pacific Ocean like a silent sentinel. The possibility of the valuable seaside land came through the friendship of board of trustees member George Evans with the Adamson family: Merritt H. Adamson, Sylvia Rindge Adamson Neville and Rhoda-May Adamson Dallas. The brother and two sisters were descendants of the family that had purchased the entire Malibu territory in 1891. Frederick Hastings Rindge bought 13,315 acres of prime coastal land that were part of the original Spanish land grant, Rancho Malibu Topanga Sequit, made to a Spanish soldier by the King of Spain in 1804. When rising taxes forced the ranch into bankruptcy in 1951, it was subdivided and parts of the original property came back to the daughter of Frederick and May Rindge, Rhoda Rindge Adamson. From there Rhoda's children, Merritt, Sylvia and Rhoda-May, became heirs to parts of the rugged land that stretched along the famous coastline.

But some at Pepperdine opposed the Malibu site, believing that the celebrity village's reputation made it an unsuitable place for a Christian college. One President's Board member resigned when Malibu was finally chosen. He was convinced that it would be far too expensive to build there.

Board members Robert P. Jones and George Evans were especially helpful in getting the offer of Malibu land. Evans, whom Norvel called the "unsung hero" of the "Malibu miracle," was financial advisor to the Adamson family and met with the various parties many times at the Jonathan Club to work out details of the land offer.

The 15 members of the board of trustees finally met to decide the future direction of undergraduate study at Pepperdine. After much discussion, they decided to decline the offer of the Malibu property because the College simply did not have the money to invest in moving the thousands of tons of earth to build on the hillsides.

All through this period, discussions on the viability of a campus at Malibu continued. Don Darnell and Henry Salvatori were very influential in steering the school toward the "seaside paradise." Walter Knott, famed founder of Knott's Berry Farm, urged the College to move forward, saying, "I have worked on flat land and had to build mountains. I'd rather have had the mountains and cut them down where needed!"

Even people beyond the usual Pepperdine circles got into the discussion. The board received a letter from Bill Banowsky, then the minister for Norvel's former church, the Broadway Church of Christ in Lubbock, Texas. Banowsky wrote powerfully on why he believed that Malibu was the right location.

In the midst of the uncertainty, President Young had an idea. He asked the board if they would approve the Malibu campus concept if he could get a gift of a half million dollars from Richard Scaife to start the site preparation process. Scaife, one of the heirs of the great Mellon fortune, had become familiar with and supportive of Pepperdine. The board agreed to Norvel's proposal.

Bill Teague flew to Pittsburgh, Pennsylvania, and returned with the money from Scaife. So, in October 1968, a special bulletin from Pepperdine College announced the exciting gift of 138 acres of Malibu land. Suddenly the prospects for the little college in south-central Los Angeles seemed exceptionally bright.

In a news conference, Merritt Adamson said that he and his sisters felt "that in making this gift of land to Pepperdine we are helping to fulfill the destiny of the property." He continued, "Our family long has felt this prime Rancho Malibu land should be held for an outstanding and special use."

Norvel responded to the statement, saying that the new site would be the center of a progressive liberal arts program serving residential students and the suburban community. "Because of the rare beauty and aesthetic qualities of the Malibu area," Norvel said, "and because the area was not being served by a four-year college, we felt that to plan and build in Malibu would give us an opportunity to establish a unique campus in which the traditional liberal arts program may be blended with the latest learning facilities and techniques."

Many people were thrilled. And, of course, many people were taking bows. And there in the middle of it all, as so often was the case, was Norvel Young, dreaming and scheming and creating possibilities while others were taking the credit. Like a basketball point guard with his team at heart, he was passing the ball to teammates and patiently waiting for the right moment. Then he made the play.

Norvel was a consummate playmaker. And in the process of creating possibilities and plays, he made everyone else a hero.

Something else happened in fall 1967, something so apparently insignificant that it was to be forgotten almost immediately. Norvel was on a trip to New York and had arrived at Kennedy Airport. He caught an airport bus to Manhattan and settled himself back into the seat for the ride into the bustling city. But right behind him was a young man, a third-year law student from Vanderbilt, who was interviewing with several New York law firms for a job. And the young man immediately recognized Norvel from the times he had heard him speak at Abilene Christian College and at church. He leaned forward and introduced himself, and a short conversation ensued.

When Norvel found out that the young man was looking for employment and life opportunities, he suggested to him that he consider Southern California. He regaled the young man with images of "the gateway to the Pacific and Asia," and painted a beautiful and exciting picture of the West Coast and the mission of Pepperdine. Then they reached their individual destinations and parted company.

But the young man did not forget the passing conversation. Within seven years or so, he and his wife and family had moved to Santa Monica, and he had joined the law firm of Latham & Watkins in Los Angeles. He was eventually added to Pepperdine's Board of Regents. And upon the death of Chairman Lloyd Nelson in 1980, he was chosen to fill that important chairmanship. He also became a leader in the Culver Palms Church. His name was Thomas G. Bost.

A CAMPUS UNDER SIEGE

In the late 1960s social and environmental pressures seemed to push toward the bursting point. There were student protests at Cal Berkeley, at Stanford, at UC Santa Barbara, at UCLA, everywhere. Each interest group demonstrated to draw attention to its list of grievances and its list of demands. For example, African American students demanded more Black Studies programs and Mexican American students demanded more Chicano Studies programs, and so on. For a while, it seemed as though Pepperdine might escape the protests. Then came 1969.

President Young was walking home from his office in the administration building. By that time, the college administration had been moved to the large building on the northwestern corner of Vermont Avenue and 81st Street. The building previously had been a Von's Market, but the college had acquired the structure so it could use the former administration building for classrooms for the expanding student body. The building had a tower on the corner nearest the intersection, and the president and other senior administrators had offices in the tower or the mezzanine leading up to it – thus the wide references at Pepperdine to the "Tower of Power."

It was about dusk when Norvel began his walk home, north a block, then westward on the sidewalk of 79th Street. Toward the end of the row of palm trees on the Promenade he could see a group gathering in front of Marilyn Hall, the women's dormitory. Then he could hear a woman scream and people yelling and running. He realized that the crowd was shocked and distraught and becoming agitated. Soon he got the terrible story.

It was a common practice for the neighborhood teenagers to use the College gymnasium to play basketball. But on this afternoon, Charles Lane, campus chief of security, had told a couple of young men that the gym was closed because of another function later in the evening. Stories differed as to what happened next. To the best of Norvel and Helen's recollection, it happened like this:

The young men and Lane exchanged words, and threats began to fly. Lane went to his car, which he had parked nearby. He opened the trunk and laid his shotgun on top of the car to show the boys he meant business. The two boys were frustrated – maybe they thought he was being unfair or something – but they became very insistent. Lane hoped he could frighten them with the gun. At one point the security chief reached for the shotgun and one of the boys jumped for it at the same time and grabbed hold of it. A short struggle ensued and the gun went off. Teenager Larry Kimmons was shot.

Norvel said, "When I ran up, Larry was lying on the ground dying. Blood was all over and around him. The woman screaming was Larry's mother, and my heart went out to her." Then Norvel began to think of the broader implications. Soon police and ambulance vehicles arrived and the scene was mass confusion with sirens and lights and gathering crowds of neighbor people.

The police began a full-scale investigation. Helen remembered the officers in the living room of the president's home talking to students and neighborhood folks, as well as with Norvel and Bill Banowsky. "It was such a strange and sad time," she recalled.

As soon as Banowsky reached campus, he and Norvel went to the Kimmons' home to express the college's sympathy to the boy's mother, to tell her of the grief of everyone at Pepperdine. The two went to the home against the advice of the police, who thought there could be racial repercussions. But Norvel and Bill thought it was the right thing to do.

There was an atmosphere of absolute shock in the home, and yet the grief-stricken mother seemed to appreciate the college's concern. But, as Helen remembered, the family's feelings soon turned to anger as others became involved. Militant groups that were eager to inflame any situation, even though Pepperdine had worked very hard at keeping good neighborhood relations. Lane was acquitted in the trial that followed, but that didn't bring back Larry Kimmons. It was a great tragedy – and also an explosive situation, because Kimmons was African American and the guard was white.

Norvel and Bill Banowsky were up all night talking with the Kimmons family and negotiating with community residents and others. There had always been goodwill between the community and the college. That goodwill helped them get through the immediate difficulty.

Pepperdine had avoided the kind of militant protests that other colleges and universities had endured. Administrators at other institutions were knuckling under to student demands in what seemed like a violent overthrow of America's institutions of higher learning. But now the tragic death of Larry Kimmons set off a chain of events that threatened to bring the same kind of confrontations to Pepperdine. A few days after the accident, a group of Pepperdine students, composed mostly of the Black Students Organization, gathered in front of the Academic Life Building (formerly the Administration Building) on campus. They chained the doors closed and staged a protest on the steps of the building. They demanded an immediate meeting with President Young in the Oasis student lounge. Norvel went by himself to meet with the students.

In the meeting, the students presented Norvel with ten demands, including several things the school simply could not do. Norvel later commented that he wished he could have done more, but it simply was not possible, in his view. The situation was made more tense in that some of the college's Student Life staff members had sided with the militants and were also pushing for certain changes.

In a hastily called meeting with some of the faculty members during the lock-out, Norvel delivered an update on the student demands and shared his own views that the college must not allow the students to run the school. He soon realized that he was nearly alone in the matter. Bill Banowsky, Oly Tegner and a few others were his only allies. Many of the faculty voted to give in to the student demands. Some of them may have genuinely agreed with the student group, but most, in Norvel's view, were simply afraid of what the volatile situation might bring.

Finally, it was time to confront the lockout so the college could get back to the business of education. Norvel, Bill Banowsky and Oly Tegner met to discuss how to bring closure to the situation. Bill told Norvel that the president should not confront the students. Banowsky said he would go himself. With a chuckle, Oly Tegner remembered, "Banowsky said to Norvel, 'You stay here. If you go over there, they might kill you. Come on, Oly. Let's go.' And I thought, 'Well, if they are going to kill Norvel, what makes you think they won't kill me?'"

When they got to the Academic Life Building, Banowsky asked the students to unlock the building and go home. When they refused, he said, "We aren't going to call the police and have you ejected. We are just going to see to it that you lose all your credits for the semester." Prospects of calling the police and having to go to jail didn't seem to frighten the students. But apparently the thought of losing credits they had worked hard for did motivate them. They unlocked the doors and the situation was defused.

After the shooting incident, strangers, non-students, began to loiter on and around the campus. At times they would be standing at the heart of the campus, in front of the gate to the driveway of the president's home. On two or three occasions, a group of angry-looking men surrounded Helen and the children as they tried to pull the family car into their driveway. Though not afraid for herself, the incidents did make Helen nervous for the children's sake.

The awful events left the campus tense and divided. Helen remembered that it was hard to feel that there was a cordial relationship with African American students. Even some of the black students who had been the best of friends with the Youngs now drew back. Everyone was grieving, and the campus was left in a very precarious state.

The Pepperdine Bible Lectures were scheduled to begin within a day or two of the problems. They went forward, but were moved to the Inglewood Church of Christ, a safer and less volatile venue.

Things gradually settled down as the emphasis shifted from the tragedy to the discussion of Pepperdine building a new campus in Malibu, with the Los Angeles campus becoming primarily a commuter campus.

11

THE MIRACLE
AT MALIBU

Both were visionaries, both were exceptional speakers,
both were motivators, both were charming promoters.
It would take all that talent and more
to accomplish the task before them.

*I*n 1981, Chancellor M. Norvel Young said, "Joe Bentley
[Pepperdine's longtime legal counsel with the law firm of
Latham and Watkins] says there have been so many
'coincidences' that he is convinced that Pepperdine has a
manifest destiny. Surely the past is prologue. A recent study made
by the educational consulting firm of Brakeley, John Price Jones,
Inc., found that the faculty, staff and Board of Pepperdine
University have 'an excitement created by a sense of destiny.'"

It is true that many people associated with Pepperdine through
the years had a certain feeling or unique sense about the institution. Some expressed it as "a calling" or "a special mission."
Others referred to it as "a destiny." However it was described, it
was the idea that Pepperdine was somehow different from other
schools. Many had the boldness to suggest that the school was
ordained by God to carry out a specific role in its society.

Certainly, some of those kinds of assertions were there from
the very founding of the college in September 1937, and they
related to George Pepperdine's great feeling of stewardship over
the money he believed God had entrusted to him. But one

cannot look at the span of the school's history without seeing a heightened sense of mission as the lives of Norvel and Helen Young become intertwined with the institution. The Youngs lived and breathed *purpose* and *mission* in all that they did. It was a part of their generation, a part of their heritage.

That is not to say that Pepperdine University's mission began with the Youngs. It did not. It began with Mr. Pepperdine's idealism and devotion to God. And that "heightened sense of mission" is not to say that everything the Youngs thought and said and did always worked out. Norvel and Helen were always quick to acknowledge their weaknesses. Yet in their humanness, their genius was the ability to focus sharply on the goals they believed were immutable, then to allow those goals to direct their energies. They were members of that "greatest generation," as television journalist Tom Brokaw called the heroes of the mid-twentieth century. The people of that generation were not contemplative idealists, though they were fine thinkers. Instead, they were doers. With sleeves rolled up, they made things happen ... beneficial things, great things. And like the generation of pioneers a hundred years before them, they had notions of a "manifest destiny" that laid before them. Like the pioneers, they saw the challenges of their lives through the eyes of faith.

As circumstance piled upon circumstance, Norvel and Helen became convinced that God was moving the college toward some wonderful goal. The Los Angeles campus seemed ready for a transformation: it was becoming more difficult to recruit typical undergraduate students to attend college in the inner city, but the campus could serve admirably as a commuter school for working adults. With the business and education departments becoming schools and with the addition of a law school, Pepperdine College was nearly ready to announce its university status.

By the mid-1960s, the leadership of the college was already considering how to accommodate the expanding student body.

Now all the pressures seemed to be propelling Pepperdine toward some new, exciting campus that would capture the imagination of the community and the nation. Norvel Young certainly agreed with the thinking of Daniel H. Burnham, who said, "Make no little plans; they have no magic to stir men's blood … Make big plans, aim high in hope and work." Norvel and Helen would be looking for nothing short of a miracle.

A DYNAMIC PARTNERSHIP

It was back in early 1958, only a few months after the Youngs moved to Los Angeles, and Norvel had traveled to the campus of David Lipscomb College in Nashville. He was attending his first ever Presidents Meeting, a regular gathering of the leaders of several Christian colleges across the nation. On this occasion, the presidents had been called together to receive a gift of five or ten thousand dollars each from benefactor A. M. Burton for their schools. And as a part of the program, a promising young Lipscomb College senior addressed the group. His name was William S. Banowsky.

During the compelling speech, Norvel felt "a strange connection with Bill," as he put it. When he got home he told Helen, "I want this young man. He's a leader!" Later, Norvel said of Banowsky, "He was obviously what we called in Tennessee 'a five-gaited horse' – a man of many talents."

When they met after the address, Norvel encouraged the young orator to continue on with his education and seek a master's degree. He did, graduating in only one year from the University of New Mexico with a master's in speech communication, while he preached for the Netherwood Park Church of Christ in Albuquerque.

It was at that point in 1959 that Norvel invited Bill Banowsky to join the administration at Pepperdine as assistant to the president. The 23-year-old quickly proved himself to be a dynamic young man who could get things done. Four years later, he had not only earned his Ph.D. in speech communication from USC, but he also had been promoted to dean of students. But in 1963, the restless young Texan decided it was time for a new chapter in his life. With Norvel's blessing and recommendation, Banowsky accepted the pulpit of the Broadway Church of Christ in Lubbock. He served there with distinction for five years, maturing and honing his leadership skills.

In 1967, Bill Banowsky and Norvel Young met again and renewed their friendship in Fresno, California, at the ranch of Marion and Lois Edmonds. Bill knew the Edmonds from the days when he served as preacher for the South Gate Church of Christ and Marion Edmonds was a leader in the congregation. Banowsky and Young were both in Fresno for a church function and were invited to the Edmonds ranch. The two tried their hand at horseback riding, and as they rode, they talked of the future. Norvel shared his dream for Pepperdine's new undergraduate campus, which he hoped would be at Malibu. And Bill caught the dream – adding that, while he did not have an interest in returning to the Los Angeles campus, the idea of building a whole new school in a place like Malibu excited him.

Always the astute observer, Norvel Young realized that, after his ten years as president of Pepperdine, the college now needed a burst of youth and enthusiasm in order to move to the next level of success. He typified the visionary leader who is great, not only because of his own talents, but because he knows his limitations and consequently surrounds himself with talented people. As Norvel settled into his saddle on a swaying horse that meandered along a forgotten road in California's San Joaquin Valley, he described his vision to his young companion. And he laid the groundwork for bringing Bill Banowsky back to Pepperdine.

After the meeting in Fresno, Banowsky returned to Texas and wrote the letter recommending Malibu as the site for the new college. Meanwhile, Norvel returned to Pepperdine to consult with Executive Vice President Bill Teague, who seemed ready for a new work. Indeed, he had often talked of running for the

United States Congress. And with support from Henry Salvatori and others, everything pointed to this being the opportune time. For Norvel, it meant that Teague's vacancy would open the way for Banowsky to return to Pepperdine.

Within a matter of a very few months, all of the pieces finally fell together. Teague returned from Pittsburgh with the pivotal gift from Richard Scaife, which was the prerequisite for accepting the offer of the Adamson land at Malibu. Then Teague resigned his position at Pepperdine to run for Congress. With the early 1968 announcement that Malibu would be the site for a new undergraduate campus, President Young was ready to appeal to Banowsky to return to Pepperdine. And when Norvel made the call in 1968, Bill was prepared to accept perhaps the greatest challenge of his life.

BIRTH OF A COLLEGE

The vision of building a beautiful new campus above the sparkling ocean in Malibu was creating an unexpected excitement among many important people. Twenty-five years later Mr. Richard M. Scaife would reminisce with Norvel, "It seems only yesterday that we climbed the fence and picked our way up the hills to look down on what is now Pepperdine University – today an impressive institution of opportunity and learning, just as you knew it would be. And it was the certainty of your convictions and remarkable energy that made it so."

Scaife continued, "Your youth and creativity are there as ever, as is the inspiration you give to others. Whether it be as a dedicated family man with a wonderful wife and children, or as a resolute man of God and defender of the faith, or as one who has endured great personal affliction and tragedy to be reborn for still greater things – you continue to leave your mark upon us."

With Banowsky's arrival in 1968, an amazing team was formed, and with it, the next historic phase of Pepperdine's history was inaugurated. Young and Banowsky were a matched pair that spanned two generations: Bill was 32, and Norvel was 53. Both were visionaries, both were exceptional speakers, both were motivators, both were charming promoters. It would take all that talent and more to accomplish the task before them.

"Dr. Banowsky was challenged to take the lead in constructing a truly innovative master plan that would directly influence the shape of brick and mortar," remembered Norvel. So while President Young ran the daily operations of the college, Executive Vice President Banowsky organized a faculty committee to plan an interdisciplinary curriculum. He also recommended the services of the architectural firm of William Pereira and Associates to create a master plan for the physical facilities of the new college. The idea was to begin with a clean sheet of paper and to create something entirely new in both academics and architecture. It was a powerful dream.

President Young later gave Banowsky the credit for obtaining the services of world renowned architect Pereira. "He sold me on him," said Norvel. "But one of the most difficult things was deciding what to do about Pereira's former partner, Charles Luckman. Pereira and Luckman had just parted ways and were not very friendly at the time. But Luckman was a friend to Pepperdine and had helped us pick the Malibu site and other things. We had to tell him that we were going with his former partner. Nobody would go with me, so I had to go see Charles alone with the news. Though it was difficult, he remained our good friend through the following years."

Norvel recalled that, not long after his return to Pepperdine, Bill Banowsky met Mrs. Blanche Seaver for the first time. Mrs. Seaver's husband, the late Frank Roger Seaver, had been president of the international oil tool firm, the Hydril Company. As he thought back over the years, Norvel said:

I will never forget the first time Vice President William Teague and I asked him [Frank Seaver] to help on a film project illustrating the difference between

Communism and the private enterprise system. Henry Salvatori had recommended that we visit Mr. Seaver. We asked his help on a $15,000 project. We were seeking 15 people to give $1,000 each. Instead he wrote out a check for $7,500 and, with a grin, handed it to me saying, "Do you think this will help?" It not only helped, it put the project over the top. We obtained additional support from Richard M. Scaife of Pittsburgh. With this assistance we launched a series of freedom seminars and summer programs for public school teachers. The sowing of this seed brought an abundant harvest. It wasn't popular then to be "Conservative" or patriotic or even "anti-Communist," but we dared to be different.

Before meeting Banowsky, Mrs. Seaver had already given money to Pepperdine College after learning that her husband, Frank, had remembered the school in his will. (Helen remembered that an excited Norvel had come home with the news that Mrs. Seaver had given the school a million dollars. To celebrate, he gave Helen a gold bracelet, which he assured her was not paid for by Mrs. Seaver's money!) But now Norvel and Bill wanted to interest Mrs. Seaver in the Malibu campus. They drove out to Malibu together in her chauffeured car – Bill and the driver in the front and Norvel and Blanche in the back. Mrs. Seaver was immediately taken with the handsome and charming executive vice president. And, as it turned out, she was also very excited about the Malibu location.

But in the late '60s not all was well for Pepperdine, nor for higher education in general. There were riots at Stanford, the University of California at Santa Barbara and elsewhere. Angela Davis, an avowed Communist, was employed by UC Berkeley as an instructor, and President S. I. Hayakawa was simply trying desperately to keep the lid on his school. In those difficult times, some donors switched their allegiance to

Pepperdine. They saw Pepperdine as a more traditional school than some of the larger schools, which they perceived as having capitulated to the student unrest.

But Pepperdine was not without its own crises. As mentioned, in 1969 Norvel and the administration had to face a tense period of student unrest on the Los Angeles campus. Somehow, the situation was defused and the power keg was not ignited.

Still, the episodes on the Pepperdine campus seemed mild compared to the major upheavals that were transpiring on other college and university campuses, fueled by the cultural and sexual revolutions. By contrast, it seemed that the most pronounced activities at Pepperdine were academic advancements.

Buoyed by the youthful support of Bill Banowsky, Norvel Young launched out in a number of entrepreneurial ways. He was approached by Edward Di Loreto and others about becoming affiliated with a small, evening law school in Orange County. President Young quickly moved the proposal forward. In short order, he had also expanded the department of business into a school of business, and moved the department of education toward a school of education. While almost no one noticed, Norvel was transforming Pepperdine College into Pepperdine University.

In October 1969, Editor Reuel Lemmons devoted an entire issue of his journal, *Firm Foundation*, to Pepperdine College. In his editorial he wrote:

> We see by the papers that Pepperdine College has acquired a law school. We have seen the beautiful newly acquired site at Malibu. We hear that Pepperdine will continue its efforts on its present campus. It has had a campus in Heidelberg, Germany, for some time. We have wind of still other plans. It all makes us wonder if we are about to experience our first multi-campus university [among Church of Christ-related colleges]. Could be. It seems obvious that plans point in that direction.

Lemmons went on in his editorial to announce that Bill Banowsky had just been named chancellor of the new Malibu campus – a campus, we might add, that boasted nothing but chaparral-covered hills at that time. In the issue was an article about Pepperdine's purpose, with a photograph and the following caption: "The Malibu land was a gift of the Adamson family, two sisters and a brother, shown here with Pepperdiners. In the picture, from left, are Charles Runnels, assistant to the college president; Merritt H. Adamson; Rhoda-May Adamson Dallas; Dr. M. Norvel Young, Pepperdine President; Sylvia Rindge Adamson Neville; Robert Jones, member of the Board of Trustees, and Dr. William Teague, vice-president."

Among the other articles about Pepperdine was one by Bill Youngs, called "The Man at the Helm." Youngs was the public information specialist for the college and the writer of volumes of information about the college's people, including a biography of George Pepperdine, titled *Faith Was His Fortune,* and a biography of Mr. Seaver, titled *The Legacy of Frank Roger Seaver*. Once when Norvel Young and Bill Youngs were together with a potential donor, the man, not catching the "s" on the end of Bill's last name, asked Norvel, "Is Bill your son?" To which Norvel responded, "No, Bill is a member of the branch of the family that didn't know how to spell."

In "The Man at the Helm," Bill Youngs offered a taste of President Norvel Young's busy schedule in the days leading up to the building of the Malibu campus. He wrote, "It's 8:30 in the morning and things are in full swing at Pepperdine College. The president parks his car – a new model he talked an auto [dealer] neighbor into providing for the college – near the administration building and walks briskly up the alley and through the mail room."

Bill Youngs continued to sketch the beginning of the frenetic day, which involved stopping every few yards to talk with secretaries, administrators, professors and students. Then he jumped to the end of Norvel's day:

A plane to catch in the night ... a meeting with Los Angeles business leaders – potential big donors for the new campus ... a wedding to perform on a Saturday afternoon at a church a hundred miles of freeway away ... a sermon to preach next morning a hundred miles of freeway in the other direction ... back home for an elders meeting, chapel at the college on Monday ... Pittsburgh in time for dinner with foundation directors that same night ... "Did I give the 20th Century Christian editorial to Helen?" He knows he doesn't have to worry about Helen – she'll find it...

How does he do it? How can this man keep up the pace he does and still find time to solve a problem for a young student secretary in the ad building?

"Norvel doesn't have any qualms about asking people to sacrifice for Pepperdine," a member of the Board of Trustees commented recently. "But the thing about Norvel is that he wouldn't ask anyone to do anything he wouldn't do himself. He drives himself more than he expects anyone else to do."

While the media and church publications like *Firm Foundation* had already picked up the story of Pepperdine's advancements, there had never been an official public fanfare concerning the new campus. The time had come to publicly reveal the dramatic architectural and academic plans for the future college. Norvel Young remembered it this way:

Plans were formulated to unveil the architectural drawings and to announce "the birth of a college." Faculty, alumni and friends were invited to a gala event at the Century Plaza Hotel. Reservations flooded in, overflowing the ballroom, so arrangements were made to simultaneously use the International Ballroom of the Beverly Hilton Hotel. Governor Ronald

Reagan spoke at both hotels, shuttling back and forth in the rain. Mr. Scaife of Pittsburgh, Mrs. Frank Roger Seaver and Richard Seaver, Fritz Huntsinger, Leonard Firestone, George Elkins, Mrs. B. D. Phillips, the John Tylers, Mrs. Margaret Martin Brock, Morris Pendleton, the Charles Paysons of New York, Clint Murchison of Dallas, Jerene Appleby Harnish, the John Stauffers, Bill and Bob Ahmanson and a host of others joined us that evening of February 9, 1970. William Pereira unveiled the dramatic campus plans, and we launched the new undergraduate college with a $24.5-million campaign. It was an auspicious beginning.

A CAMPUS BY THE SEA

About three and a half months later, on Saturday, May 23, 1970, the day dawned with a little haze in Malibu, California. By 9 a.m. or so, scores of people had finished their breakfasts and were beginning to wind their way through Los Angeles freeways to Santa Monica and from there, west along the coastline. When they reached Malibu Canyon Road, they turned north a quarter mile, then climbed a road above Pacific Coast Highway to a leveled-off hill overlooking the famous celebrity enclave, Malibu Colony. By a little after 10 a.m., an unusual assembly was taking shape against the rugged terrain of the Santa Monica Mountains. And the haze was lifting.

Many of the well-dressed people who were arriving had been at the "Birth of a College" dinner in early February. They were probably struck by the contrast between the elegance and glitter of that gala, which spanned two hotel ballrooms, and this rugged place above the ocean and below the mountains. From an evening on plush carpeting amid graceful décor, they had ventured to a bright morning in the glaring reality of sagebrush, rocks and raw earth. They parked their cars and took their places on white folding seats in long rows. Some special guests moved to a separate area where they congregated in cap and gown.

As 10:30 arrived, the robed group, representatives from many colleges and universities, proceeded in an academic procession, filling the front rows, while some moved onto the platform under the white canopy. The historic ceremony to formally dedicate Pepperdine's new campus site had begun.

There was an excellent keynote address, titled "The Role of the Private College in Today's World," by David Lawrence, editor of *U.S. News & World Report*. Lawrence noted, "Moral force has not yet reached the high point in our country or in the world, but certainly our colleges can contribute a great deal to this development, and private colleges have a special opportunity in this pursuit."

Looking back, Norvel editorialized on the message by adding, "And so at this juncture in our nation's history when college campuses were torn with the strife of riots and revolts, when students were being jailed and killed, Pepperdine University countered the tide in establishing a new campus dedicated to moral and spiritual values, to conservative patriotism as well as academic excellence. This was the beginning of an exciting and historic chapter in California independent higher education." But clearly, the highlight of the morning for some people was a short speech by William S. Banowsky. He had been executive vice president under Norvel Young since 1968, and now he was inaugurated into a new position. Around his neck was a medallion that proclaimed him "Chancellor of Pepperdine College." The honor acknowledged the important role he would play in the building of the campus that would soon rise literally beneath the feet of the attendees. Chancellor Banowsky's speech was titled "A Spirit of Place," and it would find its way into the folklore of Pepperdine. He concluded with these words:

> What we hope to create here, in these hills, is a spirit of place. A place where minds will be opened, where lives will be changed, where lasting friendships will

be formed. A college is, after all, something like a human being in that both have a soul of some kind. My deepest concern, in this hour of dedication, is for the soul of the college ... It is in this spirit that we hallow this ground and accept this challenge. These historic acres along the rim of Malibu will, from this day, never again be the same. From this day forward let it be known that, in this place, "We look not at the things that are seen, but at the things that are unseen; for the things that are seen are temporal, but the things that are unseen are eternal."

Beside the youthful Dr. Banowsky was his mentor, President M. Norvel Young, feeling proud, not displaced.

NORVEL CHOOSES A SUCCESSOR

It was Norvel's deliberate choice to share the limelight with Bill Banowsky. In fact, the new chancellor (who would soon be president), with his youth, speaking ability and charm, would soon become more widely known among the general public than Pepperdine's president of nearly 13 years, M. Norvel Young. During much of the 1970s, if a faculty or staff member mentioned the name of Pepperdine University in the Southern California area, the response was likely to be, "Oh, Pepperdine! I heard Bill Banowsky speak awhile back. He's fantastic." Norvel could have found a less flamboyant and charismatic person to help him build the new campus – and retained the limelight himself. But he knew that the task would take all of his own efforts plus the efforts of the best leader he could find. Bill Banowsky was that leader. And who got the credit was not as important as the mission itself.

Norvel often referred to Banowsky as "my best friend." The feeling was mutual. More than 25 years later, Bill would write to Norvel and say:

You came into my life, at precisely the crucial hour, like a burst of joy in a bright sunlight, bringing wisdom, experience, perspective, integrity, ambition and above all else, boundless love for everybody and everything. You gave to me everything you are! Regrettably, my container could only absorb so much ...

But, in my Being, I have been a better man because of you. ... I would never have been a university president without you! Anywhere! ... You believed in me from that moment we met at Lipscomb in the spring of 1958 ... You have been my dearest friend.

... Imagine what it meant for Plato to have had Socrates and for Aristotle to have had Plato and, excusing the grandiosity, you will know truly what it was like for Banowsky to have had Norvel Young. ... Yes, as you poetically put it, "We made music together!" In some sense, the sum total of the blending of our personalities, our strengths, our weaknesses, our energies, our visions created a power much greater than the sum of our separate parts.

What I most profoundly appreciate is your love – your deep, instant, unwavering, unconditional, life-giving love for me. Next to Gay [his wife] and my parents, you have done more to shape my life than any other human being.

Certainly, Norvel admired the talented young man for his charm and intelligence. Bill Banowsky had the poise and courage to not only make tough decisions, but also to ask friends of the university for the "big gift." But beyond mere admiration, their souls were somehow knit together. After Banowsky returned to Pepperdine in 1968, he and Norvel would work side by side in the "Miracle at Malibu" for a decade, and a lasting friendship was forged from joys and hardships, triumphs and tragedies.

Once again, Norvel's intense devotion to his mission can be witnessed as he allowed – even encouraged – another person to step to the forefront and take the lead, for the sake of the cause. It was not the first time he had done this; it would not be the last. This is one of the characteristics that set him apart from other fine leaders. Only a person with the highest ideals and a healthy sense of self is able to forsake self for the larger cause.

Norvel Young was so focused on his mission, or rather on what he believed was God's mission, that he rarely looked back. One of his favorite sayings was, "The past is prologue." Whether they were successes or failures, things of the past might be recalled, but they were not to be dwelt upon. The important thing was to move forward; the vital thing was the future.

He also liked to say, "I stand on tiptoe looking forward to what God will do in my life in the years ahead." He had a right to anticipate good things, because God had done such remarkable deeds in Norvel's life in the past. But the future, as it turned out, had both seasons of light and seasons of agonizing darkness. Yet even in the darkness, God brought goodness out of suffering.

For a dozen years Norvel had been making friends in Los Angeles and across the nation. Now it was time to call them to the cause. And with amazing clarity, he painted a picture of a great university that existed only in his mind. Often he would take a potential donor up the winding dirt road to a hill in Malibu. Then he would proceed to transfer the vision he saw into the mind of the other impressed person. But just as often, he sat in an office or restaurant with a potential donor, many miles from the wild Malibu mountainside, and wove a dream that warmed a heart.

An example: Margaret Martin Brock was an influential woman who, like many other conservative Los Angeles people, liked Pepperdine because of its Christian values. She reminded Norvel, "One meeting at the 'corner table' of the Los Angeles Country Club comes to mind. You were presenting me with the idea of doing something for the President's residence and you even had a model (which I still have) for me to take home and think about. As I am sure I have told you before, nothing has pleased me more than the results of that meeting. I am thrilled again and again every time I hear of the wonderful events that take place in the Brock House and you, my friend, are responsible."

Such is the stuff of Malibu dreams and miracles.

TRIUMPH
AND TRAGEDY

*Again and again he prayed that God would
heal the wounds of this unbelievable ordeal.
He entered the winter of his soul.*

*I*n retrospect, time seemed to be accelerating for Norvel
Young and Bill Banowsky. They were the "Co-captains of
the wonderfully imaginative and highly effective team that
put together the funding of the 'Malibu Miracle,'" in the words
of Howard A. White. "During the years beginning with his
presidency in 1957, Dr. Young had constantly improved the
school's financial position, had enlarged and activated the
University Board, and had won many friends to the university,"
continued White. "One of his most significant moves was to
bring William S. Banowsky into the administration and ultimately to lead the Board of Trustees to name him president."

In 1966 Norvel had appointed a site selection committee to
find an appropriate place for a second campus ... In October
1968 it had been announced that the heirs of the Adamsons had
given Pepperdine prime property in Malibu ... In February 1970
the historic "Birth of a College" dinner had been held ... In May
1970 a campus dedication ceremony had been conducted ... In
April 1971 President Banowsky had presided over the official
groundbreaking of the first building complex on the Malibu
campus ... And by September 1972 students were attending

classes at Pepperdine's new location. *Total lapse time from dream to reality: six years.*

To Norvel and Bill Banowsky, progress may have seemed to creep at times. But the speed at which the land was found, the money raised and the campus built was nothing short of miraculous. Many in the Southern California educational establishment had for some time viewed Pepperdine as an upstart and a second- or third-rate school.

Now they added to that epitaph "grandiose," "pretentious" and "shallow." But Norvel Young's dream from the beginning was never about beautiful buildings at the expense of inferior academics. He honestly believed that a school could be based on Christian faith and principles and also embrace excellence in academics.

A NEW UNIVERSITY, A NEW HOME

In a little more than seven months after the Malibu dedication ceremony, the next milestone was past. With the beginning of 1971, George Pepperdine College became Pepperdine University. And as the construction of the Malibu campus proceeded and William S. Banowsky garnered more publicity for the school and for himself, it seemed to make sense to name him president. He continued in many of his fund-raising tasks but added more administrative duties. Norvel Young, on the other hand, stepped aside and took on the title of chancellor, focusing all of his considerable energies in raising funds to complete the new school.

In March 1971, Young and Banowsky traveled to Sacramento to visit with Dr. Mott, director of the office of Parks and Recreation for the State of California. Their mission was to try to obtain a presence, a "beach head," in Malibu. The two knew that it had become necessary for the Adamson family to sell their historic Beach House in Malibu, which previously had been leased to people searching for an exotic place to hold a gala party. The house, with its surrounding 15 acres, had been sold to the state for about $2.5 million. Rumor had it that the state was going to tear the house down and put in a parking lot for surfers.

The Pepperdine leaders wanted to lease the property, but Dr. Mott informed them that the state could not accept rent. So an agreement was reached, whereby Pepperdine University would spend $35,000 each year in restoring the house and its grounds. And for that investment, the university would then have the use of the home and the property. It was a brilliant move. It gave Pepperdine a base of operations in Malibu, and it saved a historic mansion that reflected the colorful history of Malibu.

But in 1971, the question was, who will move into the Beach House – the Youngs or the Banowskys? The two couples got together to discuss the situation, and Norvel finally said, "I think the ones who love to entertain the most should move into the house." The Banowskys had four young boys at home at the time, which obviously made it difficult for them to do a great deal of entertaining. So the Beach House went to the Youngs, and the Banowskys moved into the president's home on Pepperdine's Los Angeles campus.

So in early 1971, Norvel and Helen moved their home to Malibu and became the advance guard of a new institution that would come to live in an old celebrity haunt. The State of California had officially allowed Pepperdine to occupy the historic Adamson-Rindge Beach House, situated on Surfrider's Beach, between the famous Malibu Pier and the mouth of Malibu Creek. And after living there 13 years, the Youngs turned over to the state a beautifully preserved landmark. Today, the large two-story house and grounds are a California State Park and Museum.

Years later, Helen remarked, "The house has been a museum for a long time now. But interestingly, we had more people come through the house when we were living there, while it was our personal residence, than visit the museum today. About 7,000 people a year would come to visit us. We would allow organizations of attorneys' wives, Boy Scouts, Webster Elementary School children – everyone – to take tours. It was wonderful public relations for Pepperdine! I'm not sure they get that many visitors today."

The house was Colonial Spanish in design, with large arching windows and terra cotta tile roof. One of the striking features of the home was the extensive use of ceramic tile, which was produced by the Ringe family's Malibu Tile Company. Though the company went out of business years ago, its beautiful tiles and tile murals are a part of the history of Los Angeles. The Beach House boasted ceramic tile hallway floors, which had been made to resemble Persian rugs. With a quick glance, one might expect to be walking on a carpeted surface rather than tile. The grounds were as striking as the house itself, with a gatehouse and a long gravel driveway that curved around to the garages on the left and the main house. Behind the house was the pool and pool house, the latter used by the Youngs as a suite for their office staff.

Life at the Beach House was both idyllic and hectic. The Youngs lived in a gorgeous, historic home in the center of one of the most famous seaside villages in the world. The front window had a view of the garden and the mouth of Malibu Creek, with the famous Malibu Colony beyond. Out of the rear window, the trademark Malibu Pier and its popular beach was like a California postcard. The south window looked out to the Pacific Ocean with its battalions of surfers. Yet the Youngs were entertaining nearly constantly. Some visitors, like famed violinist Yasha Heifitz, came just to see the Adamson Beach House, occasionally walking up the driveway uninvited and knocking on the door, expecting a tour. But usually, visitors came at the gracious invitation of the Youngs. There were Malibu neighbors to welcome, and potential donors to the university to host. And there were countless luncheons, dinners and parties. As the fundraising pace quickened, the pressure also began to escalate. In addition, Norvel and Bill Banowsky continually tried to address the problem of whether or not the university could continue to operate the Los Angeles campus as well as the new Malibu campus, as they had proposed.

But living on the beach also provided opportunities for relaxation and rejuvenation. Long walks on the sand, watching the sun set over the ocean, listening to the squawking seagull and other soothing diversions helped the Youngs deal with mounting pressures as the university grew.

THOSE IN PERIL ON THE SEA

There are times when a reinvigorating paradise can quickly turn into a terrifying nightmare, however. Late one afternoon in November 1974, Bill Banowsky suggested to Norvel that the two of them should take a 14-foot catamaran sailboat along the coast for a relaxing ride. As they moved out from shore, the wind quietly powered them forward and they skimmed swiftly over the gentle waves. Their administrative and fund-raising challenges seemed to be stranded behind on the shore as they moved away to freedom.

Near sunset they sailed back to the beach and pulled the catamaran up onto the sand. They pulled together some driftwood and made a fire, and they sat warming themselves, talking of many things. Darkness was not far from settling over the ocean as Banowsky looked at Norvel with a mischievous grin. Norvel knew what it meant. He said, "Great! One more time."

Together they shoved the catamaran back into the foaming surf. Norvel pushed from the starboard side while Banowsky pushed from the stern as they prepared to jump up onto the canvas deck that straddled the two metal pontoons. Just as they were about to mount the bobbing boat, the wind filled the sail and shot the vessel forward. Instinctively, Norvel grabbed the stern of the starboard pontoon and was immediately jerked off his feet. It happened in a split second. Bill leaped forward to catch the boat, but he missed and fell into the breakers. Norvel glanced back and saw his friend's shocked face and heard him call out, "Climb on! Climb on!" Quickly dusk began to swallow the figure on shore. And Norvel was alone, being dragged out to sea.

He tried to pull himself up onto the craft, but it was cutting through the ocean too swiftly. He could no longer see the shore and knew the distance was too great for him to let loose and swim back. He knew he would never have enough endurance to swim against the increasingly choppy sea. Blackness was now gathering around him as he sped through the water with such force that his trousers were pulled off right over his shoes. All he could do was try to hold on, his arms outstretched before him.

Later, in an article titled "Ordeal at Sunset" written for the August 1975 *Guideposts* magazine, Norvel would say, "I tried to pull myself up on the pontoon. But try as I might I couldn't lift myself even six inches. The racing water held me down and back. Panic filled me. This mindless craft would drive on endlessly, towing me like some infuriated whale."

He tried again to climb onto the pontoon, but he just didn't have the strength left. His arms were weakening by the second and pain was shooting through his shoulders and elbows. Alone, he knew death awaited him. His thoughts returned to the warm driftwood fire he had sat by a few minutes earlier. The problems they had discussed seemed so insignificant now. He could see the faces of his wife and children. And he cried out, "Oh, God, help me, help me! Give me strength."

Norvel tried again to climb up. He shoved his leg up onto the pontoon but struck a metal projection. Blood ran down the back of his knee. He slipped back deeper into the water, choking and gasping for air. By this time he was probably two miles out to sea and his hope was almost gone. How would anyone find him in the darkness even if a rescue team had been dispatched?

As the waves rose higher in the open sea, Norvel was in despair. He had often counseled people that "God is a very present help in trouble," but now his faith was weak and he was terrified. Over and over he prayed, "Oh, God, help me, help me!" Suddenly, as if it were a direct answer to the prayer, his panic left him. His mind was clear for the first time and he was able to use his always logical thoughts to carefully analyze the situation. He noticed that the bow of the catamaran would rise up on a wave, then it would dip low on the other side. On the upward movement, as the bow rose, the back of his pontoon was temporarily under the water. He waited for the exact right moment and lifted his leg over the pontoon. He now had one leg up. Again he waited. As another swell lifted the front of the boat, he pushed himself up higher. Wave by wave he moved onto the pontoon. The very sea that threatened to drown him was now saving his life.

As he clung to the cold metal top of the pontoon, the 25-mile-per-hour wind continued to push him out to sea. He found it impossible to crawl forward to the tiller. However, he found that he could reach the rod that was connected to the rudder. He pushed with all his energy – *new energy* that God seemed to give him. Slowly the craft turned toward shore. But as it came about, the wind caught the other surface of the sail with such force that the boat capsized. Somehow, Norvel held on and slipped to the flat underside of the pontoon that was now exposed. The boat lay powerless upside down in the water, now moving at the discretion of the ocean rather than the wind. "Thank you, God," Norvel repeated over and over again.

Norvel clutched the pontoon in utter exhaustion. Then he thought he heard a voice over the roar of the ocean. "Hang on, brother ... hang on!" He lifted his head and saw the vague figures of Bill Banowsky and his son sailing toward him through the darkness. They had commandeered a neighbor's boat and set out to find their friend. They pulled a thankful M. Norvel Young into their boat and headed for shore.

Shivering and utterly spent, Norvel lay in the boat with his heart singing the old naval hymn by William Whiting:

> *Eternal Father, strong to save.*
> *Whose arm hath bound the restless wave,*
> *Who bidd'st the mighty ocean deep*
> *Its own appointed limits keep:*
> *O hear us when we cry to Thee*
> *For those in peril on the sea.*

Bill Banowsky had alerted the Coast Guard, and a rescue boat had been dispatched to the Malibu area. With their lights, the Coast Guard personnel were able to find Bill, his son and Norvel making for shore. They brought them into Paradise Cove, several miles west of the Adamson Beach House. A shaken Helen Young was there to meet them. Norvel had to be carried to the car; he didn't have an ounce of energy left.

In the *Guideposts* article, Norvel wrote, "I have since thought of the many lessons I learned that day. A greater respect for the 'ocean deep' ... a deep resolve to live every day with a sense of rejoicing and thanksgiving, a deeper appreciation of our God Who hears and answers in every time of trouble. I also knew that no longer would I let problems worry me so much that I could not find their solutions."

And yet, as terrible as the ordeal at sea was, as genuine as his commitment to "no longer let problems worry him so much," that ordeal was nothing compared to the horrible event that was only a few months away.

THE SEAVER LEGACY

The decade of the 1970s would change the face of Pepperdine in more ways than one. The emphasis would quickly move from Los Angeles to Malibu with the opening of the new campus in September 1972. And the dominant influence in terms of commitment and resources would become Blanche Ebert Seaver. It was she who agreed to fund the building of the campus infrastructure. Her contributions became profound as mountains were moved, roads were cut, parking lots were paved and utilities were brought in. It was a tremendous investment. As Howard White would say, "Without her rare generosity the 'Malibu Miracle' would have been impossible."

In time, Mrs. Seaver's confidence and support of the university was acknowledged by naming the undergraduate school in honor of her beloved husband. On April 20, 1975, at a dedication ceremony President Banowsky proclaimed that from that day forward, the liberal arts college "will be known to men everywhere as the Frank R. Seaver College." Mr. Richard Seaver, CEO of Hydril Company and nephew of Frank Seaver, introduced then-Governor Ronald Reagan, who delivered the dedicatory address. Reagan mentioned, "What is being dedicated here today was made possible in large measure by the genius, the work, the thrift, and the unselfishness of a man who used to call himself 'just a plain old duffer.' Some duffer!"

Norvel Young and, especially, Bill Banowsky had a close relationship with Mrs. Seaver. She believed in Pepperdine University and in its new Seaver College because she believed in the institution's people. But President Banowsky would be moving to new challenges at the University of Oklahoma about three years after the dedication of the new college. Someone else would have to fill the gap of that key relationship with Mrs. Seaver. That person was Vice Chancellor Charles B. Runnels. Along with his charming wife, Amy Jo, Charlie Runnels would increasingly become a key person in Pepperdine's advancement.

In 1981, Norvel said, "One of the secrets of Pepperdine's phenomenal growth has been the camaraderie and unity of philosophy of a capable and dynamic administrative team. Among them, none has worked harder nor more effectively in fund raising than our Vice Chancellor Charles Runnels. Men like Dr. Runnels and Vice President for University Affairs James Wilburn are responsible for a large measure of Pepperdine's success."

As the University's "Wave of Excellence" campaign picked up steam in the mid-1980s, then as its "Challenged to Lead" campaign soared in the '90s, Norvel and Helen's admiration and appreciation for the contributions of Charles and Amy Jo Runnels continued to increase. When it was time for Dr. M. Norvel Young to pass the baton of leadership in January 1985, the University turned to Dr. Charles B. Runnels to become the University's second chancellor. Until her passing in 1994, Mrs. Seaver's closest companions were Charlie and Amy Jo.

Helen said, "Charlie and Amy Jo have become dear friends through the years. Many of the people we knew in Asia have become their friends. They are so warm and open." For 20 years, Norvel and Helen Young and Charlie and Amy Jo Runnels were a powerful "friend-raising" team for Pepperdine. When Raleigh Runnels, Amy Jo and Charlie's teenage son, died of cancer many years ago, Norvel preached the funeral. Through good times and bad, they have remained co-workers in a Great Cause.

Both Norvel and Charlie believed that, in many ways, the "Legacy of Frank Roger Seaver," about which Bill Youngs wrote in 1976, was really his wife, Blanche Ebert Seaver. "She spent her remaining years dedicated to preserving her husband's memory," said Norvel. "Frank had always said, 'If you want to do something for the future of our country, do something for the youth, for they are the future.' Mrs. Seaver made sure Frank's name would forever be associated with young people."

POISON STRESS

Beneath the seemingly glamorous life of the Youngs in a paradise setting, something terribly troubling was stirring. The stress of knowing that raising the funds for the new campus was primarily on his and Bill Banowsky's shoulders was taking a heavy toll on Norvel. His doctor prescribed Valium to help relieve the pressure. Though the tranquilizer quieted his nerves, it also took away his upbeat attitude and made him depressed. But he found a new "friend." For more than fifty years, Norvel had never touched a drop of alcohol, but now he convinced himself that taking "a little wine for thy stomach's sake," as Paul advised his young friend, Timothy, in the New Testament, might be helpful. Maybe a cocktail now and then would ease the stress and bring back his optimistic spirit.

Months went by and the drinking became regular. But somehow, Norvel was able to keep his new habit hidden. Only a few people saw the telltale signs. Once, he was arrested for driving under the influence, but a friend was able to keep it quiet. Looking back now, it may have been better for Norvel to "take his lumps" at that point, because what happened next was a tragedy of the first magnitude.

On an evening in mid-September of 1975, news reached the Youngs that a young professor at Pepperdine, Dr. Charles E. Wilks, had been riding his motorcycle on the university's rain-slick campus drive and somehow had lost control while heading downhill. He struck a light pole and was killed. Norvel was responsible for bringing the young man to the university – he was sure the new professor would be a wonderful addition. Now the young man was dead. And as Helen went to be by the side of the man's wife and daughter, a depressed Norvel turned to alcohol.

To add to his grief and stress, he was concerned about an upcoming event – the largest one the university had ever seen – which was to take place in about three days. President Gerald Ford was to visit the Malibu campus to dedicate Firestone Fieldhouse (named in honor of benefactor Leonard Firestone) and also the president's home, Brock House (named for long-time friend Margaret Martin Brock). The University had been searching for bleachers that were to go up in the parking lot of the Fieldhouse for the many thousands who were expected to attend the event. Because of a recent attempt on President Ford's life, security was to be tight. And the Secret Service was hounding Norvel and others to get the bleachers in place so that the area could be secured.

Then Norvel was notified that those running the main frame computer had just discovered that the student accounts-receivable total was about $5 million, which meant that the university was owed $5 million of uncollected tuition and other student costs. In addition, they found that the University's accounts payable total was up to about $3 million. The news was a disturbing surprise. Everything seemed to be closing in on Norvel Young's dreams. There was so much to do. Too much. And now the death of a promising young professor …

The next day, Norvel began work in his Beach House office, going about his usual routine. At about eleven o'clock, he got into his car, drove out the gravel driveway and headed south on Pacific Coast Highway toward Los Angeles. He had made the drive hundreds of times, and today he had a meeting in town with Don Darnell, who served as chairman of the Pepperdine President's Board (later, renamed the University Board).

As his car sped by the backs of the houses that lined the ocean, he was not feeling well at all. The death of the professor and his grieving family were on his mind, along with financial concerns and the anxiety over the biggest event of Pepperdine's history, hosting a sitting president. But he had also consumed some alcohol to "comfort and calm him." As he drove, his mind began to fog over Then, as he neared Pacific Palisades, he began to experience blurred vision. He tried to clear both his mind and vision … he shook his head … then there was blackness. A few hours would pass before he realized what happened next.

Near the J. Paul Getty Museum, his car struck another car that was waiting at a signal light. The violent collision drove the trailer hitch on the front car into its fuel tank, and the gasoline ignited. The car was soon in flames. Then Norvel's car also caught on fire.

The driver of the other car had her mother and her aunt in the back seat of the small two-door car. There was no escape. Both of the older women were killed. The other driver and Norvel were both injured and were transported to the hospital. In fact, a man in a nearby home ran and pulled Norvel from his burning car, probably saving his life.

The Wednesday, September 17, 1975, *Los Angeles Times* ran a story with the blaring headline: "Pepperdine's Chancellor Held in Fatal Crash." Apparently, in the reporter's mind, the thing of real importance was that Pepperdine's chancellor was in trouble – he was being "held." The opening paragraph, indeed the first seven or eight words of the article, gave the bias of the story:

> Pepperdine University Chancellor M. Norvel Young was jailed on suspicion of manslaughter and felony drunk driving after being involved in a traffic accident in which one woman was killed and two others were critically injured, the California Highway Patrol reported.

THE COMING OF WINTER

When Norvel woke up, he was in a hospital. He had facial lacerations, a brain concussion and internal bleeding. As the haze in his mind lifted slightly, he could see the face of Helen close by his side. He asked her what had happened and she told him he had had an accident and was injured. The awfulness of the situation was beginning to descend on him. It was like having a nightmare, somehow forgetting it, then remembering it again – only to discover that it was stark reality.

He later said, "I turned my face to the wall and cried. It was the worst day in my life. I knew I was completely at fault because I had been drinking, but I didn't know how disastrous my mistake had been." As the details unfolded, he began to gradually recall parts of the accident and the things that led to it.

Norvel Young was absolutely crushed by the guilt. He wondered why he hadn't just been killed in the accident. He kept thinking of the two older women and the driver. Then he thought of his family. And he pictured the hundreds of thousands of Christians in the fellowship of which he was a part. The university campus on the hills in Malibu with all of its people would come into his mind. He had betrayed the trust of many thousands of people. How could he face the world again? How could he live with himself?

News of the accident traveled fast. All the local media covered the story because of its sensational nature. Even Paul Harvey mentioned the story on his national report. And Norvel had no one to blame but himself. He knew he deserved whatever punishment came his way, even imprisonment. Perhaps as never before, he threw himself on the mercy of God. He prayed for the driver of the other car, and he prayed for the families of the two that perished. Again and again he prayed that God would heal the wounds of this unbelievable ordeal.

He entered the winter of his soul.

AFTERMATH

Certainly, the Los Angeles community was distressed by the accident. But the Pepperdine community was in a state of utter shock. And because of Norvel Young's long years of leadership within Churches of Christ, a whole fellowship of people was aghast. Some critical members condemned Norvel, but most were people of good will and they prayed for God to heal the situation as soon as possible.

Within minutes of the news, Norvel's three daughters, Emily, Marilyn and Sara, were at his bedside, along with Emily's husband, Steven Lemley. Norvel's son Matt was in medical school in Houston and he immediately caught a plane for home. The family surrounded Norvel with love. And they prayed. They knew that his soul would need more healing than his body.

Publisher Ralph Sweet, a longtime friend of the Youngs, grabbed a plane and flew in from Austin, Texas, "just to help." Another Texan whom Norvel had known since college days, Reuel Lemmons, editor of *Firm Foundation* journal, also caught a plane and came to encourage Norvel.

Amazingly, Dr. Paul Davis, the education editor of *Reader's Digest*, simply arrived with his suitcase from San Francisco saying he would stay and help deal with the situation as long as it took. The hospital put him in a room next to Norvel's and Davis spent four days talking with the press, helping visitors and assisting Helen with the whirlwind of problems.

Calls began to come in from across the nation. And more than 2,000 letters, cards and telegrams poured in to Norvel and the family. Remembering the comfort the communications provided in the terrible aftermath of the accident, Norvel said, "We received thousands of letters that were supportive and helpful. Helen still has all the letters."

He continued, "We began to get checks from people like George Elkins, David Packard and Tex Thornton. Leonard Firestone told us he had a similar thing happen to him." Suddenly the truth was apparent: for years Norvel Young had taken great pains to be kind to every person he met; now that kindness was returning to visit him.

Although everyone at 20th Century Christian Publishing was supportive, an emergency meeting was held in Abilene, Texas, and the board decided to accept Norvel's decision to turn over his editorship of *20th Century Christian* magazine. He was obviously more than willing to do that. Joe Barnett, minister of the Broadway Church in Lubbock, Texas, was asked to become the new editor in light of the situation.

As for Norvel Young, the days following the accident were filled with terrible bouts with despair and desperation. The feelings would leave for awhile, then return with a vengeance, overwhelming him. Some family members and friends were afraid of leaving him alone. As they observed his mental state, they wondered if he might try to take his own life. But they were not as afraid as Norvel himself. His entire world had shattered. Everything he was, everything for which he stood, went up in the flames of the accident. He simply did not believe he could endure the shame. He repeatedly read the book of Psalms, especially Psalm 51, and prayed over and over for forgiveness.

On October 30, 1975, there was a preliminary hearing for Norvel in the Santa Monica Court. Both he and his attorney agreed to waive the preliminary hearing, giving up his right to defend himself and to question witnesses. Later, in the Superior Court the judge asked Norvel for his plea. Norvel quietly said, "I plead guilty, your honor." The judge set December 4, 1975, for sentencing.

The December 4 date for sentencing was delayed until January 27, 1976, to allow the judge time to study the large number of letters he had received from interested people. The vast majority of the letters asked for leniency for Norvel Young because of his great contributions to society throughout his life.

When January 27 finally came, a frightened Norvel Young stood before the judge for sentencing. He had no defense. He was at the mercy of the court. The judge sentenced him to one year in jail – but immediately suspended it on the condition that Norvel take a six-month leave of absence from his duties at Pepperdine and perform public service. Specifically, he was to conduct courses for drivers who drink and do research on the kind of stress that contributed to his use of alcohol. He was fined $2,000 and his driver's license was suspended for four years.

With the sentencing past, a pinpoint of light finally penetrated his gloom. Hope struggled to the surface of an ocean of despair … and took a breath. It was like those icy-cold winter waters in Malibu, with blackness creeping over the ocean. Like being dragged through the salty sea that threatened to swallow him. And like the calm that finally came to his panicked mind. God entered. And Norvel Young was alive again.

Reflecting back, he said, "I learned how vast and how central grace is in the Gospel. I now actually *think* in terms of grace. It is wonderful that God allows us to forgive ourselves. And I have observed Him helping many other people in situations similar to mine since that time."

Indeed, Norvel's life after the accident became a parable of grace: every day was characterized by love, by fresh beginnings, by positive energy, by deep and abiding gratitude for each blessing, from the tiniest to the grandest. And his life reflected a deep, settled faith.

But there was another very tangible result of the tragedy: a scholarly, in-depth study on stress was conducted by Norvel Young under the auspices of the University of Southern California Safety Center. Research guidelines were approved by a six-person academic committee: Dr. Seymour Farber, Dr. Hans Selye, Dr. Robert Maurer, Dr. Charles Barron, Dr. Robert Canady and Dr. Meyer Friedman. Dr. John Dreher supervised the research and served as technical advisor. The resulting monograph was published in 1978 by Pepperdine University Press and titled *Poison Stress Is a Killer.*

In the preface, Dr. Norvel Young wrote, "When all these inputs are evaluated, a very clear message emerges in regard to any activity in which man must compete – the lethal effects of 'poison stress.' This is not the stress that leaves one physically tired, but satisfied – it is that self-generated reaction to external pressures which damages the biochemistry, upsets the emotions, drains the strength, and leaves its victim dangerously open to accident and physical illness."

He concludes his preface with these chilling words: "The physical and social toll of these factors is increasingly identified as a cause of extensive job-connected disability in the work force. The divorce court, the prison, the psychiatrist's couch, and the morgue bear similar testimony."

The words were not simply academic.

In the winter of Norvel's soul, in the frozen aftermath, a thought was trying to form in the minds of people who loved him. That thought would be expressed eloquently nearly a dozen years later in a tribute to Norvel at the 1987 Pepperdine Bible Lectures. Bill Banowsky quoted the "bully" President Teddy Roosevelt, who said in 1910:

> It is not the critic who counts, not the one who points out how the strong man stumbled or how the doer of Deeds might have done them better. The credit belongs to the man who was actually in the arena,

whose Faith is marred with sweat and dust and blood; who strives valiantly, who errs and comes short again and again; who knows the great enthusiasms, the great devotions, and spends himself in a worthy cause; who, if he wins, knows the triumphs of high achievement; and who, if he fails, at least fails while daring greatly so that his place shall never be with those cold and timid souls who know neither victory nor defeat.

The "strong man stumbled" and no one could believe it. Then finally, they realized that he was not a machine. He was just a man. And some were angry because he was just a man – like themselves.

But Norvel Young's time was not yet over. He would have more than 20 additional years to "spend himself in a worthy cause."

There may have been winter in his soul, but he was not a "cold and timid soul," in TR's words. The fire would return to his bones.

13

THE LONG WAY HOME

Norvel Young had allowed himself to
gradually drift far from the home of his heart.
He could not have imagined that he
would ever be in such a distant place.
But he knew the way home.

O ne of the attendant traits of greatness is the ability to make a comeback against heavy odds. There were people who thought M. Norvel Young was finished as an effective leader in the educational community and at Pepperdine University. And among Churches of Christ.

While most people reacted with compassion, a few chided him with suggestions that "the best thing for Pepperdine University was for Norvel Young to simply fade away into oblivion." But they didn't understand grace. And they didn't understand "The Heart of the Fighter," in the words of Landon Saunders. Character is not about never making mistakes; it involves the strength to confess one's sins and shortcomings, to ask for forgiveness. And to rise again to new levels of understanding and virtue.

Slowly but surely, Norvel made the return to his work. He swallowed enough internal humiliation to sink an ocean liner, but he struggled back to the surface. A lesser person would not have survived, could not have shown his face in public again. Somehow Norvel Young summoned his childlike faith. He grasped the truth of God's inexhaustible forgiveness. And he even found the grace to forgive himself – at least enough to go on.

Many people were affected by the tragedy of the accident. Certainly, family and friends were shaken, discouraged, embarrassed, as were Norvel's colleagues at the university—and the whole Pepperdine family. But one person lived every painful moment with him: Helen Mattox Young. And she never wavered. She too learned more about God's grace. And she also learned more about the vast goodness of Norvel's heart. Her strength was truly astonishing – for there were times when she had to stand tall for the two of them. When the storm finally passed, it was her victory, every bit as much as it was his.

Future years for Norvel and Helen Young would be years of triumph. For as someone has observed, "Whatever doesn't kill you makes you stronger." Norvel Young had allowed himself to gradually drift far from the home of his heart. He could not have imagined that he would ever be in such a distant place. But he knew the way home.

THE WILDERNESS

Just four days after the fiery accident on Pacific Coast Highway near the Getty, thousands of people were passing that way toward the Pepperdine Malibu campus. It was September 20, 1975, and the whole vicinity was abuzz with activity. Eventually, a crowd of 18,000 filled the bleachers that had been erected on the parking lot of Firestone Fieldhouse. President Gerald Ford's helicopter landed and he was whisked to the staging area. At the appropriate time, the dignitaries descended the stairs from the Fieldhouse to a platform that had been built above the parking lot – and to a sea of faces, thunderous applause and the music of the U.S. Marine Corps Band. In addition to President and Mrs. Ford, there was Pepperdine President William S. Banowsky, entertainer Pat Boone (who would lead the audience in the national anthem), actor John Wayne (who would lead the Pledge of Allegiance), editor Reuel Lemmons (to offer a prayer), Mr. Richard Seaver (who would accept the Fieldhouse on behalf of the University), benefactor Leonard Firestone, plus Richard Scaife, Fritz Huntsinger and other friends of the University. They were announced in twos over the public address system.

But at a certain point in the introductions, only one name was called ... Helen M. Young. She smiled and walked regally, with head held high, as she descended the staircase. Some thought the volume of applause increased as she was introduced. Nearly everyone knew of the terrible invisible burden she carried, and their admiration for her soared.

But Chancellor Norvel Young was missing from the most spectacular day of the University's history.

He was in No Man's Land, a wilderness of broken dreams. And he remained in that far country for many months. He resigned his role as the editor of *20ᵗʰ Century Christian* magazine. He resigned as an elder of the Malibu Church of Christ. In annual reports and college catalogs, he was listed as "M. Norvel Young, Chancellor (on leave), Pepperdine University." He was removed or put on leave-of-absence from several boards. He was sidelined from the Pepperdine Board of Regents. This man who had lived in the middle of the busy channels of life had drifted into the backwaters. It looked as though the world would go on without him.

But he was not forgotten.

A CONTRITE HEART

Norvel knew of only one way to do it. He traveled all over the country, speaking to people individually and in groups, asking for forgiveness. Roger Coffman, a minister in Georgia, later said, "Norvel, I cannot ever recall one human being standing any taller than you did one evening during the 20ᵗʰ Century Christian dinner at the Abilene Lectureship just after the automobile accident in Los Angeles. To address your peers as you did, candidly and honestly, without making any excuses, but simply asking for forgiveness and help, made a deep and lasting impression on me that I will never forget."

Seaver College Professor of Communiation Morris Womack visited Norvel shortly after he returned home from his hospital and recuperation period. Norvel was still staying in bed most of the time, and Womack sat with him in the bedroom of the Adamson Beach House. Norvel said to him, "Morris, I don't even remember getting in my car that day." But he never denied his guilt, never excused the drinking that led to the accident. He only asked for forgiveness. Womack assured him that he was indeed forgiven by people of good will.

On Sunday, December 14, 1975, a little less than three months after the accident (which seemed to be a long silence to some people), the following statement written by Norvel was read before the Malibu Church of Christ:

> I come before you in a spirit of contrite confession of sin. I have sinned against God, against the two whose lives were lost in the accident, against the one who was injured and against their families, against the church, against Pepperdine University and my associates here. I would give my very life to undo this tragedy, but this is impossible. I must live with the awful realization that my grief cannot bring back a human life or erase the injury to so many. I confess to you that my use of alcohol was involved in this accident. To say that I am profoundly sorry is such a feeble and inadequate expression of my stricken conscience. I have confessed my sin to God and know that he has forgiven me for Christ's sake. I now confess my sin to you and ask your forgiveness and your prayers.
>
> I want to go further in explanation, but not to make any excuse. There can be no excuse. For 50 years I abstained from alcohol and taught against its use. As President of Pepperdine, I attended thousands of

functions where it was served, but did not partake. In a mistaken attempt to relieve stress, I began to use alcohol occasionally. In 1969 I developed a heart condition which has reached the point where my heart never beats normally. Later, I had a heart attack and two small strokes. I was put on heavy medication to slow my heart and thin my blood. This medication saps me of physical energy which sometimes results in depression. One of my doctors suggested using moderate amounts of alcohol to relax the heart. I began to do so on occasion, especially in times of stress. I did not keep it at home or serve it. I did not become addicted to the regular use of alcohol, nor am I addicted now. With God's help, I will never use alcohol again in any form. I pray that my tragic experience will serve as a warning to others.

I am humbled and grieved, yet even in the midst of suffering, I know God's mercy and comfort in Christ. I want to make as frank and complete a statement of my sin as I can, taking all the responsibility and asking forgiveness, especially of my brethren.

I leave the future in God's hands. My relationship with Pepperdine University will depend upon the judgment of the court, the attitude and response of the brotherhood, and ultimately the decision of the Board of Trustees.

I sincerely thank you for all your prayers. I ask your prayers for the families of the deceased, the judge, the University, and for me.

– M. Norvel Young

The January 6, 1976, issue of the journal, *Firm Foundation*, carried an editorial by Norvel's longtime friend, Reuel Lemmons, editor of the publication. It said in part, "Here is an excellent opportunity for those of us who claim to go by the Bible to prove that we do it. We who have been forgiven so much can with grace extend it. ... The forgiven can go free; it is the unforgiving who wear chains. We have all been the recipients of unlimited grace. Now is the time to extend it." Lemmons went on to reprint the above statement by Dr. Young in its entirely.

Less than six months after the accident, Norvel wrote a long message to his beloved readers of *20th Century Christian* magazine. It is worth recording here, in part, because it says so much about the mission of the magazine, as he saw it, and about the essence of his faith. He also gives insight to his struggle and the progressing drama of his ordeal. The message appeared in the March 1976 issue of the magazine, as follows:

> To Our 20th Century Christian Family:
>
> For 38 years I have had the privilege of sharing my faith with you through the pages of this magazine. I was one of the small group of young men who founded the *20th Century Christian* in 1938, and for the past 30 years I have been its editor.
>
> The *20th Century Christian* through these years has sought to exalt Jesus Christ as God's Son and our Lord, to foster faith in the Scriptures as the inspired Word of God, to promote New Testament Christianity in the present age, to affirm the everlasting promises of God, the providence of God and the power of prayer. We have emphasized the Good News of God's amazing grace. We have tried to promote the unity of the Spirit in the bond of peace. We have encouraged the sharing of the gospel with those who have never heard it. We have stressed faith in Christ, hope in God's promises and love above all.
>
> It has been our purpose to state the message of Christ so as to interest both those who are already Christians and those who are not yet Christians. Our articles have been aimed to help the person in the pew

as well as the man in the pulpit. We have opposed sectarianism and eschewed both the extremes of pharisaical legalism and modernistic liberalism. We have discouraged a judgmental spirit and encouraged a humble dependence on the righteousness of Christ, rather than self-righteousness. In an age of sin and darkness, *20ᵗʰ Century Christian's* dedicated writers have tried to light a candle rather than curse the darkness.

Through the years I have urged our readers to rely on God in times of joy and in times of distress. Now I bear witness again to God's grace as I speak to you out of the crucible of suffering. On September 16, 1975, I was involved in a tragic traffic accident in which two women lost their lives and the other driver and I were injured. I was responsible. I have admitted my guilt to the church and to the court. I would give my very life to undo this tragedy, but my remorse cannot bring back a single life or erase the harm done.

In the midst of my despair in the hospital, I prayed for forgiveness. I praise God for the cleansing power of the blood of Christ. For 44 years I have preached the forgiveness of God to others. Now I have experienced in a deeper way the healing power of his grace. I thank God also for his love to me which has been shown through the outpouring of compassion from my brethren. Thank God for your overwhelming remembrances of me in my trouble. Your prayers have sustained me and given me courage to carry on. The judge stayed for six months a one year custody sentence. He required me to take a six months' leave of absence from Pepperdine University to give full time to a research and lecture program in traffic safety which can result in saving many lives. This project will be under the auspices of the University of Southern California Safety Center.

It is obvious from the article that Norvel viewed the changes in leadership of the magazine as permanent. He was again asking for forgiveness. And he was saying good-bye to his beloved readers. He didn't know if he would ever again be associated with the magazine into which he had poured so much of his life. He didn't know what the future would bring – but he knew that the future was in God's "all-wise and all-powerful hands." Joe Barnett, who had served as associate editor, was appointed editor. Barnett was a man of exceptional ability who was, at the time, minister of the Broadway Church in Lubbock and the president of Pathway Evangelism.

The president and publisher was to be Jim Bill McInteer, a wonderful friend who later wrote to Norvel after looking at Dr. Young's 80 years of living, "... your wisdom has been exercised in many other spheres. You've seen fit to open the door for many of us of lesser stature and ability, that opportunities otherwise denied might come to us. For the confidence you've placed in various ones of us, and the belief that your judgment prompted in 'giving him a chance,' I thank you for that perception, that courage, and that graciousness."

The vice president and treasurer was to be Winston M. Moore. Nearly 20 years later, Moore wrote to Norvel and said, "About 61 years ago, when you were 19, I had the pleasure of meeting you as you won the Founders Day Oratorical Medal at Lipscomb University (then David Lipscomb College). You have been a dear friend of me, my two brothers, J. C. and Paul, and my entire family ever since that time for which I am deeply grateful."

REBUILDING TRUST

A little more than two years after the accident, the *Firm Foundation* journal ran an article by Norvel Young in its January 3, 1978, issue. Norvel's title was "Beyond a Frowning Providence," taken from William Cowper's great hymn "God Moves in a Mysterious Way." Norvel wrote:

In my own life I have experienced how God can bring blessings out of adversity. Two years ago I was involved in a tragic accident in which two people died and I was seriously hurt. I was the one responsible. I am sharing this experience with you because I am still learning from it; and I believe my sharing will help someone who faces a similar traumatic experience to know that God cares, forgives, sustains, comforts, and empowers.

When I regained consciousness, I was in the hospital. Gradually it dawned on me what had happened. The news of the accident was on television and in the press. I was overcome with shame. Questions hit me like knives. Why, why, why? What would happen to my family? Would I ever be able to face life again? I even indulged in enough self-pity to wish that I had died in the accident too. But more than all was my desperate constant prayer, "God help me!"

I confessed my error and repented. I prayed earnestly over and over again. My wife, four grown children, and my son-in-law came to pray with me. Close friends and co-workers came and prayed. Others called and over two thousand sent telegrams, cards, or letters. Strangers expressed their concern. ...

Gradually I began to accept personally what I had preached for forty years. I realized that God loved me in spite of all and that he had forgiven me for Christ's sake. He was loving me through the concern of my family and friends and even through strangers.

Norvel went on to write about a few of the lessons he was learning: "God knows me and loves me just as I am." "God's compassion is seen also in the forgiving spirit of Christian friends." "God is alive and at work today. He has not left us alone."

He concluded, "There are other lessons too numerous to mention – a more acute sympathy for others in trouble, an overflowing heart of thankfulness for the simple, daily joys. Surely 'behind a frowning providence, God hides a smiling face.'"

It was so very appropriate for Norvel to use a line from the English poet William Cowper's hymn. Cowper, too, was in terrible straits and on the brink of self-destruction when God broke through. And it was in that brilliant moment of divine sunshine that he wrote:

> *God moves in a mysterious way*
> *His wonders to perform;*
> *He plants His footsteps in the sea,*
> *And rides upon the storm.*

For Norvel, God had indeed "ridden upon the storm" of his shattered life. But Norvel's title for the article came from the fourth verse of Cowper's hymn:

> *Judge not the Lord by feeble sense,*
> *But trust Him for His grace;*
> *Behind a frowning providence*
> *He hides a smiling face.*

Some may have wondered about the sincerity of Norvel Young's repentance. But it is hardest to fool those who are closest to you – and his family embraced him even more as he endeavored to do the right thing. They knew the accident and Norvel's guilt could not be swept under the rug. The accident and the root problem had been a public thing. Now they supported him as he struggled to rebuild trust in a public way.

Nearly 20 years later, in June 1994, Norvel's daughter, Marilyn Stewart, wrote an article for *21ˢᵗ Century Christian* magazine in which she discussed the outcome of the great tragedy in her father's life. Marilyn titled the article, "The Most Optimistic Person I Know." In part, she wrote:

"Isn't it great to be alive?" he asks the man running beside him on the track. His friend is a little taken back. "Well, yes, it is. I just hadn't thought about it." But Norvel Young had thought about it this morning and every morning. He is excited to be alive and to have the gift of another day. Optimism is his way of life. He is always upbeat, always cheerful, always enthusiastic. ...

Is this man for real? Does he not know about the homeless, about violence, about Bosnia? Has he never seen hunger, disease and poverty? Has he avoided personal troubles?

He has held a starving child in his arms in Ethiopia. He spends hours at the Union Rescue Mission serving the homeless and drug and alcohol addicts. He is on the phone with a friend who has AIDS. He has given months to raising funds for the hurting in wartorn Europe. He has lain awake countless nights figuring out how to make a small, poor Christian college survive.

In his own life he has experienced the most hideous personal tragedy. Nearly twenty years ago he was involved in a terrible automobile accident in which two people were killed. At the very time he was supposed to be welcoming the President of the United States to the campus, he was in the hospital, charged with driving under the influence.

He had known the thrill of success. Now he knew the agony of defeat. Some thought this was the end of his career. But others rallied to him with forgiveness and support. And God was gracious. God gave him the strength to admit his guilt and repay his debt to society as best he could. God forgave him, and he was able to forgive himself. He found Christ his ever-present help in time of trouble, turning back to life with a deeper dependence on God, a life of constant, believing prayer, and a trust that God *does* work all things together for the good of those who love him.

Perhaps it is because of this pain that he is today even more loving, understanding and forgiving. Perhaps this is why he cherishes each day as a precious gift. Perhaps this is why he finds such joy in every experience of life. Perhaps this is why he is the most optimistic person I have ever known.

Norvel's family and friends were very conscious of the fact that the tragedy brought Norvel to a deeper dependence on God. It became evident in the way he began to pray out loud every day with those he loved. Every time Helen and Norvel heard some special request for prayer, every time they heard an ambulance, every time they walked around the track, every time they said good night . . . they spontaneously prayed. Especially when family or friends or any visitors were about to say goodbye, Norvel would say, "Let's pray before you leave," and everyone would clasp hands, bow their heads and he would pray for God's watchful care over them.

As time passed and people watched the inner qualities of Norvel's life rise to the surface, he slowly began to re-enter the stream of activities in the community, at the university and in his church. He had humbled himself, done the best he could to repair his transgressions. He had learned much about living – even at 60 years of age. Now it was time to live again.

He resumed his duties as chancellor at the university. He was welcomed back to the Pepperdine Board of Regents. Other corporate boards asked him to remain as a member. He became deeply involved again in 20th Century Christian. And he began to serve again as an elder of the Malibu Church and did so until the end of his life.

It was fortunate for Pepperdine that Norvel had struggled back to his key place in the university. Because he was there in time to become a major player in confronting the next major challenge. Howard A. White wrote, "Although there had been many rumors through the years that President Banowsky would enter politics or take another post, the university community was somewhat shocked when he called the regents together on August 16, 1978, and tendered his resignation in order to accept the presidency of the University of Oklahoma."

In early August Norvel and Helen had taken a trip to Asia, but even then they knew that Bill Banowsky was considering some career offers. Before they left, however, Norvel made the president promise that he would make no decisions until the Youngs returned. But in the Hyatt Hotel in Hong Kong, a phone rang in the middle of the night. When Norvel answered it, he heard his friend's voice say, "Norvel, you're speaking to the next president of the University of Oklahoma." Shortly, the world, and the regents, would hear the news.

The Youngs returned as soon as possible. They began working behind the scenes with board members, including Board Chairman Lloyd Nelson, Tom Bost and others. By the time of the August 16 meeting of the Regents where President Banowsky announced his resignation, they were ready to propose that Howard White become interim president. White, who had served as executive vice president under President Banowsky, was on vacation in Dublin, Ireland, when he received a call from Chairman Nelson inviting him to become the University's fifth president. As the months went by and everyone realized the phenomenal job President White was doing, support was gathered to name him permanent president. Nelson later said that the board's executive committee had considered conducting a nationwide search for a new president but had decided that "Dr. White is here and he's our man, an extremely capable man."

Within just a few years, a constellation of people and organizations were again depending on the wisdom and judgment of Norvel Young.

About a dozen years after the accident, Norvel was passing through Arizona on his way to or from some meeting. He stopped in Phoenix and looked up his friend, Edwin White, who preached for the Eastside Church of Christ in that city. Norvel was interested in seeing an art exhibit in some neighboring town. White asked him to preach for the church on Sunday, and Norvel was eager to do so. But his time with White turned out to be more than casual conversation.

Years later, White remembered, "Norvel may have seen some attitude or tendency in me, I don't know. But he bared his soul and told me the details of his accident and the things that led up to it. Then he warned me ... he said, 'I thought everything depended on me. I saw myself as carrying this heavy, unbearable load. I began to drink to relax and escape from the pressure. Edwin, don't make the same mistake. You can't do everything. Share the vision, share the work. Depend upon God.'"

White never forgot the conversation.

FOUR DECADES TOGETHER

With their 40th anniversary only about eight months away, Norvel gave Helen a beautiful New International Version of the Bible for Christmas 1978. In the front of the Bible, he carefully wrote, "To my dearest Sweetheart – You are my living epistle and I know this new version will bless you and those who "read" you. May each page become alive through the revelation vouchsafed by the Holy Spirit. Never forget how much I love you and know that God loves you infinitely more — Devotedly, Norvel."

In early summer of 1979, Jerry Rushford, who was minister of the Malibu Church of Christ at the time, noted that Norvel and Helen's 40th wedding anniversary was approaching in August. He asked the Youngs for permission to plan an evening of celebration and they gave their approval. The event was hosted by members of the Malibu Church, and Howard White, who was one of the elders of the church and was in his first year as president of the University, offered his residence, the Brock House, as an appropriate setting for the memorable occasion.

On Friday evening, August 31, 1979, Norvel and Helen Young celebrated four decades of marriage in the presence of their four children and many longtime friends, including Hugh and Lola Tiner, Don and Louise Miller, Walter and Anna King, William and Ruby Green, Glenn and Shirley Boyd, Helen Pepperdine, Dot Moore and Howard White. As the guests entered the Brock House, they filed past long tables laden with old photographs that chronicled 40 years of memories. Royce Clark, professor of religion and member of the Malibu Church, served as photographer, helping to preserve the memory of the evening. Several days later the Malibu Church presented Norvel and Helen with a photo album of Clark's pictures to commemorate the occasion.

A large part of the celebration was devoted to reminiscing, and with Rushford acting as master of ceremonies, person after person stood to share his or her various "Norvel and Helen stories." Some of the stories even predated the Youngs' wedding day. In the relaxed comfort of the Brock House, Norvel and Helen Young took a 40-year stroll down Memory Lane in the presence of some of their oldest and dearest friends.

The high point of the evening occurred when several friends encouraged Helen to return to her home and see if she could still fit into her wedding dress. Moments later, she dramatically reappeared in the gown she had worn in Oklahoma City 40 years earlier! Following the applause and spontaneous roars of approval, Norvel was jokingly asked if he could still fit into his wedding tuxedo. With a twinkle in this eye and an impish grin, he admitted that it was impossible. But the fast-thinking Dr. Young had a logical explanation: "You know," he reasoned, "we've had four children."

Sometime later when President White reflected back on his seven years of residence in the Brock House, he concluded that the most enjoyable evening out of many wonderful evenings was the night the Malibu Church hosted the Youngs on their 40th anniversary. It was the kind of occasion that lifted the spirits of everyone present. Three months after that special night, in November 1979, the Malibu Church of Christ asked Norvel Young to begin serving again as one of the congregation's elders. After more than four years of recovery from his tragic accident, he was once more laboring in something he loved, the familiar role of servant leader. He would fulfill the responsibilities of an elder in the Malibu Church for the next 18 years.

14

A WOMAN FOR
ALL SEASONS

She was like the proverbial "Jewish mother,"
who was the sustainer of her family, who always was
there with a word of sage advice, who was nearby with
"chicken soup for the soul," as well as for the body.

I t seems evident that there would never have been the
M. Norvel Young so many thousands respected and loved
without a woman named Helen Mattox. Conversely, there
would never have been the Helen M. Young so many thousands
admired and adored without a man named Norvel Young. They
were a matching set, a priceless pair.

But make no mistake, Helen Mattox Young was much more
than simply an assistant or a supporter who stood behind Norvel
as he accomplished great things. She was a full partner in many,
many ways. And she was an outstanding leader in her own right.
In fact, there may never be another first lady of Pepperdine
University like her. There may never be another leading
spiritual woman among Churches of Christ like her. She was
one of a kind.

Dr. Richard T. Hughes, church historian and distinguished
professor of religion at Pepperdine University, wrote in his book,
Reviving the Ancient Faith: The Story of Churches of Christ in America:

> Helen M. Young ... perhaps the most visible and
> influential woman among Churches of Christ in the

second half of the twentieth century, has spoken regularly since the late 1940s for women's classes in local congregations and on lectureships sponsored by Church of Christ-related colleges. With deep roots in the Stone-Lipscomb tradition of Churches of Christ, she has emphasized practical Christian living, the spiritual life, and the role of the Christian woman in the modern world.

Another historian, Robert E. Hooper, said of Helen Elizabeth Mattox in his book, *A Distinct People: A History of the Churches of Christ in the 20th Century*, "In her own right she has had a tremendous influence as a writer in *20th Century Christian* and *Power for Today*. She remains in demand as a lecturer and speaker for women's meetings."

It has been mentioned that Helen's mother was a bright, talented woman who participated in civic affairs, founded benevolent works, and made her impressive presence felt in the local church and the community. Upon her death, the *Christian Chronicle* newspaper ran a photograph of Irene Mattox under the headline, "Christian Woman of the Century." Helen seemed to have inherited her mother's outstanding intelligence and talent, but also her father's irenic spirit and kindness.

Perhaps the first of her wonderful traits to emerge was her graciousness. Even as a very young woman she had the ability to put people at ease, make them feel welcome. From the moment she and Norvel were married, she emerged as a consummate hostess. As the wife of a young professor, she was called upon to host both formal and informal occasions. And through the Lubbock years, she served as a minister's wife at a time when that was a very demanding role. Helen prepared endless dinners and luncheons and entertained countless guests in her home. She created a warm, gracious environment in which Norvel could serve and succeed.

When they moved back to Pepperdine in 1957, the hosting took on grander proportions. Now she was entertaining the wealthy and influential and powerful as well as the ordinary staff member or church member. And she moved with astonishing grace among this great variety of people.

HOSTESS PAR EXCELLENCE

One of the earliest actions that Norvel undertook when he assumed leadership of Pepperdine in 1957 was to reinstitute the annual Pepperdine Bible Lectures, which had been discontinued. And for many years, the Youngs hosted a gathering of Bible Lectures participants in the evening after the last scheduled event. Usually referred to as "Afterglow," it was a time for people to relax and discuss the stimulating truths they had encountered during the day. Or just visit and enjoy one another's company. Somehow, Helen always managed to provide the "glow" for such occasions. She was there to greet each guest to her home and make him or her feel welcome. She continually supervised the refreshments to insure that everyone was well cared for. She would introduce newcomers and see to it that no one was left out of the festivities and discussions. Her eyes continually moved throughout the guest area as she circulated, always a smile on her lips, always a desire to make every guest comfortable.

Professor Morris Womack tells of one of his earliest memories of Helen Young in the late 1960s when he arrived as a new administrator and faculty member on the Los Angeles campus. "It was a faculty Christmas party as I recall," he said. "There was sort of a receiving line and with every new arrival, Helen would turn and introduce the person or the couple to the ever-larger group. My wife, Ada, and I had been with Pepperdine just a short time. But to my amazement, Helen turned and introduced both of us as she had all the others, as if she had known us forever."

Norvel moved from the presidency of Pepperdine to the office of chancellor, then chancellor emeritus, but the Youngs continued to host a holiday open house reception in early December as they had since their earliest days in Lubbock, Texas. The timing itself of the later receptions was indicative of their creativity and sensitivity. They knew that the president and other university officials would be hosting holiday events near Christmas, so they planned their open house for early in the month so as not to interfere with the plans of others. They also knew that friends of Pepperdine and colleagues from the university would receive many Christmas cards during the middle of December, so they decided to create a "Thanksgiving card." Timed to arrive in homes a week before the Thanksgiving holiday, it seemed only fitting for Helen and Norvel to send such a greeting card: it always expressed their gratitude to God for all of life's blessings and their thanks to the recipients for their friendship and love. And included in that greeting card was a small card inviting folks to the "Holiday Open House at the Youngs." Once again, Helen was the "general-in-command" of the daunting task of hosting a steady stream of visitors who filled the Young home with laughter and conversation.

Already described were the many receptions at the Adamson Beach House in the late 1960s and early 1970s. Helen and Norvel loved to bring visitors to the wonderful and historic seaside home. In fact, it has been noted that, even though the home became a California State Park open to the public, there were probably far more visitors to the home when the Youngs lived there than in later times when it reverted to the State of California. Helen herself hosted the annual women's retreat during the Pepperdine Bible Lectures. But even more, there were nearly constant dinners and receptions at the home.

And as mentioned earlier, people often wandered back down the long, curving driveway from Pacific Coast Highway, knocked on the door, and asked about the house. Nearly always, Helen would invite the curious strangers in to see the details of the home. Retired Judge John J. Merrick wrote Norvel in 1995 and said, "As Past-President of the Malibu Historical Society and the Malibu Lagoon Museum, and an on-going member of the Board of Directors, I remember so well your loving tenure as

Lessee of the historic Adamson Beach House while awaiting completion of your campus quarters. I know how much you and Helen enjoyed living in the house and walking the beach with your hound dog, and I know how beneficial it was to have you two as 'caretakers' of this jewel."

The Youngs did indeed think of themselves as caretakers of the Adamson Beach House. They never forgot that the old house belonged to the people of California. Come to think of it, that is also the way they viewed the President's Home on the Los Angeles campus ... and their own home, wherever that may have been. They may have called it "our home," but they treated it as if it belonged to the public. "Come see us!" was always their parting call. And many people did just that. Often, they would see visitors on campus and say, "If you need to relax, go on up to the house. The door is always open. Just go right in and make yourself at home!" Although Norvel was always gracious and welcoming, this open feeling came primarily from Helen Young, the hostess par excellence.

WOMAN OF MANY WORDS

In her early years, Helen was tentative and unsure of herself. Perhaps because of the great talent of her mother, Helen felt that she had not been blessed with speaking ability or intellect. But as the years passed, even though she did not promote herself as a speaker, she increasingly became in demand because of her eloquence and her insightful messages. She began speaking at Abilene Christian College Lectureships as early as 1949, on the subject, "The Role of the Preacher's Wife." Eventually, she would teach on all of the Bible lecture series at colleges affiliated with Churches of Christ, as well as countless women's retreats. Through the years, Helen taught Sunday morning Bible classes for women in Nashville, Lubbock and Los Angeles. She also began to write and edit. On the Los Angeles campus of Pepperdine College, she served as an instructor in the Home Economics and Sociology departments, teaching "Marriage and the Family." Later at Malibu, she taught a course in Pepperdine University's Religion Division called, "The Bible and the Modern Woman." She was also asked to speak at civic functions and schools.

In 1985, Helen's book, *Children Won't Wait*, was published. After several printings, Brownlow Publications stepped in and completed two more printings. The foreword for the book was written by the famous Dale Evans Rogers.

Zondervan Publishing House published the widely read *Time Management for Christian Women* in 1990, which Helen co-authored with her niece, Billie Silvey. The book is filled with helpful advice like:

> We always have time for what's essential. The key is to sift out the essential from the myriad demands each day brings. ...
>
> The past is irretrievably gone and the future doesn't yet exist. But how many of us waste the precious present living in regret over the past or in anticipation of the future. ...
>
> Time constraints cause us to make mistakes which actually slow us down. They lead to stress-induced ailments, such as heart trouble, strokes, ulcers, and migraines. And they cause us to get so wrapped up in the urgent that we neglect the things – and people – we value. ...
>
> I still have occasional lapses, but I have discovered that the time I spend with God is not time away from my other tasks. It is time that gives me the perspective and power to meet the demands of life.

But in terms of writing, Helen may be best known as an editor. For many years she was consulting editor and a senior editor for *20th* (and later *21st*) *Century Christian* magazine. Even earlier, she was co-founder and co-editor of the devotional guide, *Power for Today*. She and Norvel edited the devotional guide for 20 years before putting it into the able hands of their daughter and son-in-law, Emily and Steven Lemley. Today the circulation of *Power* is approximately 50,000, but the readership is far beyond that number. It is estimated that each magazine is seen by three people, thus each issue may be seen by more than 150,000 individuals.

A MOTHER IN ISRAEL

In the book of Judges in the Old Testament, the Song of Deborah includes these words by the famous female judge: "Village life in Israel ceased, ceased until I, Deborah, arose, arose a mother in Israel." Deborah sat daily and heard the disputes brought before her, wisely judging each and every case. She also was a prophetess, a spokesperson for God. And she was a great leader of her people, riding out in a chariot with Barak and his men to oppose the armies of the enemy. It is fascinating, therefore, that she chose to refer to herself as "a mother in Israel." Apparently for her to arise as a mother in Israel was to serve as a mender of village life, as a healer of societal and spiritual ills. It was to be a nurturer of her people.

If that is true, then Helen Young can certainly also be thought of as a "mother in Israel." She was like the proverbial "Jewish mother," who was the sustainer of her family, who always was there with a word of sage advice, who was nearby with "chicken soup for the soul," as well as for the body.

For example, in her book, *Children Won't Wait*, she wrote, "There is a time to ponder what a child is – not a pet nor toy, but a person, an individual – a soul made in God's image." She added, "There is a time to answer questions, all their questions, because there may come a time when they will not want our answers."

Then she said, "There is a time to treasure every fleeting minute of their childhood. Just eighteen precious years to inspire and train them. We will not exchange this birthright for a mess of pottage called social position, or business success or professional reputation." Her concluding prayer was:

> God, give us wisdom to see that
>   *today* is the day with our children.
> That there is no unimportant
>   moment in their lives.
> May we know that no other career is
>   so precious,
> No other work so rewarding,
> No other task so urgent.
> May we not defer it nor neglect it,
> But by thy Spirit accept it gladly,
>   joyously, and by thy grace realize
> That the time is short and our time
>   is now,
> For children won't wait!

Helen later said, "My greatest joy has been my husband and my children – and now my precious grandchildren. This is where my heart is."

Proverbs asks the question, "A wife of noble character who can find?" Then, among the enumerated descriptions of such a woman, it says, "Her children arise and call her blessed; her husband also, and he praises her." Certainly, Helen's children have arisen to call her blessed.

Each of the Young children embraced their parents' belief in the importance of education. Marilyn and Sara laughingly said, "We thought we would have to have a Ph.D. before we could think of marrying!" In fact, Sara completed her master's degree in marriage and family counseling. Marilyn earned a Ph.D., also in marriage and family counseling. Matt became an M.D., specializing in serious burn treatment. And after Emily raised her children, she went back and completed a Doctor of Education degree. The same emphasis on education extended to the husbands of the daughters. Emily's husband, Steve Lemley, finished a doctorate in Communications at Norvel's irresistible encouragement. Marilyn's husband, Stephen Stewart, already had a law degree (and didn't have to agree to complete his education before he received Norvel's daughter's hand in marriage!). Sara's husband, Sam Jackson, completed a doctorate in Educational Psychology, with Norvel's encouragement.

Emily Y. Lemley met her husband, Steve Lemley, at Lubbock Christian College where Steve later served as president for 11 years. Emily is the teaching director for Community Bible Study in Malibu, and she and Steve edit *Power for Today* devotional guide. Steve is now provost (chief academic officer) for Pepperdine University and they live in Westlake, California. They have three grown children.

Matt Norvel Young received his medical training in pediatrics and has practiced with the Grossman Burn Center for the last 15 years. He is a well-known burn specialist and was a speaker on a Los Angeles radio program on health. He was married to Flora Lanners and they have four children. He is now single and lives in Topanga Canyon near Malibu.

Marilyn Y. Stewart is a professional counselor. She married Stephen Stewart, who is the financial officer and legal counsel for his family's drilling business in Grants, New Mexico. Together they have four children and live in New Mexico.

Sara Y. Jackson married Sam Jackson, who is a graduate of Pepperdine. He is director of Corporate Relations for World Vision International, where he has served for 12 years. Sara is assistant director of the Center for the Family at Pepperdine. She and Sam have three children and live in Agoura, California. Helen added, "My sons-in-law are the finest in the world." As a true grandmother, she was devoted to her grandchildren, as they were to her.

Not only did her own children call her blessed, but countless others also called her blessed because of her Christian example. They saw her tremendous talent, yet they knew of her true servant heart. They saw her strength in times of testing, yet they knew of her gentleness and love. It is no wonder that, in 1992, the American Mothers Inc. named her "California Mother of the Year."

American Mothers board member Lu Dennis said, "Mrs. Young is a lovely lady, who has done very well by her children." Kanet Thomas, who was president of Associated Women for Pepperdine at the time, nominated Helen for the award. Kanet said, "Helen Young is an author, lecturer, teacher and editor. She is a leader in educational, religious, philanthropic and civic groups. But in no area does she excel more than in her role as a mother."

The May 1992 issue of *The Christian Chronicle* newspaper ran a color photograph of Helen surrounded by four of her grand-children: Monica Young, Jessica Jackson, Ethan Young and Joseph Jackson. The caption mentioned, "Helen Young, founder of the Associated Women for Pepperdine University, Malibu, Calif., will celebrate a special Mother's Day this year as the 1992 California 'Mother of the Year.' Young was named to the honor by American M~thers Inc. in February."

Inside the issue was an article on Helen that mentioned, "Mrs. Young believes the honor she received underscores the vital role of mothers." Helen was then quoted as saying, "This is one more effort to call attention to the role of mothers, which should not be neglected in our society. All mothers face different problems and challenges, and we all do the best we can."

THE MANTLE OF LEADERSHIP

Helen Mattox Young developed not only into a gracious hostess, a remarkable woman of letters, and a beloved matri-arch for multitudes, but she also developed into a true leader.

During the mid to late1940s and the early 1950s, she began developing leadership skills as Norvel served as the minister for the Broadway Church in Lubbock, Texas. She worked side by side with her husband, and he shared most of the details of his work and his vision with her. She participated in the planning for the new church building, for the new children's home, for the new college. All their married life, she kept the family financial records and saw that the income taxes were prepared correctly. Norvel took the lead in deciding on investments, but she handled all details after a decision was made.

By the time she and Norvel and the children headed for California, she had become his major asset. Only a year after their arrival, as Norvel struggled with the various public relations problems and, especially, with the financial woes of Pepperdine College, Helen met with Mrs. Pepperdine and a group of women and formed the Associated Women for Pepperdine. They insisted that Helen serve as the founding president and she immediately went to work, building the organization into an army of supporters who would eventually become "Pepperdine's Million-dollar Endowment" through the scholarship money they raised. She placed AWP on such solid footing that the organization was still a vital part of Pepperdine after more than four decades. As the organization approached the new millennium, the Evelyn Clark Endowment Fund for AWP had more than $1 million used exclusively for student scholarships.

But AWP was more than a fund-raising organization. It fostered love and friendship among its members. As one member who was also a civic leader said, "I have never been in an organization with so little envy, jealousy and back biting as AWP."

From 1968 to 1972 Helen served as a member of the Pepperdine Board of Regents and she continued to serve as a Life Regent.

When Dan Anders, longtime minister for the Malibu Church of Christ, tendered his resignation because of ill health in 1998, the church asked Helen to serve on the search committee for a new minister. Such was the respect for her judgment that the church wanted her to be involved in selecting the next person who would feed the church from the Word of God. For she herself had fed many women and men from the Bible that directed her own life.

In Lubbock, Helen had been a member of the Library Board and president of Lubbock Women's Forum. Now in Los Angeles, she served on the boards of directors of a number of civic organizations including Town Hall of California, United Way Region IV, American International Bank, The Muses of the California Museum of Science and Industry, the Los Angeles County Chapter of Freedom's Foundation at Valley Forge, the Women's Division of the Los Angeles Area Chamber of Commerce, the Excellence in Media Advisory Board, International Christian University, Otis Art Institute and others.

Because of her many years of selfless service, Pepperdine University bestowed a number of honors on Helen Young. Not long after the founding of AWP, the Alumni Association presented her with the Alumni Service Award for the year 1959. It was the twentieth anniversary of her graduation from George Pepperdine College. As her work for the University mounted, the Alumni Association again honored her with the Alumni Service Award in 1986. A decade earlier, in 1976, she had received the Christian Service Award for her spiritual contributions. In 1985, Pepperdine's Graduate School of Education and Psychology presented her with its Dolores Award for special service. And in 1987, on the University's 50th anniversary, she received the Pepperdine Medal of Honor.

Helen participated in several Founder's Day Convocations at Pepperdine University. Sometimes it was a dramatic reading or an open discussion. On one occasion, she was given the honor of reading the Founder's Address, in which Mr. Pepperdine dedicated his college – an address that she had actually heard in September 1937. The dedicatory address became the centerpiece of the special Founder's Day Convocations in September of each year, in which the entire university community gathered to welcome a new academic year – with robed professors in procession and appropriate speeches and festivities.

Lubbock Christian University awarded Helen Young an honorary doctor's degree in 1980 when she delivered the

Commencement Address, and the Children's Home of Lubbock gave her the Friend of the Child Award in 1985. The Excellence in Media organization, on whose board she eventually sat, gave her the Angel Award in 1987.

One could sense that Helen didn't handle the honors too well. They made her feel awkward, uncomfortable. They embarrassed her to some degree, because she was used to serving behind the scenes.

Through the years Helen served as a mentor as well as a mother to her daughters. And she also mentored (and mothered) the dozens of students who lived in their home through the years. Even after the passing of Norvel, she continued to have two women law students in her home. Countless students came to her for advice and counsel.

What image might we conjure up to illustrate the importance of Helen as a leader? Perhaps it might be the picture of Helen Mattox Young on September 20, 1975, descending the stairs from Firestone Fieldhouse to the platform where the President of the United States would give an address. When her husband was in the pit of despair after his accident, she was there to comfort and support him. Then she was there to proudly walk for him – when he could not walk. On one of his proudest days, it was Norvel's beloved mate, his other self, who represented the two of them. The Young name was present and well accounted for.

THE
FRIEND-RAISERS

*One of the Youngs' children commented,
"Daddy and Mother were like Will Rogers:
they never met a person they didn't like."*

T hrough the years, Norvel and Helen Young proved
themselves to be one of the most dynamic fund-raising
couples ever. But perhaps they were so successful
precisely because they did not set out to simply raise money.
Their central focus was always on some mission, whether it was
sharing the good news about Jesus, building a children's home,
founding or strengthening a college, promoting a rescue
mission or some other good work. "Focusing on some mission"
must not be understood as an abstract principle, as opposed to
being involved in the betterment of individual persons. The
Youngs believed in the biblical first and second "great command-
ments": to love God and to love one's neighbor. They understood that to love means *to serve.* And so they served both God
and people through missions of various kinds that touched
individual lives.

They considered themselves "friend-raisers," rather than
fund-raisers. It wasn't simply a play on words. Neither was it a
public relations ploy. Their goal was to make friends for
Pepperdine University, for Lubbock Christian University, for

Abilene Christian University ... and the list went on and on. Beneath it all, they hoped to make friends for God. And they made friends wherever they went. They befriended those who could never help their causes. In other words, they made friends just to spread peace and friendship. If some specific good came from it, fine. If not, that was fine too.

We might say that Helen and Norvel, in a general way, had four motivations – they loved God, they loved people, they loved to travel and they loved to give gifts. They combined the latter two loves and purchased small gifts as they traveled. When they returned from their trips, they kept a supply of gifts on hand for birthdays, anniversaries and other occasions. They liked to surprise people with some exotic gift from Korea or Thailand or Hong Kong.

Whether it came naturally or was learned behavior, it was nevertheless amazing how easily they made friends. How many people around the world, some who didn't even speak English, have heard the words, "Hi, I'm Dr. Norvel Young from Pepperdine University"? Or, "Hello, my name is Helen Young. I'm glad to meet you!" Somehow their friendliness was never misunderstood as salesmanship or manipulation. Their sincerity was transmitted through their eyes, their faces and their body language. They posed no threat. They were genuine.

The friends of Norvel and Helen Young were legion. And they came in all ages, shapes, sizes and colors. They were kings and presidents and statesmen. They were renowned educators and financiers and internationally known writers. Some were living legends. But others were housekeepers, custodians, gardeners and ordinary people. All were loved equally.

Dorothy Belk began working with the Youngs in 1977 while they still lived in the Adamson Beach House. She would travel from Los Angeles to cook, keep house and help Helen prepare for guests. "At the Beach House, we had no caterers," Dorothy said, "we had to prepare the food ourselves."

As she reflected on Norvel, she said, "Dr. Young was very appreciative of anything you did for him. If you gave him a bowl of oatmeal for breakfast or a Diet Coke for a snack, he was always thankful. He would say grace, even if it was just him and me."

"I never saw him angry," she continued. "In fact, I never knew anyone like him. He got his strength from God. It was wonderful to see Dr. Young enjoy Christmas. He never wanted to take the Christmas tree down. He kept wanting to keep it up for one more day."

Dorothy Belk came to the Youngs through an employment agency. But she stayed for more than 20 years, beyond her retirement age, because of her love for them. Even after Norvel's death in 1998, she still came to help Helen one day a week. Dorothy added, "Mrs. Young is a very sweet person. Maybe too sweet. She doesn't know how to say, 'No.' She and Dr. Young were the ideal couple. This would be a beautiful world if there were more people like Dr. and Mrs. Young. You won't find nobody like the Youngs."

A NEW CENTURY

One of the things Norvel and Helen loved to do was take their friends with them into new adventures. There were longtime fellow world travelers, like Oly and Allie Tegner, with whom they shared many wonderful trips. And there were many colleagues and friends of Pepperdine who accompanied them to Europe or Asia. From the time their children were in their teens, they accompanied Helen and Norvel on overseas trips. After the children were grown and married, they went with their parents to points around the globe. And even some of the grandchildren went traveling to the Olympics in Barcelona or to preaching and teaching meetings in Russia.

But sometimes the adventures weren't travels at all. The Youngs liked to paint a dream and take their loved ones and friends to some new mission or cause – whether it was building a university or feeding the poor. How many people did Norvel Young invite to his January 1, 2000, party? He wanted to go into the new millennium with his friends, those he had known all his life and those he had known for five minutes.

In October 1988, Norvel was in a reflective mood as he wrote his editorial for *20th Century Christian* magazine. He also had an important announcement to make. He and his readers were about to embark on a new adventure. He wrote:

> Thanks for the memories of fifty years of service by wonderful people who have made this magazine possible – editors, writers, artists, printing directors, business managers, secretaries and so many more. Thanks for the memories of thousands of readers, some of whom have traveled with us all the way from our beginnings in 1938. We celebrate the achievements of the past, and we pause to give God the glory for all the good accomplished. It has been a happy journey.
>
> But yesterday is only to be used to shape a better tomorrow. One thing that all those who worked closely with the magazine have had in common has been vision. We look to the future with hope and optimism. If God permits the world to stand, the magazine will celebrate its 62nd birthday when we cross the threshold into a new century and the third millennium.
>
> It is my pleasure to announce the decision of our editorial and publishing co-workers to change the name of the *20th Century Christian* to the *21st Century Christian* beginning January 1, 1990.
>
> Our name will change, but not our message. The magazine was begun to share the message of Christ with contemporary men and women. May God bless us as we seek to continue to be biblical, attractive and appealing. May we be loyal to our trust to communicate Christ, to uphold his authority, to promote his

abundant life of faith and love, to spread the word of his salvation which alone can save the world.

The best is yet to be.

Our gratitude to Dr. Jerry Rushford, our guest editor, for this watershed issue, which is real in the history of a movement.

The first of the articles that followed in that issue was one by guest editor Rushford, entitled "A Magazine and a Movement: Reflections on a Half Century." He began his article with these words:

> It is not often that we are privileged to celebrate the fiftieth anniversary of a Christian magazine. A grateful brotherhood congratulates the *20th Century Christian* on the completion of fifty years of positive and encouraging leadership in the field of Christian journalism. The Restoration Movement has produced nearly 2,000 different periodicals in the past 165 years, but only a few have survived a half century of continuous publication. For a journal to last that long, it must develop a clear identity and cultivate more than one generation of readers. The *20th Century Christian* has accomplished both elusive goals.

"Cultivate more than one generation of readers" is another way of saying that the Youngs made friends for their magazine for nearly three generations. And the new title of the magazine was another way of saying, "Come with us into the future. For the future is as bright as the promises of God."

In the following year, 1989, the Youngs shared a special celebration with family and friends. As their 50th anniversary approached, the Young children began planning a celebration for their "larger than life" parents. Eventually, three receptions were held in four days in the cities that were important in the lives of

Helen and Norvel: Nashville, Lubbock and Los Angeles (Malibu).

The Nashville celebration was the first, and it was held in the home of Norvel's cousin Annette Johnson. From there the Youngs flew to Lubbock, where the Broadway Church hosted a reception that included hundreds of well-wishers. The Young daughters and their families were able to be present for that gala gathering. Finally, the marathon celebration culminated on Pepperdine's Malibu campus, where all the children and grand-children were joined by friends and colleagues in a wonderful occasion.

Helen wore her wedding dress at all three parties, and Norvel again told his well-worn joke about not fitting into his wedding tuxedo because they had had four children. The napkins were imprinted with the words often repeated between the two: "I love you more than yesterday, less than tomorrow." Helen and Norvel were always thinking about today ... and tomorrow.

YOU MUST COME SEE US

From the earliest days of their marriage, Helen and Norvel subconsciously considered themselves hosts. That's just who they were. Helen said, "We both got that from our mothers. Mrs. Young always had young people meeting in her home. Every-one was welcome, and everyone came! The Youngs often had a 'lonely relative' living with them – someone who was in need of help. Mallie Young Webb, whom they called 'Sister,' was Dad Young's sister, and she lived with them several years." Helen added, "Mallie was Norvel's greatest influence, spiritually, and when Norvel was eleven, she was his school teacher."

Helen continued to reflect, "My mother was always hospitable. If there were people who visited our church, they would invari-ably be invited home for dinner at our house."

Then with a laugh, she said, "I can remember my brother and I kicking each other under the table and snickering because of the strangeness of some visiting missionaries. When we mentioned it to Mother, she said, 'Until you are ready to go [into the mission field], don't criticize those who do.' Anyway, we did have lots of company."

J. P. Sanders lived with Norvel and Helen as they began their marriage in Los Angeles in fall 1939. Probably few newlyweds would be so hospitable today. It has been mentioned that Helen's determination to be hospitable prompted her to invite Mr. and Mrs. Pepperdine over for dinner during the first month of her and Norvel's marriage. And, of course, one of her first purchases was a *Better Homes and Gardens* cookbook, because she wasn't an experienced cook. Helen didn't let her embarrassment over the big rolls deter her. She also remembered having Jimmie and Vivian Lovell and Don and Louise Miller, members of the Board of Trustees, for dinner as well as faculty wives and students.

When the Youngs moved to Lubbock, Texas, there was nearly a constant stream of visitors in their home. "Lubbock was a good stop on the way from Dallas to California," recalled Helen. So their home became the N&H Young Motel.

"Norvel was always having workshops or lectureships of some kind," said Helen. "Naturally, the speakers or some of the participants would stay with us." Of course, many friends would come and stay for a few days to be "recharged" by the hospitality and enthusiasm of the Youngs: Frank Pack, Batsell Barrett Baxter, Ira North and many others dropped in for a day or a week. The last house in which they lived in Lubbock, at 3210 West 27th Street, had a guest house in back specifically for visiting preachers and others, so that relieved the pressure a little on the family.

The Youngs were well known for their holiday open houses. Their first Christmas reception was held not long after arriving in Lubbock, and they continued for 54 years, including those at Pepperdine University. A remarkable record! Helen remembered, "Norvel would always say, 'Let's do one more.'" Even without Norvel, Helen did "one more" on her own in 1998.

When the Youngs moved from Lubbock to Pepperdine's Los Angeles campus, entertaining moved up a notch or two. The President's Home was stately and spacious and had a guest suite on the other side of house, so it was convenient for hospitality. They began having prospective faculty stay with them. Then visiting speakers and others would stay in their home during the Pepperdine Bible Lecture in Los Angeles, and the tradition continued on for more than 40 years.

As the fund-raising efforts increased, the Youngs would have 20 or 30 people for dinner in the President's Home in Los Angeles or, later, in the Adamson Beach House in Malibu. They remembered hosting Margaret Brock, John Tyler, Morris Pendleton, George Elkins, Fritz Huntsinger, Don Darnell, Pat Boone, Bryant Essick, S. I. Hayakawa, Richard Scaife, Mrs. Payson, Hubert Humphrey, Ed Pauley and many others.

One day at the Adamson Beach House, Ronald and Nancy Reagan came to lunch while he was governor of California. The next day, the governor showed up at the front door with a small tree in a tub to express his appreciation for the Youngs' hospitality.

Many well-known people visited the Youngs at their beach home: Lowell Thomas, Gene Autry, Arthur Burns, Loretta Young, David Packard, David Lawrence, Art Linkletter, Malcolm Muggeridge and many others.

At their home on campus just above the Brock House, Helen and Norvel continued to welcome people from far away and near by. Hari and Padma Harilela of Hong Kong, the Honorable and Mrs. Praman Chansue of the Thailand Supreme Court, Dr. and Mrs. Chatri Sophonpanich of the Bangkok Bank and many other international friends, including an Indian governor and an Eastern European princess, were their guests. Christian college presidents famous attorney and author Louis Nizer, editor and writer Norman Cousins and the Russian/American writers conference all enjoyed the Youngs' hospitality.

Norvel loved to tell a story of Helen's gift for making new friends:

> An international businessman, a potential donor to the University, arrived at our home for a scheduled meeting with me. Because of a conflict in my schedule, I was delayed for about an hour. Helen invited the man in and served him tea. Then she sat down and said, "Tell me about yourself."
>
> When I finally arrived for the appointment an hour later, Helen politely excused herself. When she was gone, my guest exclaimed to me, "Your wife is the most interesting conversationalist I've ever met!" Helen later told me that she hardly said a word after asking her initial question. She just spent the time listening and nodding her head.

Of course, Helen was really interested in the businessman's story, as she and Norvel were always interested in the lives of people they met. They didn't have to feign interest – they were truly fascinated by individuals and their unique stories. Norvel and Helen's genuineness and gracious people-skills blessed and multiplied their friend-raising.

Sam Jackson, husband of the Youngs' daughter, Sara, loved to tell about an incident that happened during a trip he and Norvel took to Africa in support of World Vision, an international relief organization for which Sam was an executive. They traveled deep into the bush to visit the Masai people. And as usual, Norvel pulled out his Pepperdine University printed material to make conversation. Sam thought, "What is he doing? Doesn't he know he's with people who have never even heard of Pepperdine?"

Undaunted, Norvel spread open his brochure and began to point at the beautiful pictures of Malibu and the university. Suddenly, a woman became animated. She began jumping up and down excitedly and yelling in her native language. Sam thought they had inadvertently insulted or offended her in some way. But they soon understood what she was trying to say. She had recognized her relative in one of the pictures of students in Norvel's brochure! With Norvel Young, it *truly was* a small world!

On one occasion, Norvel and his son-in-law, Stephen Stewart, had been invited to the floor of the New York Stock Exchange. They were traveling on the subway from their hotel to Wall Street when Norvel began conversing with the person next to him. "I have an MBA from Pepperdine," she replied, "and my friend sitting next to me went to Pepperdine, too." Soon a man sitting across the subway car perked up. "Did I hear somebody say Pepperdine?" he ventured. "I have a law degree from Pepperdine." By taking the initiative, Norvel had brightened a dull ride on the subway – and made three new friends. There was no telling what you might learn when you were with Dr. Norvel Young.

For more than 30 years, the Youngs opened their home to students – not merely to visit for a luncheon or a dinner, but to take up residence in a spare room. Today, those students are college professors, medical doctors, distinguished lawyers ... all with gratitude and devotion for the Youngs.

"You must come see us." It wasn't an empty invitation. The Youngs meant it. It was common to hear them say to some visitor on campus, "We have a meeting to run to right now, but go up to the house and make yourself at home. The door's open." Since they intended for people to accept their invitation, only once in awhile would they be surprised when someone took them up on it. For example, a young boy of eight received a Pepperdine key chain as a gift from Norvel during one of his African trips. Norvel said to the boy, "Study hard and you may be able to come to America and go to Pepperdine." Ten years later the Youngs answered a knock on the door, and as the door swung open, it revealed a smiling young African man holding up a key chain.

CAUSES AND FRIENDS

In 1987, at an occasion of tribute for M. Norvel Young, former Pepperdine President William S. Banowsky said,

> More than any other person, Norvel Young has been the glue which has held Pepperdine together. More than any other person, he is the bridge from the present to the past. He, alone, is the only man present today who was a close personal friend of both George Pepperdine, the founder of the college, and Frank Seaver, the maker of the university. And perhaps it is only Norvel who worked closely with both Batsell Baxter, the founding president, who was born in 1884, and David Davenport, our sixth president, who was born in 1951. Norvel Young is the only man to have served as president of the institution on both the Los Angeles campus and the Malibu campus.
>
> It is his warm, gregarious, effusive, and impulsive spirit which has set the tone for this place called Pepperdine. If Norvel were dean of admissions, every student would get in. If he were in charge of student aid, most would get a scholarship. If he were the dean of students, nobody would get kicked out. I have felt that if Norvel were the Lord, nobody would go to Hell. He would try to find a way somehow for the Baptists and the Buddhists, as well as for Ivan Boesky. Obviously, today's great Pepperdine draws its quality from tidier and more exacting standards. But it also draws much of its character from the approving, including, affirming, all-embracing love, which is the heart of Norvel Young.

Former Pepperdine President Howard A. White called Norvel a person "with prodigious energy." The same was true for Helen, of course. The Youngs were bridge-builders, always trying to span some distance between disparate ideas or people. That is not to say that they didn't have strong convictions. They would not embrace a "tolerance" without backbone that accepts anything and everything and stands for nothing. They knew exactly what they believed and stood for, but they also knew that they were not the appointed judges of all people – God would handle that awesome task Himself – and their task was simply to encourage people to love one another and encounter Deity.

The Youngs made friends at every level of society. Former chairman of Arco (Atlantic Richfield Company) Lodrick M. Cook said to Norvel:

> In his remarkable work, *Valley Forge*, playwright Maxwell Anderson says, "There are some men who lift the age they inhabit, till all men walk on higher ground in that lifetime." He was speaking, of course, of George Washington, but I think the words apply to you with equal logic.
>
> Is there anyone connected with Pepperdine University who does not walk on higher ground thanks to all you have done to build it into one of the finest institutions of higher education in the United States and, indeed, the world? All of us are beneficiaries of your work – from the community whose life is enriched by all the influences of the University to the newest freshman whose entire life will be shaped in important ways by the experience he or she will undergo in Malibu.

It was a great compliment to Norvel Young, but also to Pepperdine, Norvel's cause. Lod Cook was one of a host of Norvel's friends who caught the vision, the great cause that Norvel championed way back in '57 when few people knew or cared about Pepperdine.

Another friend was Robert R. Dockson, former chairman of CalFed Inc. Bob wrote:

> Norvel, we first met many years ago when I was Dean of the USC School of Business Administration and we both were active in Rotary. I remember how you impressed me at that time with your tremendous drive, deep religious convictions, and great love for Pepperdine. Your devotion to Pepperdine is well known and greatly appreciated by those of us who have watched you work over many years. Your contributions are legendary and will live on for as long as man is committed to institutions of higher learning.
>
> ... You have never failed to speak out for those things in which you believe and you have never failed to convince others of the great benefit that comes from a very strong belief in God and religion.
>
> Having said all of the above, I have left out, probably, the most significant achievement in your life. You married Helen, a lovely person who has made it possible for you to be who you are.

While some people drift through life never having found anything to challenge them or call them to action and devotion, the Youngs found countless causes, all involved in making life better for people. Having found a new cause, they would then set out to find friends for the cause. Or they would find friends for no reason at all, except that they wanted to be friends with the world.

One of the Youngs' children commented, "Daddy and Mother were like Will Rogers: they never met a person they didn't like."

ALWAYS A WELCOME GUEST

One of Norvel's earlier friends in California was George Elkins. George had been a friend of Matt Young, Sr., Norvel's father. When the Youngs returned to Pepperdine in 1957, Elkins became a staunch friend of the college. Years later, George's son was killed in an accident and Norvel spoke at his funeral. It would be one of dozens of eulogies Dr. Young would deliver for colleagues and friends of Pepperdine. As the new Seaver College campus was built in 1971-72, George Elkins would donate the funds to build a 350-seat auditorium that would bear his name.

Norvel "inherited" a number of friends from the Hugh Tiner years. His predecessor had developed the President's Council (later called the President's Board) to advise and assist the College in the early 1950s. But little was accomplished until deeper friendships were created in the late 1950s under President Young. Bryant Essick, president of Essick Manufacturing Company, was the first chairman of the President's Council. He, Don Darnell, J. Leland Atwood, Charles Fleischman and other board members became long-term friends. Others friends included Fred Llewellyn, Richard Ralphs and Henry Salvatori, stalwart citizens who attended the Freedom Forums conducted by Pepperdine and became friends of the College along with others.

These friends brought more friends to Pepperdine. For example, Richard Ralphs introduced the school to Leonard H. Straus, who became a lifelong friend, a treasured member of the Board of Regents and a benefactor. Richard Ralphs' family owned a large number of supermarkets in California, the Ralphs Market chain. A building that had been a Ralphs Market on Vermont Avenue adjacent to the campus was given to the school by Morris Pendleton. The building was converted into a recreation center and bookstore for the college. Len Straus was the president of Thrifty Drug Stores and Big 5 Sporting Goods. Among his many gifts to Pepperdine was the Ralphs-Straus Tennis

Center and an endowment for the Straus Institute for Dispute Resolution.

Today a part of this friend-making might be called "networking." When he arrived to become president, Norvel Young had to learn his way around the big city and L.A. society. He became a member the L.A. Chamber of Commerce and of Rotary Club (no. 5) that met at the Hilton Hotel downtown. There he met influential people like Carl Miller, editor of the western edition of the *Wall Street Journal*.

As the college moved into the final years of the '50s, Norvel began to see that he could not administer the school and also be the only one raising funds, so he brought in people to help with that work. First he hired O. T. Shipp, whom everyone called "Skipper Shipp," to serve in a development role. Then later, in the 1960s, William Teague would join the staff as vice president and serve in an important development role. Teague would go on to become a corporate CEO and, later, president of Abilene Christian University.

By 1970, Norvel had added other important members to the President's Board, including Merritt Adamson, Edward Di Loreto, Leonard Firestone, Walter Knott, Richard Scaife, Richard Seaver, Alton Watson and Palmer Conner. A crucial person in the building of the Malibu campus was Mr. John Tyler. His gifts would make possible the Tyler Campus Center, and upon his death and the death of his wife, Alice, a very large part of his estate went to Pepperdine, making their contributions truly profound. Other key people were Jerene Appleby Harnish, Morris and Gladys Pendleton, Fritz and Marianne Huntsinger, Leonard and Dorothy Straus and Joan and Charles Payson. Later they would be joined by Regent Flora Thornton (whose husband, Tex, had been Norvel's friend in Texas), George Page, Odell McConnell, Ed and Mary Currivan, Leon and Margaret Rockwell, Henry and Ginny Braun ... all instrumental in building the Malibu campus. A walk through the Malibu campus brings back memories of good friends, many of whom have passed to another life. Their names grace buildings, auditoriums, rooms, many special places: Elkins, Phillips, Smothers, Ahmanson, Stauffer, Weisman, Joslyn, Fouch, Lindhurst ... and others. Together they built a "shining city on a hill."

At the top of the Pepperdine hall of fame were the Adamsons, Richard Scaife, George and Reva Graziadio, Odell McConnell, John Drescher and John C. Tyler.

But the central figure of that time and the decades that followed was Mrs. Blanche Ebert Seaver. Along with Bill and Gay Banowsky and Charlie and Amy Jo Runnels, Norvel and Helen were great friends of Mrs. Seaver. She was, in fact, loved by the whole Pepperdine community. In return, Blanche Seaver's gifts to Pepperdine became the largest of any single donor in University's history.

In 1960, Norvel had met Blanche's husband, Frank Roger Seaver, who was owner and developer of the Hydril Company. And as mentioned, although he didn't know much about the small college, Mr. Seaver become interested enough to leave a gift to Pepperdine in his will. When he died in 1964, Blanche began to investigate Pepperdine. And the rest, as they say, is history.

Noted earlier, two who emerged as dear friends of the Youngs were George Eltinge and George Graziadio, entrepreneurs and founders of Imperial Bank, on whose board Norvel served as a director. While both Georges gave significant gifts to Pepperdine through the years, George and Reva Graziadio moved into the elite ranks of the foundational benefactors of the university with their gift of endowment for The George L. Graziadio School of Business and Management. The Graziadios and the Youngs grew closer and closer as friends as the years went by.

With the distinguished members of the President's Board (soon to become known as the University Board) in place in 1970, Pepperdine had the support it needed to begin its daring move into the future. As mentioned, Norvel Young was behind the scenes of this dramatic development, like an invisible symphonic maestro without sheet music, building the instrumental sections, then raising his baton and hoping all the pieces made beautiful music with the first downbeat. They did.

Norvel's approach to fund-raising matured over the years. Looking back, perhaps it was his experiences in Lubbock, Texas, having to raise money for Christian causes, that gave him such a good foundation. He found that one could not badger people into building a house of God, or building a Christian children's home, or constructing a college center for biblical studies. One had to encourage people to look within – toward noble and spiritual motivations. After all, at that time most people in his particular fellowship were not blessed with much money. Whatever they gave to Christian causes was usually sacrificial and had to come straight out of their modest living funds.

Norvel also discovered a wonderful truth: people who hoard money and things are usually miserable; people who give away money and things are usually happy and free. He began to see his role as helping people who had been blessed with financial resources to find true happiness by sharing with others. He knew from experience that it worked: the giving he and Helen had done in their lives brought them the greatest happiness. He would say, "When you ask someone for a gift for a noble cause, you do two good things for them. First, you compliment them because you recognize that they have either the financial resources or the personal abilities to make a significant gift. And second, you offer them the honest opportunity to enrich their lives through giving to an important cause." He believed that because he believed the biblical injunctions, "It is more blessed to give than to receive," and "Ask and ye shall receive."

For Norvel Young the Fund-raiser, this meant, "Do not *pressure people; no hard sell.*" He believed in simply presenting the vision and making a friend. Whether the friend decided to give to the cause or not, you had still gained a friend. And friends were better than wealth. Other fund-raisers were more direct, and Norvel himself became a little more direct as he grew older, probably because he felt the pressures of time, the urgency – life was getting away from him and everyone else. But there was always earnestness in his voice ... and a sense of friendship mingled with dreams of a better tomorrow.

One of Norvel's mentors in fund-raising was George Benson, who served for many years as a foreign missionary, then as president of Harding College in Arkansas. Benson developed a series of patriotic programs in the '50s and '60s that encouraged the participation of conservative donors at Harding College. He helped Norvel start Pepperdine's Freedom Forums program that brought nationally known political speakers to Los Angeles hotels under the auspices of the college. The forums increased the school's visibility tremendously and attracted community and corporate leaders to Pepperdine.

Norvel's message to potential donors was and continued to be: "We have a vision of producing students who are a credit to America. Our students are a cut above others; they are academically excellent and their moral standards, on the average, are higher than those of their counterparts on other campuses." And he truly believed what he said.

In many ways, Norvel Young sought to establish a "brotherhood" of those who were concerned about the direction of American higher education. He built deep friendships with people who had similar concerns, on a different basis than his religious brotherhood, but not completely unlike it in intensity and devotion. With some people he shared religious conviction. With other people he shared a vision of education and America. Love and trust were integrally involved in both realms of relationships.

He and Helen never gave up on a person, either religiously or in regard to giving to Christian education or some other cause. He seemed to have infinite patience. Some with whom he worked would encourage Norvel to concentrate his efforts on those who were more certain donors. These fund-raisers would drop someone from their thoughts if that person had not given after a reasonable time. Norvel would never drop a person. Again, it was more about friendship than funds, and he refused to abandon a friend. He would think, "Someday that longtime friend will give a marvelous gift to Pepperdine, and everyone will be surprised but me." In the end, how correct was he? Helen estimates that Norvel was right between 80 and 90 percent of the time on people he said would someday give a significant gift.

In the heyday of fund-raising for the new Malibu campus, Bill Banowsky and Norvel Young made a good team for several reasons. Bill was younger and more aggressive. Norvel was experienced and more human. Bill had urgency. Norvel had patience. It was a good combination.

In the last 15 or more years of his life, Norvel became friends with fund-raising professional Jerald Panas. Undoubtedly, it was because their philosophies on giving were so similar. For example, Panas agreed with Norvel that it was unwise and unethical to drop and forget people when they had given all of their money to a cause. Indeed, Norvel believed it was a Christian attitude to not neglect those who had given in the past. So like Charles Runnels, Larry Hornbaker and other Pepperdine advancement officers, Norvel and Helen Young maintained friendships for life among those who had little or nothing left to give except their love for Pepperdine.

CITIZENS YOUNG

Both Helen's mother and Norvel's father had been active in community affairs. So it was natural that the Youngs would be favorably disposed to involvement in service clubs, boards, benefits and other community projects and organizations.

Norvel was added to his first corporate board of directors in Lubbock, Texas. He was well known in town, and R. W. Pullen became a friend of Norvel's. When Pullen moved to Charleston, South Carolina, as president of Public Savings Life Insurance Company he asked Norvel if he would serve on the board of the company. Norvel agreed, but his motives were not simply to advise the company. He was praying that his president friend would become a Christian. Both men got their wish: Norvel served commendably on the board until the company was sold in 1984, and years later, Mr. Pullen became a Christian.

As Norvel participated on more corporate boards, he found it to be stimulating and a pleasure. He had always been interested in business. Perhaps it was the influence of his father, who was a successful businessman. In addition, when he became president of Pepperdine College, he decided that being involved in businesses in the community was good public relations.

Norvel served on the boards of Forest Lawn Memorial Parks (of which his friend, Fred Llewellyn was president); Lockheed Aircraft, until 1976; 21st Century Christian, Inc., and was chairman for many years; and Imperial Bancorp, of which George Graziadio was chairman and CEO. For nearly 10 years Norvel served as chairman of the Audit Committee for that board. He also served on the board of GCG Trust, a subsidiary of Bankers Trust of New York, which was later purchased by Mutual of Iowa.

But Norvel was also quite involved in civic organizations. He was on the Board of Governors of the L.A. County Museum of Natural History. He served as secretary of the L.A. County Museum of Natural History Foundation for 20 years. In addition, he was a director of the L.A. Area Chamber of Commerce and was a Chamber of Commerce Associate. Norvel was on the L.A. Chapter Honorary Men's Committee of the Freedom's Foundation of Valley Forge and the advisory board of Excellence in Media.

One of Norvel's favorite interests was the Union Rescue Mission in downtown Los Angeles. He served on the board from 1981 until his death and was vice chairman of the board during the period of construction of it's new building. He served other benevolent organizations such as M-2 Sponsors, which aided prisoners. He was on the National Advisory Council of Project Drug Free! and on the National Board of Advisors for the Washington Legal Foundation. And on the list could go: the

Newcomen Society in North America, the Bohemian Club, the Jonathan Club, the California Club, Rotary and many others.

Dr. Norvel Young was a member of several educational organizations. Governor Reagan appointed him to represent all private colleges and universities on the Coordinating Council for Higher Education for California. He was also a member of the Independent Colleges of Southern California organization, Phi Delta Kappa and Pi Gamma Mu. He was a board member for Abilene Christian University until he moved to California, was on the Advisory Board of Lubbock Christian University (of which he was co-founder) and was on the board of International Christian University.

For all their work and service, Helen and Norvel were often awarded high honors. Some of Helen's awards were mentioned previously. Norvel was awarded honorary doctorates by the University of California, Irvine, College of Physicians and Surgeons; Lubbock Christian University; and Pepperdine University. He was the very first Alumnus of the Year at Abilene Christian University and an Alumnus of the Decade at David Lipscomb University. Twice he was awarded the George Washington Medal of Honor by the Freedom's Foundation of Valley Forge.

One of the greatest honors for the Youngs came in 1992 when the funding was completed for an endowed chair in their honor at Pepperdine's Graduate School of Education and Psychology. Appropriately, it was called the M. Norvel and Helen M. Young Chair in Family Life. It was made possible by a major gift from longtime friend George Evans. Many of Pepperdine's other friends made significant contributions toward the chair.

Helen said at the time, "We heartily agreed that of all the things that might be done, the study of the family was our favorite." Norvel added, "Establishing endowed chairs is a successful and time-honored tradition of assuring high-caliber educational opportunities. As the University grows academically, it's very important to develop chairs and professorships not only at GSEP, but at all the schools."

The endowed chair enabled the University to attract a recognized expert in the field of family life. The first person to fill the position, in September 1993, was Dr. Dennis Lowe, respected not only as an academician and family counselor, but also as a longtime friend of the Young family. By February 1996 the Young Chair had evolved into the Pepperdine Center for the Family, directed by Dr. Lowe. Lowe was able to develop the idea of an institute that plans and holds conferences, brings noted experts in family life to Southern California, coordinates parent mentoring programs and in other ways assists people in having better marriages and families. This had originally been a dream of Helen and Norvel. Sara Young Jackson joined Lowe as associate director of the center.

When the chair was first established, Helen commented, "Norvel and I have been together for many wonderful years. Our strong marriage has weathered difficult times and provides great joy and satisfaction. Many of the strongest families I know are Pepperdine families. I believe that in this area we really have something to teach."

Norvel and Helen Young spent a lifetime making friends for the church, for Christian education, for Pepperdine University and for a host of other causes ranging from improving families to feeding the poor. The Youngs were successful in raising huge sums of money for those grand projects. But the passionate effort was never just about money. It was about vision. It was about making things better, about doing the most good in the least amount of time.

Those who knew them well always wondered how the Youngs could maintain such a long list of friends from such diverse backgrounds. Those friends included people from every ethnic group, every religious persuasion, every nation and every economic and educational status. They were on a first-name basis with poor missionaries and multi-millionaires. They socialized with uneducated workers and brilliant academicians. They hosted students from third-world countries and powerful politicians.

How does one develop such a breadth of personal relationships? The answer is that one must love people deeply and be a genuine friend to each person. Norvel and Helen had legions of people who believed that they were not merely acquaintances, but close personal friends of the Youngs. That is because when someone was with Helen or Norvel, there was no one else in the universe at that moment in time: all of Norvel's or Helen's attention and care was focused on that single conversation. The eyes were focused, the attention intent. They honestly wanted to know what each person was thinking. They cared.

They were able to raise funds. But they were successful because they first raised friends. They raised friends because they dared to be vulnerable and dared to be a friend.

16

TRAVELS WITH NORVEL AND HELEN

*When the door opened, a bare-footed
Mother Teresa of Calcutta stood smiling at the trio.
Helen and Norvel were stunned and honored.*

A s a 22-year-old young man, Norvel Young was already a seasoned traveler. He and his cousin, James Baird, had traipsed around the world while most young men their age were still trying their solo wings away from home in college. However, Helen had traveled very little when she and Norvel were married in 1939. Most of her trips were by necessity, traveling to the homes of relatives or away to college, or more regional leisure trips.

They were married in Helen's hometown, Oklahoma City, and Norvel had a job to which he was returning at Mr. Pepperdine's college in Los Angeles. So their honeymoon was really a trip back to Southern California where both of them had been, Helen as a recent Pepperdine College graduate and Norvel as a Pepperdine professor.

They traveled through the farmlands of Kansas and stopped off in Denver. They drove through the Rockies of Colorado and relaxed in the Grand Tetons and Yellowstone National Park areas of Wyoming. In California they marveled at Yosemite Valley and soaked in the charm of San Francisco.

It probably was appropriate that their honeymoon didn't consist of a two-week resort vacation to Hawaii or the Bahamas.

Instead, it was a *journey* — a 2,000-mile trek. And for the rest of their lives, Norvel and Helen would journey together on a great adventure. They never seemed to stop for long; they were always on the move. Certainly, the term "journey" was figurative or metaphorical. Their life together moved through space and time, had a beginning point and a final destination. But quite regularly their journeys were literal and took them to ports of call around the world. Both of them dearly loved to travel, so that became their avocation. And the more they traveled, the broader became their vision. After more than five decades of journeys, they had friends virtually spanning the globe. They were in love with the whole world.

ANNUAL PILGRIMAGES

While they would travel to exotic places and new frontiers, the Youngs maintained a regular schedule of annual trips. Every year, in the third week of February, they traveled to the annual Abilene Christian College (later University) Bible Lectureship. Abilene Christian was Norvel's alma mater, so his allegiance to the school drew him back year after year. He loved the school of his youth. Looking back, he and Helen thought that the only year they missed the Abilene Lectureship was 1997 when they took a final around-the-world tour after Norvel had his stroke.

But in addition to the call of his alma mater, there were other reasons they went to Abilene. They were always anxious to renew friendships with Christians from Lubbock and other Texas cities, Christians from Nashville and Oklahoma City (their hometowns), and folks from across the nation. Then there were the contacts they made for various causes they supported. In addition, the Youngs regularly hosted a *20th Century Christian* and *Power for Today* breakfast or luncheon every year during the lectureship to promote those publications. If that sounds a bit promotional at first hearing, one must remember that neither publication they edited was a moneymaker. Far from making a profit, both were "profit-losing" enterprises. The Youngs never really made money from the publications, nor was it their intention to do so. To the contrary, they spent large amounts of their own money keeping the magazine and devotional guide going through the years. The pages of those periodicals were simply one of their many ministries, their way of encouraging Christians and others. They were always gratified when they heard of some person in distress or in a difficult situation or in prison who was uplifted by one of the publications.

The breakfasts or luncheons would feature a talented speaker delivering a spiritual message, and nearly always a Christian service award would be given to a worthy person. Sometimes, it would be a "Woman of the Year" award, a journalism award or a Christian lifestyle award. And the Youngs invariably encouraged the attendees at the meetings to give them their suggestions on how to improve the periodicals.

After 1957, when the Youngs moved from Lubbock to Los Angeles, Norvel would usually be asked to stop by the Broadway Church of Christ in Lubbock on the way to the Abilene Lectureship to preach for the church. He and Helen were always happy to renew loving relationships and make new friends at their former church. Naturally, they were always given a warm reception. The church never forgot the "Young Years" at Broadway.

At Christmastime, Norvel's parents, Matt and Ruby Young, customarily traveled to Norvel and Helen's home for a holiday visit. Then, in the summer, Helen and Norvel almost always went back to Nashville to visit the senior Youngs. On those summer trips, they also would spend some time in Oklahoma City with Helen's parents, J. P. and Irene Mattox. The summer Oklahoma-Tennessee trek was another of their annual rituals.

In the last 20 or more years of his life, Norvel also made an annual pilgrimage in July to the Bohemian Grove, north of San Francisco. The Bohemian Club was a men-only association, similar to the Jonathan Club in Los Angeles, that was founded with the purpose of bringing men from the arts, entertainment and literature fields together with men from the business and political worlds. While there was a building in San Francisco for the club, it was more widely known for the club's annual July meeting at the Bohemian Grove.

The grove was in California's coastal mountain range beyond Santa Rosa (north of San Francisco) and consisted of a series of rustic lodges with quaint-sounding names nestled among the majestic redwoods. The gathering of men centered mostly on large meetings of all the participants, but in addition, each lodge also had its own discussions and activities. The meetings drew top executives like Steve Bechtel of the Bechtel Corporation, builders of monumental projects worldwide. Bechtel was the one who succeeded in getting Norvel into the Bohemian Club in a faculty-category membership. Later, Pepperdine presidents William Banowsky, Howard White and David Davenport, along with Pepperdine's Chancellor Charles Runnels, became members in the same category.

It was an exciting experience to interact with famous artists, musicians and ctors, along with national and international figures like Ronald Reagan, George Bush, Henry Kissinger and various presidential Cabinet members. But the central attraction was the programs that featured everything from lectures on economics by leading economists to jazz combo, symphony music and plays — plays in which the club members themselves played roles. It was an opportunity to become acquainted with outstanding men from diverse fields in a relaxed, rustic atmosphere.

The Youngs also made a yearly trip to Yosemite National Park in California. Members of the Churches of Christ on the West Coast gathered each year for a week in July to enjoy a spiritual retreat in one of the world's most beautiful places. Called the Yosemite Family Encampment, the event began in 1940 and the first featured speaker was Pepperdine College's President Hugh Tiner. When Norvel Young became president in 1957, he continued the tradition of Pepperdine's involvement in the encampment, as did Howard White and David Davenport at a later time until the encampment was discontinued in the mid-1990s.

Norvel and Helen began staying in one of the rustic, some would say primitive, housekeeping units in Yosemite Valley. The units had wooden floors and half walls, with canvas tent-like tops. It was much more like camping than staying in a cabin. But they seemed to enjoy "roughing it," at least for a week. (And it was the most inexpensive living quarters in the valley!) They tried to reserve the same unit each year if possible.

Sometimes Norvel would serve as a featured speaker or teacher. And Helen, too, might teach a class, but she was always busy at the Yosemite Family Encampment with a meeting of the Associated Women for Pepperdine. She would host a large meeting of women as they discussed or reported on their work of raising funds for the college. Since the Bohemian Grove meeting was the week prior to the Yosemite encampment, Norvel would often go directly from one meeting to the other, and Helen would meet him there in Yosemite. The stark contrast of the two meetings was illustrative of Norvel's life. He would participate in the cultural activities and surroundings of the Bohemian Grove, rubbing shoulders with corporate magnates, virtuosos and presidents; then he would drive to Yosemite and camp in a rustic tent unit and attend outdoor religious lectures with his brethren. And he felt perfectly at ease in both settings.

JOURNEYS OF ENCOURAGEMENT

While most people plan their travel agendas with key points of interests in mind, Helen and Norvel nearly always began their planning by asking themselves which missionaries they could visit. They saw their journeys as golden opportunities to visit friends and encourage those who were a long way from home doing the Lord's work.

That approach to traveling originally began in 1937 when Norvel Young and James Baird began their around-the-world tour. They planned how they would contact all the Americans of whom they knew; then they hunted down missionaries and others to encourage them in their work. They also tried to meet as many respected leaders as possible. One of Norvel's great regrets was that he missed seeing such influential people as Christian apologist C. S. Lewis in England and Mahatma Gandhi in India.

From that early time on, Norvel and his beloved travel partner, Helen, planned their trips so as to get the most accomplished, whether making friends for their various causes, recruiting students for Christian colleges, establishing contact with international alumni or encouraging ministers, missionaries and others.

It is difficult for most of us to imagine the life that the Youngs lived. In our view, people travel for one of two reasons: for business or for pleasure. Occasionally we might mix the two together. But Helen and Norvel never traveled for just one reason. A business trip always involved some side excursion to see new sights and meet new people. A pleasure trip always involved some social contact for Pepperdine, or 20th Century Christian, or the church, or the American ideal. They believed that one of their missions was to bring together people and ideas and causes.

Helen's first trip abroad was the 1949 journey to Europe, including Germany. She and Norvel left Lubbock to visit missionary efforts in Europe and to see firsthand the food and supplies distribution in war-torn areas. It was a sobering journey. But once again, they managed to do some sight-seeing after the work was done. Norvel was anxious for Helen to experience the charm, beauty and heritage of lands that were old when America was young.

From that first international trip together, the Youngs have found ways to profoundly enrich their journeys by establishing personal contact with old friends and with new ones.

In 1993 they had a golden opportunity. Their trips were always filled with occasions to accomplish worthwhile tasks.

But during August of 1993, only four years after the fall of the Berlin Wall and the resulting collapse of the Soviet system, Norvel and Helen were invited to Russia to speak to groups of non-Christians about Jesus and to encourage the Christians there. They decided to take with them two of their grandsons, David Lemley and Chris Young.

By prearrangement, they met a lovely Christian woman, Natasha Golos, from Belarus, who traveled with them for weeks as their friend and interpreter. They journeyed to St. Petersburg and prepared for the first speaking sessions. The grandsons stood at the bottom of subway escalators and passed out flyers advertising the speech, titled "Why I Believe," at the Cultural Center. Norvel spoke for about 20 minutes and that was followed by a very engaging question and answer period. The people were hungry to explore Christianity and faith.

A few days later, a woman interviewed Helen and Norvel for the St. Petersburg radio station. She asked, "Why are you here on vacation instead of going to the beaches of Hawaii?" A good question. The Youngs replied, "We love the Russian people. We have been here eight times before, but this time your religious freedom allows us to speak freely. We brought medical supplies and we came to share hope – Christ."

During their travels, they met many ordinary Russian people and were saddened at the lack of food and necessities they endure. But they were able to deliver six large duffel bags full of medical supplies to Wesley Jones, the American director of the World Christian Broadcasting operation in St. Petersburg. Jones and Lydia Logievona, the Russian director of the operation there, took the supplies to a local hospital where their friends worked. The doctors and nurses obviously were thrilled.

Jones took the Youngs and their grandsons to a lovely building that had been used by an indigenous movement of Churches of Christ in the late 19th and early 20th centuries. He told them how the movement had prospered in the 1920s, despite the Russian Revolution, and followerrs had numbered in the thousands. In those difficult days, there were several million evangelical Christians who eventually went underground as atheism became the national religion.

In Moscow, the Youngs met with Christians and had Bible studies with new converts. On Sunday Norvel preached on "Faith that Moves Mountains," and Helen taught a women's class on "Faith Basics." Then they were bound for Kiev, Ukraine, where they wanted to worship with a small group of Christians there. When they and the others arrived at some rooms that had been rented for their service at the Technical Institute, a sign announced, "The Believers May Not Meet in this Room Tonight." Undaunted, they walked outside to a nearby park and stood in a circle and worshiped. And they thought of how faith reaches beyond even nationalities.

Their final destination was Minsk. Once again they had the opportunity of meeting Americans who were working to bring hope to the people of the former Soviet Union. As they returned home, they hoped they could return to Russian soon "and work longer in one place." They said that their prayer was, "May God encourage many to go and many to send and all to pray."

Every trip for Helen and Norvel was a journey of encouragement. They knew no other way to travel.

AMBASSADORS AT LARGE

During their married life, Helen and Norvel made nearly 40 international trips. And always they represented their nation, their institution of learning and their faith in a noble way. Even in the age of the "Ugly American," they made friends for America. They felt that they had been appointed ambassadors to the world. Who appointed them? Nobody. They surmised that you don't need any special authority or dispensation to do good.

A dozen or more of their international journeys were taken with the companionship of Oly and Allie Tegner. Since Oly was in charge of teacher training (he eventually would be founding dean of the School of Education), the trips had that semi-official sense that the Youngs journeys always did, even when the four of them were enjoying themselves to the fullest. Probably the majority of the trips were to Asia – Thailand, Taiwan, Korea, Japan and other eastern nations. Although Norvel never lost his love for Europe, he seemed to become more fascinated by Asia as the years went by.

Somehow, the Youngs (and the Tegners when they were along on the trips) managed to turn nearly every journey into a diplomatic mission. Most people would undoubtedly want to escape normal responsibilities when on a trip to some exotic place. But a large part of the pleasure of the adventures for Norvel and Helen seemed to be meeting and visiting with dignitaries in faraway places. They would drop in on U.S. ambassadors, international banking moguls, kings, supreme court justices, writers and countless minor officials. Norvel knew that he wasn't a "Personality," that is, an internationally known movie star or musician or artist or athlete. But he was the president of Pepperdine College, and later he was the Chancellor of Pepperdine University … and he found that his identification with the institution opened doors for him and Helen.

Norvel would introduce himself in such a grand way – "Hello, I am Dr. M. Norvel Young, chancellor of Pepperdine University in Malibu, California" – that no one would ever think to say, "So what?" His manner was so confident and he was so proud of the university, that international dignitaries would never admit that they hadn't the foggiest notion of what "Pepperdine university" was. Chancellor Young would leave the subtle implication that any educated and refined person of the world would know of Pepperdine. But in time, word got around. Because Norvel and Helen Young got around. And nearly every educated and refined person in Asia *did indeed* know about this California university that looked out across the Pacific Rim from Malibu toward the Asian economic tigers.

There were some trips in which Norvel traveled with others beside Helen. That was especially true when their children were younger and Helen determined to stay close to home. And then there were other trips in which Helen was asked to speak overseas, such as the one in summer 1985 when she spoke at a German women's lecture series in Europe.

Oly Tegner loved to tell about one trip in the mid-1960s that he and Norvel took alone. They traveled throughout much of Central and South America. The purpose of that trip later escaped Oly – maybe it was purely pleasure (but with Norvel's curiosity, it would most certainly have been educational as well). Before they headed out, Ken Davidson, who headed up the Pepperdine Alumni Association, decided that it would be a good idea to take out an insurance policy on Norvel. After all, he was key to the work of the college, and the itinerary of the trip seemed a little beyond the usual pleasure cruise. They would be passing through some countries prone to civil wars and dangerous travel. Davidson made the policy for one million dollars.

In each country, Norvel insisted that they visit with the local missionaries (he just couldn't break the habit). Then in Quito, the capital of Ecuador, they decided they wanted to visit the Inca ruins of Machu Picchu, high in the Andes of Peru. They had to first fly to Lima, Peru, then take a train from there to the base of the mountain area where the remains of the famous ancient city were situated. They boarded a Fawcett Airways airplane, a propeller-powered craft which was not pressurized. However, part of the flight took them to altitudes where oxygen was necessary. For the convenience (?) of the passengers, the airline had installed four-foot long rubber oxygen hoses for each person. When one had the sensation that the air was too thin, a few sucks on the hose was supposed to remedy the problem.

Sure enough, as they reached higher altitudes in the plane, the two Americans grabbed for the hoses. Oly remembered wondering who had been the last person to suck oxygen from his hose. But he was feeling lightheaded, so he put his mouth over the end of the hose and inhaled. Norvel did the same. But with different results. No matter how hard Norvel sucked, he couldn't get any oxygen from the tube. He started turning blue. Then he looked down, turned to Oly and said in a weak voice, "You're standing on my hose."

Soon they had enough air to laugh about the incident. But forever after, Norvel jokingly accused Oly of trying to put the college on better financial footing by collecting on the million-dollar policy.

Oly Tegner remembered another trip with Norvel, this time a journey by four buddies: Kenny Hahn, Bill Stivers, Oly and Norvel. Hahn, Stivers and Tegner were Pepperdine alumni, and all four had become great friends through the years. Their trip took them to the Mediterranean region, India and other areas.

In a city in India, the four were approached by hoards of vendors, but one pitchman was a little unusual. He badgered them to have their picture taken with his boa constrictor. Three of the men would have nothing to do with the man or his reptile. Only Norvel stepped forward and allowed the man to wrap the huge snake around Norvel's neck and body. The pitchman snapped the photograph and removed the boa before it could squeeze the life out of President Young. And they went on their way laughing.

On the same trip, the four visited Vatican City in Rome. Kenny Hahn, already a respected Los Angeles County supervisor, had made arrangements for the distinguished quartet to have an audience with the Pope. But when they arrived at Vatican City, an official appeared and told them that the Pope was ill with the flu, and sent his regrets. However, the official said he would be happy to provide a private tour of the Vatican. Though disappointed, the four decided that they had come quite a distance and at least they could see the place revered by millions of Roman Catholics worldwide.

During the tour of the stunning art treasures of the Vatican, the official took them to a place above the private garden and pointed out the beauty of the place. He also pointed to a gleaming white Cadillac and told the Americans that a wealthy Texas oilman had given the limousine to the Pope as a gift. As they moved on in the tour and left the Cadillac behind, Kenny's disappointment at not seeing the Pope surfaced momentarily as he muttered to Norvel and the others, "Jesus walked."

During their journey they did in fact visit the land where Jesus walked. It was a wonderful pilgrimage through Israel's Holy Land. After visiting Jerusalem and other historic places, they traveled out to the Jordan River as it winds its way down from the Sea of Galilee to the Dead Sea. They stood gazing at the legendary river, discussing how John the Baptist had dipped hundreds, perhaps thousands of people in these waters not far from this very place. Who knew how many Christians had been baptized there? Norvel turned to Oly and said, "Oly, would you like to be baptized into Christ in the Jordan River?" Oly thought about it for a moment and then said, "Yes, I would."

Norvel and Oly went down into the river, while Kenny Hahn and Bill Stivers stood on the shore. After Norvel said a few words, he began to lower Oly into the water. And at that moment, Kenny struck up a chorus of "Shall We Gather At the River." It sounded so comical, that Norvel began to smile and Oly worried that if he started to laugh, Norvel might lose his grip and drown him rather than baptize him. Fortunately, they composed themselves and the baptism in the Jordan River was completed – and remained an extremely memorable moment in the trip for the men, especially for Oly.

In 1977 and 1978, Norvel and Helen served not only as ambassadors but as fund-raisers as well. They traveled to Iran with Bill and Gay Banowsky, Oly and Allie Tegner, Mr. and Mrs. Richard Seaver, Dr. Chilingar and others to have an audience with the Shah of Iran. They conferred an honorary doctorate on the Shah in a solemn ceremony where neither the Shahbanan, his wife, nor any other woman was permitted by Iranian custom. Amazingly, Norvel insisted on the presence of the American women (the wives of the university officials). He argued that the women were academic officials and should be allowed into the ceremony. The Shah finally agreed. And eventually he gave a million dollars to Pepperdine to endow a chair in education named in honor of his wife, Empress Farah.

Around 1980, the Youngs stopped off in England to visit the famous satirist and editor Malcolm Muggeridge. They found his country cottage and spent several hours in pleasurable conversation with him and his wife. Muggeridge was the featured speaker at a downtown Los Angeles luncheon for business people in the late '70s.

ENCHANTMENT OF THE ORIENT

Norvel Young and James Baird had traveled beyond Europe to the Middle East and Asia on their around-the-world trip in 1937. But Norvel and Helen confined their travels to Europe and the Mediterranean world. Helen's first international journey was in 1949, with Norvel, Wanda and Batsell Barrett Baxter, Mother Ruby Young and Lillian Burton. They went through Europe and dropped into Eygpt and the Holy Lands.

It was seven years before Norvel and Helen traveled beyond the borders of the United States again. In 1956 Helen and Norvel taught in the European Bible Lectures in Frankfurt, Germany, and took time to do some bicycling in Scandinavia. Norvel and Lee Sparks went to Australia and Japan in 1959. Then in 1963, Norvel traveled to Russia with an educational fraternity. On that trip he traveled with Paul Davis, education editor for *Reader's Digest*, and the two became lifelong friends.

Five years later in 1968, Norvel and Helen were guests of U.S. Ambassador Bill Heath in Stockholm, Sweden. And once again, they enjoyed the great western European cities. But five years after that, in 1973, the Youngs and two of their daughters, Marilyn and Sara, who had been in the Pepperdine program in Heidelberg, traveled together to Italy and Greece. Helen and Norvel then traveled on to Kenya, Ethiopia and Tanzania in Africa. There they visited the wonderful game preserves of the Serengeti. Other parts of the world were beginning to call to Norvel and Helen. And they were enchanted.

The very next year they took a grand tour of Asia, again with daughters Marilyn and Sara. And after that time, though they returned periodically to Europe, their emphasis shifted significantly toward the Far East.

George Page, benefactor and namesake of the Page Museum at the La Brea Tar Pits, was a wonderful friend of Pepperdine University and of Charlie and Amy Jo Runnels. He was also a great friend to the Youngs – and a renowned traveler. Understanding that travel was one of Helen and Norvel's real loves, he encouraged them to not put it off till later. "You need to travel now, as often as you can," he told them. "Someday you will be alone like me, and you won't want to go on those adventures anymore." In truth, George Page traveled fairly often with various Pepperdine people, even as he moved into his 90s. And one of his favorite destinations was Asia. But his wife had died many years before, and that undoubtedly diminished his joy in seeing what was around the next corner.

Perhaps some of the interest in Asia began in the 1960s when George Hill was the admissions director on the Los Angeles campus. Norvel had hired Hill, who served previously as associate minister with Burton Coffman at the Manhattan, New York, Church of Christ. As the school sought to increase its enrollment, Hill began recruiting international students, especially Asian students. Even after George left the admissions office and began serving in the development area, he traveled to Asia and made contacts for Pepperdine. Soon there was a wide network of alumni and supporters throughout many Eastern nations and city-states such as Hong Kong and Singapore.

Norvel and Helen eventually took other university administrators such as Chancellor Charles Runnels and his wife, Amy Jo, with them to Asia and introduced them to the loyal Eastern alumni and supporters of Pepperdine. In May 1995 President David Davenport and his wife, Sally, traveled to Thailand with the Youngs, where President Davenport addressed a legal conference and met many Thai dignitaries. Several years before, the Youngs had visited with the King of Thailand and awarded him an honorary degree. Pepperdine had many Thai students, and Helen and Norvel were anxious to meet business people and make contacts in that country.

One of Helen's favorite outings in Asia was shopping. "Even Norvel would go shopping," she said. "Here in America, I couldn't get him close to a store. But there, it was different somehow." The two things that seemed to attract Norvel in Asia what but not in America were the unusual and exotic variety of things to buy, and the good prices. Norvel loved a bargain. And their home was filled with lovely Asia furniture and art.

There was a little woman in Bangkok that made nearly all of Helen's clothes for her. The woman not only made the clothes, but also she designed them. This was also a practical traveling consideration. Helen didn't have to pack huge, heavy suitcases. She would wait until her trips to buy clothes, especially suits, then simply buy a bag there in which to bring her new fashions home. Norvel loved to buy his suits and shirts in Hong Kong.

One year, as flames threatened Pepperdine's Malibu campus and their home, Helen and Norvel were half way around the world in Bangkok, Thailand. It was a strange sensation, they reported, sitting helplessly in their room at the Holiday Inn Crown Plaza and watching the drama back in California unfold on television. They prayed for the University's people and their Malibu neighbors and for all the firefighters. They also prayed that the homes, including their own, would be spared.

In a somewhat somber mood, they went downstairs to meet their host, Kumar Harilela, for dinner. Kumar was a Pepperdine alumnus, a member of the distinguished Harilela family who owned the hotel. The Harilela family boasted more Pepperdine alumni than any other family of which university officials knew.

Kumar knew of the wildfires and the natural concern of the Youngs. But he said, "Before we go to dinner, I have someone

I'd like you to meet. This guest has been in the hotel for a week or so, resting."

Helen and Norvel got into the elevator with Kumar, and they were deposited on the top floor. They walked down the hall past their room, the presidential suite (Kumar had insisted they occupy the suite), to one of the smaller rooms. Their host knocked on the door.

When the door opened, a bare-footed Mother Teresa of Calcutta stood smiling at the trio. Helen and Norvel were stunned and honored. She invited them in and spoke with them about half an hour. It turned out that she had come to Bangkok to rest. For her health's sake, the only way she could really recuperate was to leave the missions. So, with one assistant, she had traveled to Thailand to try to recover her strength. She asked about the Young family and Norvel showed her the family portrait he always carried in his coat pocket. She gave him a medallion for each child. Norvel was impressed by one statement she made that summed up her life. She said, "I'm just so thankful to be able to help the poor."

Mother Teresa mentioned that she had seen the fire in Malibu on television and had been praying for those in danger. It made the moment even more surreal for Helen and Norvel—thousands of miles away from their home, watching the university community being threatened by fire ... and talking about it with perhaps the most respected and revered woman in the world.

Before the Youngs left, Mother Teresa told Norvel she wanted to show him something. She reached out and took his right hand and said, "You remember the words of Jesus, 'Inasmuch as you do it unto the least of these my brethren . . .'" She paused, then pointed to each of Norvel's fingers as she finished the five-word quotation. "'... you ... do ... it ... unto ... me,'" she concluded. He would never forget the encounter with the tiny woman in the blue and white Indian sari. And he would never forget her five-finger exercise.

They said good-bye to Mother Teresa and walked toward the elevator. Norvel was curious why their host had introduced the Youngs to the great lady. He told them that, knowing their Christian faith, he thought they would be pleased to meet the legendary nun. He was right. Norvel asked Kumar why he had not put his most distinguished guest in the presidential suite. He answered, "I tried to, but she didn't feel that she deserved it."

In retrospect, Norvel and Helen decided that they had not found Mother Teresa to be extraordinary, in the strictest sense. Physically she was not impressive, her intellect seemed average, her speech common. She was, in fact, very ordinary – a simple woman. What was extraordinary was her passion to serve her God among the poorest of the poor. "She has dedicated her life to doing good. That's all. And people everywhere want to be like her," said Norvel.

It was a precious half hour. Helen and Norvel went away from the small room amazed at Mother Teresa's humility, quiet confidence and inner strength. And they were even more convinced that ordinary people can do extraordinary things when they are used by God.

17

ONCE MORE 'ROUND THE WORLD

*Now they would circumnavigate the globe
as friends of the earth, "stopping to smell the roses" . . .
and the breezes in Bangkok, the fragrant tea plantations
of Sri Lanka and the aromatic plains of Africa.*

Norvel Young's last two and a half years were filled with joy, pain, love, service, excitement ... all the things that comprised his full life from the beginning. Those who lived with him, those who worked with him, those who knew him – none of them ever saw a "retired" or retiring Norvel Young. He wore the university title "Chancellor Emeritus" during his dozen years. But to him that did not mean "has been" or "used to be." He was still making friends, encouraging people, helping individuals have more joy in their lives by supporting a noble cause as he had done for six decades.

He often told people that he would never retire. "That's what heaven is for," he would tell them. And he truly believed it. Until he became an octogenarian, he refused to even allow anyone to know his age. He wasn't ashamed of his age – he said, "If you tell people how old you are, they will treat you that way." And that certainly seemed to be true. He outworked people half his age and everyone forgot that he was a "senior citizen." He was just "Dr. Young doing what he did best" – creating a better world. However, as autumn came in 1995, friends convinced Norvel to relent and allow an eightieth birthday party to go forward. For one thing, they told him, it is time to allow people the opportunity to tell him what he has meant to their lives. After all, at 80, life is a little more tenuous. And expressions of appreciation are needful, good-byes are crucial. Words need to be spoken.

No one knows how long he or she will live. If we did, we would all plan our lives better. But perhaps it was the genius of Norvel Young's life that made it seem that he actually planned his last years in great detail. Had he known he was going to die, he certainly would have planned to work hard for his causes until his last breath. He would have expressed his love to everyone. He would have written a book that embodied his philosophy of life. He would have traveled extensively and seen the green earth a last time. And those very things, he did! He did them all, and more.

BEYOND FOURSCORE

Thursday, October 5, 1995, was a special day for Norvel Young: it was his *eightieth* birthday. The word "eightieth" is significant not only because it attests to his longevity, but because Norvel finally admitted to his age! However, the celebration of his birthday came three days later on Sunday afternoon, October 8. A birthday party was held at the Jonathan Club on the beach in Santa Monica, with a lovely buffet luncheon for family and friends. The youngest grandchild, Josiah Malcolm Norvel Stewart, made one of his earliest social appearances, at age six months. All four of the Youngs' children and spouses and their children were present, as well as Chip and Sharyn Moore, Jerry and Lori Rushford, Terry and Susan Giboney, Bill and Laurette Henegar and a few other friends. Chip Moore (James C. Moore, III) was the son of J. C. and Dorothy Moore, lifelong friends of the Youngs. Especially after the death of J. C., Chip became nearly like a son to the Youngs, and he and Sharyn were invited to be present for many family affairs.

Tributes to Norvel by colleagues and friends, in both humorous and glowing terms, were spoken and read, including one tribute in verse by Terry Giboney. Norvel enjoyed opening his birthday presents, but mostly he enjoyed being with people he loved.

In addition to the party at the Jonathan Club, there were other private birthday celebrations. Norvel concluded, "It was the greatest celebration of a birthday I've ever had. I enjoyed every minute of it. Helen says we have pieces of three birthday cakes in the refrigerator, and every one meant a party and a happy celebration." Then Norvel confessed to a friend, "We wouldn't have had any of them if you had not been so insightful as to see how much an 80th birthday would mean to me."

The birthday greetings poured in from across the nation and around the world – not merely birthday cards, but personal letters, sometimes with only a couple of carefully crafted sentences, sometimes with two or three pages of memories. The many dozens of letters were placed into a beautifully decorated box that Norvel kept near his bed, and he would periodically open the box and read a letter or two in the evening, "the way one might sip a fine wine," he once said.

In his birthday greeting, Norvel's dear friend, J. P. Sanders, said, "You have become a powerful influence in shaping the church of this century and are a legend in your own time. And Helen has become the best known woman in the church in this generation."

Bill Banowsky wrote to his mentor, "You are the best friend of my entire life and we did our best work together. As you put it: 'We really made music together.' I love you with all of my heart and respect you as one of the very greatest personalities I have ever known."

The impact that Norvel and Helen had on the students of Pepperdine, even as octogenarians, was profound. Andy Wall, who received both bachelor's and master's degrees from Pepperdine ('85, '89), became a minister in Costa Mesa, California. On January 7, 1996, Wall wrote an article in his church bulletin in honor of Norvel's eightieth birthday. About two weeks later he sent a letter to Norvel that included the bulletin article, with a note introducing it that said, "Thank you for the impact you have made on my life and on so many others. ..." The bulletin article followed:

As an undergraduate student at Pepperdine University, I often heard school Chancellor and church elder M. Norvel Young make announcements at worship services. He almost always began with the exclamation, "Isn't it a great day to be a Christian in Malibu!" Initially, I scoffed at what I assumed was this man's phony enthusiasm, dismissing his statement as empty bluster. Besides, I could almost always think of some reason why it wasn't such a great day to be a Christian in Malibu.

Between my freshman and senior years, my attitude subtly shifted. During that time, I learned more about Norvel and Helen Young's life story, about the tragedies and hardships they had endured, about their faith and perseverance. I also observed that Norvel Young was consistently upbeat, buoyant, and optimistic. Perhaps he really did mean what he said. As my graduation day drew near and I again heard Dr. Young exclaim, "Isn't it a great day to be a Christian in Malibu," I thought, "Well, come to think of it, it is."

From the famous founder and president of Campus Crusade for Christ International, Bill Bright, came these words:

How grateful we are to our wonderful Lord Jesus for the marvelous ways He has and is using you as His bondservant over these many years. You have been a magnificent role model to young Christians for years, and we feel honored to call you "friend." You have been a great source of challenge and inspiration to me ever since we met almost 40 years ago. We are so very blessed by your theological and Spirit-filled influence in Christendom.

Life Regent and former vice chairman of Crocker Bank John V. Vaugh wrote to Norvel:

> You have acquired in your 80 years something that cannot be inherited – a myriad of friends and admirers! So I congratulate you more for how you have lived your life than for having attained a few more years than average!
>
> I have many pleasant thoughts about my association with you, such as your great sense of humor and your thoughtfulness in always remembering by card or note my birthday or anniversary. I used to look forward to the meetings of the University Board primarily to hear your always up-beat, dramatic and humorous closing comments! You have been an inspiration to me, Norvel, and I shall always cherish your friendship.

Mary Dorr, president of Excellence in Media, wrote to her friend, Norvel Young:

> You have been a role model not only for thousands of young people at Pepperdine but also for all of us who have known and admired you so very much.
>
> As a member of Excellence in Media's Advisory Board, you have been a supporter through the years of the International Angel Awards, and because of your lifelong work for our Lord and our love for you, we conferred on you a Gold Angel for a Lifetime Achievement Award.

But while any number of outstanding achievements have been credited to you, we have discovered that the "little things" you have done in helping so many add up to a great glory in themselves. You have so faithfully followed in the path of Jesus in your day-to-day life and touched others in a way that you probably never knew.

Mary Dorr mentioned the "little things" Norvel had done in helping people. That was often the theme in the birthday letters. Vergil and Vesta Warden wrote, "We will always remember how wonderful you were to come get us, stranded along the highway in Malibu in the middle of the night, when we were taking my father to the airport for his summer trip to Oklahoma. This was in the Seventies! When we tried to thank you, your simple statement was, you appreciated the opportunity we gave you to help us! We'll never forget it!"

Norvel later said, "The greatest gift we received was the book of letters. They are priceless and precious to me ... I know I will find myself reading them often. They bring back so many happy memories of people I have not seen and some I have not contacted for many years." He called the book of remembrances for his birthday "the defining moment for 1995."

A SOBER WARNING

Every year Norvel received a thorough physical examination provided to the directors of Imperial Bancorp, on whose board he served for 20 years. In early February, on schedule, Norvel would make his annual foray to Dr. Michael Mellmann, famed physician to the Los Angeles Lakers and Kings athletic organizations.

After the tests were completed, Norvel would return for a report, at which time Dr. Mellman would present him with a letter giving a glowing account of Norvel's good health. That letter was usually photocopied and shared by Norvel with those he loved, who loved him. He wanted those who were concerned for him to be put at ease by the outstanding check-ups he was receiving.

Just days after his February 1996 physical examination, Norvel and Helen traveled to the Abilene Christian University Lectureship and Norvel spoke at the 21st Century Christian breakfast, as was his custom. Others may have been unaware, but Helen noticed a lack of sparkle in Norvel's voice, a certain dullness that she had begun to hear in the last few weeks. She began to watch him more closely and confided her observations to the children.

On March 13, the day before the Youngs were scheduled to travel to New York for Norvel's quarterly board meeting for the GCG Trust, Helen sat down and wrote a note to Dr. Mellmann. In it she thanked the doctor for all he had done for Norvel, then continued on to tell him of her concerns. She wrote:

> Sometime between Norvel's check-up and his appointment to get his report, he began to evidence such lack of energy. If it were any other 80-year-old, this might go unnoticed, but Norvel is so optimistic, enthusiastic and exuberant that the change was noticeable not only to the family but to several others who asked, "Is Norvel well?"
>
> Is it possible he might have had a slight stroke? Can one have a stroke that would affect emotional energy and not mental clarity?
>
> He has been extremely busy during this period and under more than usual stress, but he says he is not depressed. He is more passive, quiet – doesn't initiate conversation as much. And he has had unusual professional successes in this period – helping to bring in a 15 million endowment gift and the next day a 1.1 million one! He's pleased but not thrilled as he would normally be.

313

He seems unaware of any change in himself. I haven't discussed this with him except to ask if he is depressed – for I don't want to worry him. But this morning he told me you had called for me, so I explained.

I do believe he is more like himself today than in the last three weeks. So perhaps he will gradually regain his WOW personality. If he doesn't, when we return next Wednesday from New York, will you please see him or refer him to a neurologist? Thanks for listening.

(signed) Helen M. Young

She never mailed the note. Norvel seemed improved and things got busy, preparing for the flight on the next day. Then in New York and in subsequent days, Norvel was almost his old self again.

But as summer arrived, Norvel again seemed to slow down. Helen was privately concerned that the usual optimistic letter from Dr. Mellmann didn't quite square with her own observations. She noticed that Norvel had again "become very quiet." This outgoing, gregarious man seemed to sit idly detached. He just wasn't himself.

On August 26, the Youngs hosted an afternoon visit from a Russian couple brought by Rich Dawson, director of the university's International Student Services office. Ralph Beck, a minister in the Denver area and alumnus of Seaver College, had recommended to the Russians when he met them that they should visit the university if they went on to Los Angeles. Sure enough, they showed up at Pepperdine and were entertained by the always-hospitable Youngs. However, it was an unfortunate time for a visit. Norvel was in bed because he didn't feel well. Nevertheless, he dragged himself out of bed, dressed and went downstairs for the visit. He spoke to the people but it was clear that he wasn't his usual outgoing self.

During the visit, Helen "saw Norvel's expression change," as she put it. She said a hurried good-bye and suggested to Norvel that he go back to bed right away. Rich Dawson later said, "I looked over and Norvel was just 'out of it,' disconnected and staring down into nothing. I knew something was wrong."

But Norvel said he was so very tired that he could not make it up the stairs. With the help of Rich Dawson, she was able to get him to his bed. He went right to sleep. However, by the next morning he was no better; in fact, he was worse. With the help of Dorothy Belk, the Youngs' longtime housekeeper, Helen got him down the stairs and into the car. Then she drove him to St. John's Hospital in Santa Monica.

The staff at St. John's confirmed that Norvel had suffered a stroke. And the effects of the stroke were continuing to disable him. For 20 years, he had experienced arrhythmia, an irregular heartbeat, but the use of Coumadin and regular monitoring of his blood were controlling that condition. He made monthly visits to Dr. Stephen Berens, a fine cardiologist, who had cared for him for 25 years. The news around campus was that "Dr. Young had suffered a slight stroke." It was becoming apparent, however, that it was not a minor health problem. He stayed at the Santa Monica hospital for two weeks as they endeavored to stabilize his condition.

The three Young daughters planned an anniversary party for Norvel and Helen in the hospital. Marilyn arranged for a special room, had balloons and a cake, and brought some of the grandchildren and a few nurses in for the celebration. It was a happy time with the family gathered around Norvel. They were so thankful he was improving.

With the improvement, Norvel was transferred to Daniel Freeman Memorial Hospital in Inglewood for physical rehabilitation. He never lost his ability to speak, but he could not walk without help. At first, the progress was slow as the therapist "taught him to walk again." But over all, he responded very well to the physical therapy and in near-record time the attendants in charge were ready to let him go home. They might as well release him, they probably thought, because after a little more than two weeks of rehab, he had convinced someone to help him arrange a conference call for a quarterly meeting of the board of directors of the GCG Trust. He participated in the board meeting from his hospital bed and thoroughly enjoyed every minute of it.

The staffs at both hospitals were very kind to Norvel, but the nurses and therapists at Daniel Freeman Memorial were especially good to him. Norvel's good friend, L.A. County Supervisor Kenny Hahn, had been there for rehab after his stroke. Hahn had become friends with the sister in charge, the vice president of sponsorship and mission of Daniel Freeman Memorial, which is run by the Sisters of St. Joseph of Carondelet. That same sister took time out to stop by and meet and chat with Norvel. A year later, Norvel returned to the rehab section of the hospital with flowers for the kind nurses. A "little thing" like a stroke was nothing more to Norvel than a new way of making friends.

September 21 was "coming home day" from the hospital. It was like a rebirth to Norvel. After all, he still had many things to do, many "deals cooking." Still, those difficult four weeks or so – really, the past eight or nine months of sub-par health – were a sober warning to him. The truth was even more apparent: he was not immortal. It was entirely possible that he would not make it to his well-publicized "Celebration of the New Millennium" on January 1, 2000.

RACING THE SUN

Pepperdine's President David Davenport suggested that, after his stroke, perhaps Norvel would want to take a sabbatical leave. Amazingly, Norvel had never had a sabbatical in all his years of higher education administration. He always took his vacations, and sometime extended vacations, but never had he had four straight months away from responsibilities. Chancellor Charles Runnels and others encouraged him, too. It sounded like a good idea. And there was something else …

If the clock was ticking (and Norvel certainly knew it was), how did he want to spend his final years or months or days? His answer to that question became obvious only three months or so after his release from rehabilitation. In January 1997 he and Helen took that long-postponed sabbatical and set out on an around-the-world tour.

A defining moment in Norvel's life came when he and his cousin traveled the world as young men. Now, at age eighty-one, he wanted to do it again. But this time, it would be quite different. First of all, he would travel with his lifelong companion by his side – his beloved Helen, the one he loved more than life itself. Together they had climbed incredible mountains of achievements. Now they would circumnavigate the globe as friends of the earth, "stopping to smell the roses" ... and the breezes in Bangkok, the fragrant tea plantations of Sri Lanka and the aromatic plains of Africa.

Another thing: that first trip, in 1937, was in the direction that seemed normal to European Americans: eastward to New York, the edge of the New World. Then across the Atlantic to the Old World. On through the Middle East, across India and into China, Japan and other Asian regions. Finally returning to America across the broad Pacific.

On this last tour, however, they would *travel west*, not east. They would not fly into the settling darkness. Instead, they would fly with the movement of the light. They would race the sun.

Norvel and Helen packed light. They were very experienced travelers and knew not to take several heavy suitcases. But on this trip, after the stroke, they were even more conscious of how much the two of them could carry, or rather pull on little wheels. "Packing light" was somehow symbolic of this chapter of their lives.

They left on January 9, 1997. First stop was Bangkok, Thailand; and though they planned to have many moments of relaxation and sightseeing, they could not break themselves of their habit of trying to make their trips productive. They had made several appointments to see old friends and officials on University business. Among the people they visited was their friend, the Honorable Praman Chansue, Chief Counsel to the Prime Minister. Praman had been president of the Thai Supreme Court and was greatly respected. He and his wife, Ampansie, were lovely and hospitable people. The Youngs had a visit with Prime Minister Chavalit Yongchiyuda, also friends of 20 years, Bangkok Bank Chairman Chatri Sophonpanich, Major General Sornchia, Kumar Harilela and Vanchi Propanet. Norvel also spoke one morning to the Justices' Training Session on Pepperdine's Dispute Resolution program. Helen was thrilled to see him so well and articulate. On Sunday they worshiped with a wonderful Thai church and old friends Kelly and Sara Davidson and Larry and Pam Henderson. Once again, their visit was rewarding, and after a few days they pressed on.

From Bangkok they flew to Colombo, the capital of Sri Lanka. Sri Lanka, formerly known as Ceylon, is a large island off the southern tip of India with a population of 17 million. To many people who think of Sri Lanka only as a place of horrible flooding and deadly devastation, it was a strange choice for a destination. But Norvel had never been there before, and in his youthful curiosity, which never left him, he wanted to see new countries. In addition, it was on the way to South Africa, where they planned to spend an extended time.

The first thing they did when they got into Colombo was to see if there was a Church of Christ there. As a matter of fact, there was, and they called the minister, a native Sri Lankan named Nigel, and he met them for brunch at their hotel, Taj Salumbra, overlooking the Indian Ocean. Nigel had already received his "green card" to enter the United States with his family. Later that evening, the Youngs had dinner with Nigel, his wife, Lydia, and their daughter, Esther, at a restaurant where most visiting Americans ate. Interestingly, Sri Lankans eat with only their right hand, with a finger bowl handy for washing.

They had a pleasant visit with the family and were delighted and somewhat surprised to see them show up in Malibu at the Pepperdine University Bible Lectures just a few months later in April.

The Youngs had a more extensive itinerary than on many previous trips. Donna Lindsey of Corniche Travel had journeyed with the Youngs and a group of Pepperdine Associates to China several years before, so she knew Norvel and Helen well. Donna arranged for a Sri Lankan travel representative, Miranalas, to meet them and provide a car and driver with an itinerary to see the major sights of this ancient and historic island. The representative was well informed and efficient. Norvel was eager to see the tea plantations in the mountains. He had heard about the hillside farms and wanted to see tea growing. So after touring the city, they set out by car and drove to a fine international resort hotel in the mountains, which became their headquarters. Then they journeyed out to see the beautiful sloping tea fields and the workers tending the delicate plants. They also were able to see the ruins of ancient Sri Lankan capitals dating from before the time of Christ, including amazing archaeological remains of temples and palaces.

They were in Kandy, their resort city headquarters, when Sunday arrived, so they decided to try to go to church in the beautiful area. Their investigations found an interdenominational, evangelical Christian church not far away, which had services in both Sri Lankan and English. The minister and his family spoke English well. When they arrived for the English worship service, they discovered that all the people were Sri Lankan, but they did conduct the second service in English. Even the singing was in English. Many who apparently did not speak English chose to remain just outside the building to listen to the English service.

When Norvel and Helen arrived, they were quite an oddity to the local people. The Sri Lankan Christians didn't have many American visitors, since there was a civil war being waged at that time. The people were very gracious to the Youngs. Perhaps the thing that struck Helen the most powerfully was the prayer service that followed the regular worship period. The congregation surrounded those who needed prayer and, one by one, sang to them. They would repeatedly sing, "I am the Lord Who healeth thee, I am the Lord Who healeth thee," in a beautiful melody. Then they would move on to the next person and repeat the song. It was an unforgettable time.

The Youngs were in Colombo for two days and in the mountains for another three. Fortunately, in their travels in Sri Lanka they never came in contact with either rebel or government forces that were fighting in the northern part of the country. The thought of avoiding the country because it was embroiled in a civil war never seemed to occur to Norvel.

From Colombo the Youngs flew to the city of Dubai in the United Arab Emirates. There was no civil war in Dubai, but a quick glance at a map reveals that the United Arab Emirates is a small nation on the eastern side of the Saudi Arabian peninsula on the Persian Gulf. Of course, not too many years earlier, the Gulf had been the scene of a fierce war when Iraq's Saddam Hussein attacked Kuwait, not far away. And that region of the Middle East had remained volatile with cat and mouse military encounters, including air and missile strikes from U.S. Navy warships cruising not far from the vacationing Norvel and Helen Young.

Dubai, near the Straits of Hormuz, had the reputation of being the "golden city." If one wanted to buy gold in any "size, shape or form," this was the hot spot. The city was beautiful, sparkling and clean. Though the Youngs were fascinated by it, the real purpose for stopping off there was to shop for Winston Moore, who had ask them to buy a gold bracelet for his wife, to be given to her on the occasion of their 50th wedding anniversary. Of course, for Norvel and Helen, it was an excuse to get a few gifts for their daughters as well.

The city had dozens of shops with gold jewelry displayed. The Youngs selected the bracelet for Winston and enjoyed visiting with the efficient salespeople in their flowing white robes. Interestingly, the jewelry is sold by weight in Dubai. After the purchase, Helen and Norvel saw the sights of the city, went to the museums and walked along the bay – all in a day. The next morning they were on their way to the fascinating continent of Africa.

They flew southwest over Somalia, Tanzania and Mozambique. Their destination was the beautiful Republic of South Africa – again, a place the Youngs had never before visited. They landed at the airport that services Johannesburg and vicinity, in the city of Benoni, about 20 miles east of Johannesburg. Al Horne, the administrator of the South Africa Bible School in Benoni, and his wife, Donna, met the Youngs at the airport. Horne, a native of South Africa, was educated in the United States where he met Donna, a Texan. They are a capable and dynamic team, having served the school and the church for 38 years.

After a few days with the Hornes, Norvel and Helen traveled to Swaziland, which is a nation within a nation, surrounded as it is by the country of South Africa. Once again the Youngs combined travel and sightseeing with a real mission. They had been asked by administrators at World Vision, an international Christian relief organization, to investigate a large farm that had been offered as a gift to World Vision. Norvel was to give his judgment as to whether or not the land might be developed and might support about 240 employees, providing a living for a large number of families. The cost of developing the project would be considerable, so the question was an economic one.

They were in Swaziland two days. "The country is very poor," they said, "and one of the reasons is the 'royal properties.' The previous king added a new wife each year and, obviously, had dozens of children. So more and more of the land was in the hands of the king's relatives. There was little productive industry or farming for the average citizen."

While there, the Youngs visited those who could give them insight into the possibilities. They met with the Episcopal bishop and other religious leaders, as well as with the heads of the labor and agriculture departments, as they studied the proposed World Vision plan. In the end, Norvel's report was that the project ought to go forward.

While in Swaziland, the Youngs visited a Bible school, operated by Churches of Christ, that trains preachers and teachers. They were impressed that the school for adults had several adequate buildings equipped with computers and other learning tools. There was also some housing available for students with families. Once again, Norvel and Helen stopped by a distant and remote place to encourage the Christians to continue with their good work.

The Youngs returned to Benoni, and to the home of the hospitable Hornes. They visited the South African Bible school operated by Churches of Christ and were impressed with the caliber of the students and the instruction led by Horne. "The school trains preachers," the Youngs reported, "and they are doing a great job. They have four or five buildings and the students live at the school. It is very impressive."

In the midst of the effective work there was an element of uncertainty. Helen commented, "South Africa is very beautiful, but parts of it are still dangerous, with much violence and robbery." She added, "The Hornes' home where we stayed had multiple locks on the doors and tall wrought iron fences and gates. But it is amazing that apartheid has ended without more violence. The church where Al Horne ministers is ahead of its time, a racially integrated, loving congregation, and has been so for years."

One of the highlights of their trip to South Africa was the exhilarating journey they took through Kruger National Park, a famous wild game reserve near the Mozambique border. They flew into the park from Benoni, and despite his stroke just five months earlier, Norvel was able to rent a car and drive it across the wilds – the speed limit was a breakneck 25 miles per hour in the park (because of the abundant wildlife).

Throughout the area, there were modern, tiny houses available for rent that were fashioned like grass huts, with all the conveniences of a good hotel. The Youngs spent four wonderful days and nights in the park in the little houses. The huts hearkened back to the cabin on the lake at the Grand Tetons in Wyoming as they began their honeymoon, nearly 58 years earlier. They prepared breakfast in the outdoor kitchen and watched for the occasional hippopotamus to appear in the swift-flowing river just 10 yards away. For dinner, they went to one of the lovely restaurants in the park. It was like camping out in a zoo without cages, but being able to go to dinner in a fine restaurant.

Every day they were treated to the sight of giraffes, elephants, antelope, impala, zebra and other exotic African animals in their native habitat. One day as they roamed the park they spied a pride of lions sunning themselves near some trees. Norvel cruised closer. As they got to within about eight feet of the closest lion, Helen leaned slightly out of the window to snap a picture of the huge carnivore, which she could almost touch. Suddenly the lion lifted its head and let out an ear-splitting roar. A rattled Helen rolled up her window in record time, as Norvel hit the gas and quickly drove on his way. One has to wonder if the lion was left chuckling at his clever tourist tactic.

They returned to Benoni one more time. In all, the Hornes had been gracious friends and hosts for 11 days. Norvel was asked to preach for the Church of Christ where the Hornes are members in that city. Then it was to the airport for another leg of the journey.

Their last stop in South Africa was the very southern tip of the continent. The Youngs flew to famous Cape Town, overlooking the Cape of Good Hope that all the historic circumnavigators rounded in their world explorations. Norvel and Helen found it to be a very beautiful city, with less of the racial tensions that they had sensed in other areas. There were 32 Churches of Christ in the state, and Norvel was asked to preach at a suburban church that had an American minister. While in Cape Town they were hosted by Dr. Des Strumph, a South African physician and church leader who drove them to where Norvel was to preach. Dr. Strumph had given up a fine practice to open a medical clinic in an interracial area because he wanted to serve the poor. He arranged a dinner for the Youngs and included Jean Strumph and Oscar and Dawn de Vries and others, all native South African professional people and church leaders They ate at a beautiful restaurant on a wharf that reminded Helen of the Fisherman's Wharf area of San Francisco.

After five days in the Cape Town area, it was time to leave Africa. Through the night, the Youngs flew north across the Equator and angled northwest toward England. They spent more than a week in one of their favorite cities, London. Norvel's friend, Massoud Kadessi, had a home there and told the Youngs they should stay with him. Instead, the generous man rented them a very lovely flat (apartment) not far from Piccadilly and Hyde Park. And they had a truly delightful time. From the vast, open wild places of Africa, they suddenly found themselves in the hustle and ' ustle of one of the most exciting cities in the world.

Every morning was spent working on Norvel's book, *Living Lights, Shining Stars*. He was nearing the deadline for getting the manuscript to the publisher and London was an extraordinary place to relax and write. But the afternoons were free for shopping and riding the tour buses around town. They were able to take in three or four operas, attending some three o'clock matinees. They also attended a performance of *Hamlet* at the Shakespeare Theater. And somehow they managed to squeeze in a visit to the British Museum.

On Sunday they took the Tube (London's famous subway) to the town of Wembley, outside of London, to attend church. Helen said, "The Wembley Church of Christ is a very fine, interracial church. And some Americans who have attended there claim it is the best church they know of. That's pretty high praise."

Helen and Norvel took time to visit the students, faculty and staff of Pepperdine's London international program on Princes Gate in the Kensington section of London. And in the evening, they had the opportunity to take some of the students to dinner. When it was time to head westward across the Atlantic, they had spent ten wonderful days in the place Helen called "such a fascinating city."

Their last stop before returning home was New York City. Norvel had to attend a board meeting there and they spent a couple of days in the "city that never sleeps" before flying to Los Angeles. Amazingly, Norvel felt good during the entire trip. The stroke seemed to slow him down only a little. In fact, Helen thought he "thrived on the trip." Not a small part of the joy of traveling for them was the opportunity to encourage Christian and other friends around the world. In all, the Youngs had traveled perhaps 30,000 miles and had been on their tour for more than two months.

But they weren't finished just yet. They still had a few weeks left in their sabbatical, so they decided to do one more thing they had never done before. They booked a cruise. After being home for about three weeks, they flew to the Caribbean area to catch the Holland American cruise ship, *MS Ryndam*. For 11 days they sailed softly among the emerald islands in the sun. It was a touch of paradise ... a lavish crescendo to their four months of befriending the world.

A TURNING POINT REMEMBERED

The annual Pepperdine Bible Lectures were held less than two months after Norvel and Helen returned from their world tour. The theme for the Lectures was one that Norvel warmed to immediately: "The Imitation of Christ," borrowed from the legendary devotional writer Thomas á Kempis.

While few attendees at the Lectures remembered or ever knew, 1997 was an anniversary year for two important events. First, Pepperdine College was founded in 1937, 60 years earlier. But secondly, in 1957, 40 years earlier, board chairman Don Miller had been instrumental in bringing Norvel Young and J. P. Sanders back to Pepperdine to help change the direction of the school. One person who *did* remember the significant anniversaries was Dr. Jerry Rushford, director of Pepperdine's Church Relations office and director of the Bible Lectures.

Rushford made sure that Don Miller, J. P. Sanders and Norvel Young would be in attendance on Tuesday, April 29, at seven in the evening, opening night of the Bible Lectures at Firestone Fieldhouse on the Malibu campus. And as John O. York's keynote message concluded, Rushford took the podium to tell more than 4,000 attendees the story of how three men saved Pepperdine from financial disaster and, more important, how they rescued the school from losing its way spiritually in 1957. It was a dramatic tale and the audience was spellbound.

Then Rushford announced that, 40 years later, those same three men – Don Miller, M. Norvel Young and J. P. Sanders – were there in the Fieldhouse. He called them forward to the platform in order that the audience could express its appreciation for their monumental work. They moved slowly up the steps of the platform to thunderous applause. Sanders was nearly 91, Miller was 90 and Norvel was nearly 82. They embraced and locked arms behind the podium, and were joined by Pepperdine Board of Regents Chairman Thomas G. Bost. The audience had long since risen to its feet as the prolonged applause filled the Fieldhouse. Norvel was the spokeman for the three men and said:

> Pepperdine is so insightful to see that these two men are worthy of great honor tonight. Don Miller took the initiative, as chairman of the board, to save the school's meager endowment by refusing to let promoters steal it for a mining venture. He also took the initiative to recruit a new administrative team that would lead the school back to its original purpose.

> J. P. Sanders was God's man for the task of rebuild-
> ing a faculty. He left the deanship of Lipscomb for an
> uncertain future in what many considered an impos-
> sible task.
>
> I see the hand of God in the courage and strength
> and dedication of both of these men. For me it has
> been one of life's greatest privileges to work with
> them. Pepperdine University owes them a great debt.
> I know of no two men whom I love so much. God
> bless you, Don and J. P.

In his typical vocabulary that made it impossible for him to openly acknowledge his own contributions, Norvel never mentioned the central role he played in the saving of the school. Finally, Tom Bost stepped to the microphone in the center of the pioneers and prayed a prayer of thanksgiving for the lives of the three. And the night ended.

It was a touching beginning to a profound week of lectures. And as always, the Young home on campus was filled with visitors from far and near.

Several people who attended the 1997 Bible Lectures later commented that Norvel was unusually emotional and sentimen-tal. Edwin White, minister for the Eastside Church of Christ in Phoenix, Arizona, said, "The last time I saw Norvel, at the '97 Lectures, he embraced me for a long time and wept. Then he said, 'I love you, Edwin.' He seemed to have known that the end was not far away." Others have similar recollections.

Is it possible that Norvel Young, the one who revived the Bible Lectures in 1958, sensed that the 1997 Bible Lectures would be his last?

A HOME-RUN FINISH

Norvel had always kept an astonishing schedule. He had board meetings, community volunteer work, social gatherings, church functions and always the friend-raising activities on which he thrived. The stroke slowed him down for awhile, but the around-the-world trip rejuvenated him. And the recognition at opening night of the Pepperdine Bible Lectures encouraged him to press on.

Helen thought it unwise for Norvel to drive in the Los Angeles traffic – the stroke had left a slight residual unsteadiness. So when he picked up his appointment pace again after the Bible Lectures, Norvel asked Jim Huffman, director of Pepperdine's Public Safety operation, if Jim could occasionally allow him the use of an officer to drive him to the Los Angeles area. Huffman was happy to help and assigned Officer Hank Gamboa to the task.

For the next ten months or so, Gamboa was the regular driver – and companion – of Norvel Young, except for a couple of times when a substitute driver filled in for him. It turned out to be Hank's most enjoyable duty ever.

He remembered the time in November 1997 when he drove Norvel for a cardiologist's appointment in Santa Monica. As they left a parking structure on the way home, Hank rolled down the electric window on the driver's side at the attendant's window, just as Norvel was saying, "Don't roll down that ... uh oh, that thing is broken and won't roll up." It was a cold winter afternoon and they had no choice but to drive home with the window wide open. Hank found a blanket in the back seat and Norvel threw it over his side that was receiving the blast of arctic air. So there they went down Pacific Coast Highway, freezing from the open window. And as cars passed them on the left, Hank remarked, "Dr. Young, people are probably thinking, 'Those old guys are tough!'" To which Norvel added, "Or crazy!"

In December Hank drove Norvel to an appointment in Santa Monica where Norvel had volunteered to give some advice to a non-profit organization. It was a "halfway house" for people trying to make comebacks from drugs, alcohol and prison. As they turned into the neighborhood, Hank locked the car doors. It was a bad area. He became even more worried when he pulled up in front of their destination.

A gang of men was standing around the front of the house, sporting a wonderful array of scars and tattoos, including teardrop tattoos that Hank had heard was a favorite with convicts. Norvel seemed oblivious to the apparent danger. He got out of the car and approached the largest of the men, who was wearing a bandana around his head. Hank saw Norvel stick out his hand and begin talking to the man. The man took the arm Norvel offered him and, with a smile, guided him toward the house. Hank bounded out of the car, brushed past the group and caught up with Norvel and his guide. He wasn't about to stay in the car alone. It turned out that Norvel had a great two-hour meeting with the director. Hank decided that the place was clean and doing a good work ... "but scary." He marveled most, however, at how unafraid Norvel was. "He seemed to know God would take care of us," Hank said later.

Trips to the Union Rescue Mission were somewhat the same. Norvel was on the board of directors and had to attend regular meetings. The mission was in downtown Los Angeles, in the midst of the population it served: skid row. Hank always went inside to wait for the meetings to end. "You wouldn't catch me hanging around outside," he said. And wherever they went, whether to a Union Rescue Mission board meeting or an Imperial Bank board meeting, Norvel would introduce his friend, Hank Gamboa, to presidents, directors, everyone.

Norvel would often call the Public Safety office, and Hank's home, two days in advance of a scheduled busy day to ensure that he got Hank as a driver. A special bond had developed between them: Norvel was careful to have everyone make Hank feel welcome, and Hank was devoted to Norvel's welfare.

Hank remembered a meeting at the home of Norvel's long-time friend, George Evans. Norvel was delivering a gift, a beautiful crystal vase, to Evans. Norvel briefed Hank on how instrumental Evans was in securing the land for the Malibu campus. When they arrived, Evans asked Norvel to sign one of his new books (*Living Lights, Shining Stars*). And while he did, Evans took

Hank for a tour of the house. "I could see the love and respect all these important people had for Dr. Young," Hank said. "He would always give thanks for all his work. Never taking credit for anything himself. He would say, 'We are so blessed to be doing the Lord's work.'"

On February 5, 1998, Norvel and Helen received the sad news that James O. Baird, Norvel's cousin who had been president and then chancellor of Oklahoma Christian University, had just passed away. About two and a half years earlier, James had written Norvel a sentimental letter, in which he said:

> Dear Norvel:
>
> As our mothers were especially close as sisters, you and I have been close through the years, more as brothers than cousins.
>
> Recently, I was rethinking the significance of our trip around the world together as young men and was impressed again with how much your foresight and Christian thoughtfulness have impacted my life. Not surprisingly for you, our decisions during that trip were made with a Christian concern which has blessed me so much. From our Sunday worship together, the Bible verses you encouraged me to memorize, and your determined effort for us to visit our missionaries along the way, I now see that all of this was moving me closer to a life for Christ rather than being an attorney as I had planned.
>
> In effect, I have patterned my life after you in so many ways. The desire to preach, the pursuit of the terminal degree in education, an interest in writing are all, in great part, due to your influence. Your role in helping me become a part of your own household after my mother's death, the consistency of your friendship and love and the number of times you have gone "out on the limb" for me I do not accept thoughtlessly.

In recent years I have had to look death in the face several times. I believe if it had not been for your Christian influence I might have had to do that without Jesus. So thank you much.

> I love you greatly,
> (signed) James O. Baird

February 15 would prove to be Norvel Young's last Sunday on earth. He spent the morning worshiping with the Malibu Church of Christ. Of course, he didn't know it was his last Sunday. But it wouldn't have mattered if he had known it was his last – he still would have been there in his regular place with Helen and his Christian brothers and sisters.

Providentially, Norvel was asked to say the final prayer that morning. And as he brought the prayer to a close, he paraphrased Bernard of Clairvaux's 800-year-old lyrics in the hymn, "O Sacred Head." He concluded by praying, "Lord, let us never, never outlive our love to Thee. In Jesus Name, Amen."

When the end came two days later, M. Norvel Young's prayer was answered. He indeed had not outlived his love for Christ. Nor had he outlived his love for his wife, his family, his friends and all people everywhere.

Norvel called on Hank Gamboa's driving services on the average of twice weekly. Typically they would leave at 8 a.m. and return about 4 p.m. That is the way it was on Tuesday, February 17, 1998. As they drove along Pacific Coast Highway, Hank set the speed of the car so that they wouldn't have to stop at the signal lights. And once again, Norvel said, "You do such a good job of driving." Hank was used to Norvel's compliments. "He always seemed to notice and appreciate the little things," Hank said.

Their first stop was Santa Monica Hospital where Norvel saw his cardiologist and got some good news. His heart was doing well. From there they drove to Inglewood where Norvel received an accupressure treatment. The regular therapy seemed to increase his circulation. For several days he would "feel looser," Hank remembered.

Then it was on to get a haircut at the Third Street Promenade in Santa Monica. Suddenly Norvel noticed that something about Hank was different. "I shaved off my mustache," Hank confessed. "Somebody told me it makes you look younger." About that time a woman greeted Norvel and said, "Oh, is this your son?" And Hank said to Norvel, "See, it's already working!"

After the haircut, the two drove to Brentwood for lunch at one of Norvel's favorite restaurants. The owner recognized and greeted Norvel as they sat down to enjoy a fine meal. Soon Norvel was eyeing the custard pudding, which he loved. "Guess I better not have that. My doctor wouldn't approve," he said. Hank replied, "How about sharing it?" That pleased Norvel, so they each had half of a pudding. They drove to one last appointment in Brentwood, and when that was concluded they headed back toward Malibu. It had been a fine day. As Norvel stepped out of the car in front of his home, he was feeling well and he said, "We done good!" It was his usual summary of the day.

Later Officer Hank Gamboa said, "I felt very privileged to be with Dr. Young so often. He was a wealth of information for me regarding Pepperdine. He had so many close friends that knew and loved him. Now, I wish it had been Mrs. Young that spent his last day with him. I didn't deserve to have that honor."

Helen and Norvel had dinner together, then a little later he decided to get some exercise on the treadmill upstairs. After all, he had received a good report from the cardiologist. He was feeling good and walking in solid, regular steps on the machine. Helen was close by. She glanced away for a moment but the sound of him falling jerked her head back. Although the paramedics rushed him to the Santa Monica Hospital, he never revived. He was gone.

Norvel often mentioned to Helen, "I hope yours will be the last face I see." The God he worshiped graciously granted his prayer.

18

THE GIFT OF
A LARGER LIFE

*M. Norvel Young left a cocoon behind,
but he himself has flown away on the wings of hope
to another of his fabulous adventures.*

R ains had pelted Southern California for days, with only
brief respites, as the state and the nation experienced
some of the worst weather of the century. Thursday
was one those days about which commuters traveling the
canyons and coast highways are always concerned. But Friday,
February 20, 1998, dawned bright and beautiful, as if a special
dispensation from the four winds had been granted for the occasion. Pepperdine University's Malibu campus had never
sparkled more brilliantly.

Pepperdine's President David Davenport arose early for a
special kind of pilgrimage. He knew of Norvel Young's profound
love for the seaside campus. He smiled as he remembered
Norvel's promotional-brochure kind of description of the
University's location: "Pepperdine Malibu ... smog-free, sun-
kissed, ocean-washed, island-girded, and mountain-guarded."
Like everyone else, Davenport knew that only Norvel Young
could get away with such blatant hyperbole. If anyone else were
to use such language it would be laughable, but when Norvel
used the phrase – repeatedly – he was greeted with cheers.

Davenport thought of the life of the chancellor emeritus, this
mentor, friend and phenomenon, as he walked to the locations

where the day's activities would take place. He walked past Thornton Administrative Center and watched the Pepperdine flag wave gently in the breeze, lowered to half-mast in honor of a beloved leader. He visited Stauffer Chapel, where the body would lie in state. He paused to study the soaring collage of color in the stained glass, and absorbed the cool silence of the place. He walked into Firestone Fieldhouse, usually echoing with the screech of athletic shoes and the yells of excited players and fans. Today a stage had been erected and large sprays of flowers would soon arrive for a very different kind of event. He walked across the campus that Norvel Young was so instrumental in building. And with each step, he permanently etched into his mind images of this man who we thought would be with us always.

A CELEBRATION OF LIFE

The memorial service began at 1:30 p.m. and lasted nearly two hours. Approximately 1,500 people – family, friends, students, co-workers, faculty, staff, the wealthy and prominent, those with only modest means – gathered, seemingly drawn by a common hunger to remember one man.

Thirty minutes before the service began, Seaver College's magnificent 60-member concert choir, under the direction of Milton Pullen, began filling Firestone Fieldhouse with melodious hymns, preparing the way for the most memorable event, in the minds of many, ever to take place in the arena. The formally attired students raised their strong, young voices in praise to God ... and in honor of one, without whom they probably would not be in Malibu in February 1998. It was a most fitting prelude.

Even before the choir entered, people had begun to drift into the Fieldhouse and quietly find a place to sit and reflect. Before them was a stage with a backdrop of deep blue and huge sprays of flowers. A closed casket was centered just below the stage on a one-step riser. By the appointed hour, the room was pressed with pensive people.

President Davenport rose from the platform party and welcomed the assembly. He related a story or two that brought knowing smiles and even some chuckles to his audience as he introduced the program. Then Pepperdine's Chancellor Charles B. Runnels approached the microphone to pray. His beautiful and gracious prayer invoked the attention of God on this special moment and on the family of his dear friend.

Thomas G. Bost, chairman of Pepperdine's Board of Regents, followed Runnels to the podium to present the obituary. He gave an outline of a life well lived, with intimations of the extraordinary breadth of that life. Those words were followed by Dan Anders, minister of the Malibu Church of Christ, who read several passages from the Bible, knitting them together into a comforter to chase away the chill of death.

Henry Price, associate professor of music at Pepperdine, rose to lead a congregational hymn, "It Is Well With My Soul." The voices swelled to nearly an angelic crescendo, causing several people to later express amazement at the beauty and choir-like quality of the singing. Perhaps they had forgotten or not realized that Churches of Christ, of which Norvel was a lifelong member, regularly worship with acappella (unaccompanied vocal) music.

After the hymn, several remembrances were introduced. The first was delivered by Norvel's longtime friend, George L. Graziadio, chairman and CEO of Imperial Bancorp and namesake of Pepperdine's Graziadio School of Business and Management. He said, "The heart is truly a mysterious thing, isn't it? Regardless of circumstances that may separate us, and irrespective of the differences that bond us, all those differences mean naught – because friends remain friends; and they remain strong friends. Above all, the spirit of mutual respect prevails, and friendship of this kind is, without doubt, one of life's supreme treasures. This was the kind of friendship that my wife, Reva, and I have had, and with my family, and in a business way, with our company, on whose board Norvel sat. This was the kind of privilege that we were allowed to share with Norvel and with Helen. And Norvel has left us for a higher calling. But the love he showered on all of us will endure."

Following Graziadio was Dr. Prentice Meador, editor of *21st Century Christian* magazine and minister for the Prestoncrest Church of Christ in Dallas. "We will remember Norvel because he raised the quality of our Christian journalism," he said. And he spoke of the encouraging magazine, *20ᵗʰ Century Christian*, that Norvel co-founded in 1938, and the devotional guide, *Power for Today*, Norvel and Helen founded in 1955. He said, "Norvel loved the Lord's people, and he dreamed as he built."

Norvel's friend and colleague, Dr. Olaf H. Tegner, dean emeritus of Pepperdine's Graduate School of Education and Psychology, was next. He began, "Norvel and I were friends for 59 years. He was my closest friend and he was my best friend." And he concluded by saying, "I'm going to miss him very, very much. Whenever he called, even late at night, his last words were, 'I love you, brother.' And I close with those words to him, 'I love you, brother.'"

After Tegner, Dr. William S. Banowsky rose to address the gathering. Banowsky, former president of the University of Oklahoma, served as fourth president of Pepperdine and was, in many ways, not only Norvel's great friend, but almost like a son to him. He said, "Like Oly, Norvel has been my best friend. … and I'm sure that's Norvel's magic. And there may be several of us here who feel like Oly and I do today." Then he said, "In my opinion, Norvel is the greatest single personality in the entire history of Pepperdine University … Norvel is the captain who saved this ship."

Each of the speakers also touched on personal, beloved aspects of the man being honored, a man each of them had known in special ways.

After the singing of the majestic hymn, "How Great Thou Art," there was a beautiful reading by Hydril Company Chairman Richard C. Seaver, nephew of Frank and Blanche Seaver, benefactors of Frank R. Seaver College at Pepperdine. Then three more remembrances were offered.

The first was by Quayla Barnett and Agi Nagy, who approached the podium together. The two women were Pepperdine law students who were exceptionally close to the Young family, having lived in Norvel and Helen's home while attending law school. They spoke of the impact Norvel had on their lives and on the lives of other students. Quayla said, "On behalf of the students of Pepperdine University, I speak today for each and every student whose life has been permanently touched and imprinted by Dr. Norvel Young. ... I will remember him most not as an educator and not as an administrator, but as a personal guide and hero for my life – personally, professionally, and most importantly, spiritually." Agi, who was a native of Budapest, Hungary, told how she wanted to go to law school but, financially, it seemed hopeless. She got a call from a stranger, Dr. Norvel Young, and he told her hope was not lost. "But it was more than just encouraging words," she said. "He backed those words up with a plane ticket to California and a place for me to live – that place was his own home. ... Since meeting Dr. Young, my life has been permanently changed – I have learned how to love more ..."

Then the legendary Dr. J. P. Sanders, former president of Columbia Christian College who co-founded *20th Century Christian* magazine with Norvel in 1938 and who joined him at Pepperdine as dean in 1957, moved slowly to the podium. At age 91, his deep baritone voice still resonated through the room as in bygone days when he had been a popular preacher of the gospel. He tried to summarize "70 years of friendship in two minutes," as he said. He reminisced about the Christmas of '38, when Norvel stopped by Dallas to tell him he had met Helen. And he concluded by saying, "And so, Norvel, we thank you for this: we realize all the great good you have done by your example as well as by your teaching."

AN EMPTY PLACE AGAINST THE SKY

Finally, it was time for the eulogy. The Young family had asked Dr. Jerry Rushford, professor of religion and director of church relations at Pepperdine, to offer the central message because of Rushford's background as a church historian and as editor of Pepperdine's fiftieth anniversary pictorial history, *Crest of a Golden Wave*. Bringing both laughter and tears, Rushford reminded everyone of the sheer genius and the obvious humanity of the man who was being honored.

At one point, Rushford said,

> Why was he so different? Why was he the most remarkable, the most unique man we every met? We've each had our own conclusions. Mine is this: he did not belong in this century. He lived in this century. God placed him in this century from 1915 to 1998, but he was not a part of our age.
>
> He was, I think, maybe from the sixteenth century. He was a Shakespearean character. And his tragedies and his triumphs were of such epic proportions that they were staggering. His tragedies were so withering and so devastating and so overwhelming that you wondered how anyone could have the character to lift himself up and see through the fog and get back on the road. And his triumphs were so amazing that he didn't have to dwell on them. We all knew them. We all acknowledged them.

Rushford went on to say,

> When James Russell Lowell heard about the death of Abraham Lincoln, he walked out of his front door in Cambridge, Massachusetts, looked up into the heavens and penned that incredible line. "It seems to me," he wrote, "that there's a great empty place

against the sky." And today we know how he felt. Today as we emerge from Firestone Fieldhouse and look into the Pepperdine heavens, if we look with discerning eyes, we will see that there's a great empty place against the sky.

MEMORIES OF DADDY

After Rushford's remarks, the children of Norvel and Helen – Emily, Matt, Marilyn, and Sara – offered a response from the family. It was the appropriate, articulate, and memorable crescendo of the service.

First to speak was son Matt Young. He said of his father, "It says in Genesis that there was a time when giants walked on the earth, and certainly he ... was a giant. He learned a lot from his father, who was also named Matt Norvel. And one of the things that was important to Dad, that he tried to teach all of us, was, 'You can't be big and little all at the same time.'"

Sara Young Jackson read from a letter she had written to her father on his birthday. "My daddy gave me gifts that money could never buy," she read, "gifts that have shaped the way I look at the world, gifts that have shaped my attitude toward life itself. My daddy has given me many gifts. Today I give him the gift of saying 'Thank You' for all he has given me. My daddy gave me the gift of believing that life is good. Life is not a trial to be endured or a cross to be carried or a sentence to be tolerated. He woke up each day with an enthusiastic, 'It's a great day to be alive!'"

Marilyn Young Stewart remembered her father as a "dispenser of grace, extending to others the grace he had received and painting a picture of God's unconditional love and compassion." She mentioned, "One reason Daddy could extend grace to other people was because he didn't allow bitterness to grow in his soul." And she said, "My father showed me what God was like and laid the foundations for my relationship with my Heavenly Father."

Finally, Emily Young Lemley remembered, "His hands were always open and inviting. I never saw him point a finger. I never saw one finger – his hands were always open. And they were beautiful. They were always outstretched. Those wonderful hands were just outstretched to grandchildren, to kings, to waiters, dishwashers, everyone."

Following the response from the family, Seaver College alumna Jessica Rivera's perfect voice punctuated the moment with the beautiful strains of "The Lord's Prayer." Then President Davenport stood to conclude the service, and he briefly reflected on the memories of the past two hours. His wavering voice betrayed the emotion that everyone shared. He said, "We do think of the party he invited us all to many, many times; the party on January 1, in the year 2000, here in Firestone Fieldhouse. I'm confident that it will still take place. I'm confident that he, in spirit, will be with us. But one of the pictures I have of Norvel this afternoon is that he knew there was a larger party – that God has a larger party for His people. And just as he invited every one of you, I'm sure, that he ever met or spoke to, to come to his party on January 1, 2000, I think his life was really about inviting all of us to God's larger party. And one of the pictures I have is that when the party begins, Norvel will probably be the greeter and certainly the chairman of the hospitality committee."

Finally, Professor of Law Harold Bigham, who was also an elder of the Malibu Church of Christ, commended his fellow elder to God in a final meaningful prayer.

Flanked by grandsons, the casket was slowly moved out of Firestone Fieldhouse. Perhaps it was the realization that, for the last time, M. Norvel Young was leaving the arena he loved so much that brought such emotion to so many. It was in this room that he had so often cheered his beloved Waves to victory. It was here that he had attended and participated in scores of Founder's Day convocations, dinners, and other special events. Countless memories interlaced with Norvel seemed to be suspended from the rafters of this sports arena.

In a few moments, the casket would be transported to Stauffer Chapel, where friends and loved ones could view the earthly body one last time in the place where Norvel worshipped regularly. The family received well-wishers in the Ralphs-Straus Tennis Pavilion.

BEYOND THE SUNSET

The next day, Saturday, February 21, Helen and the family and friends gathered at Forest Lawn Memorial Park, Hollywood Hills, at 10 a.m. to commit to earth the body of Norvel Young. Each of the three sons-in-law, of whom Norvel was so proud, spoke briefly. Steve Lemley read the 23rd Psalm from the old Bible that had been given to Ruby Young, Norvel's mother, when she was just a girl. It undoubtedly was the very Bible that was first read to Norvel as a little boy. After his remarks, Stephen Stewart spoke about his love and respect for his father-in-law. And then Sam Jackson reminisced about this wonderful man with whom he had traveled to Africa. When asked if any of the grandchildren would like to say a few words, Joseph Jackson bravely spoke about his friend and grandfather. And Chris Young eloquently told what his grandfather had meant to him. Helen concluded the graveside service with some special thoughts that touched everyone present.

In the months that followed, the family carefully chose a grave marker, had it engraved and set in place. There were two plaques, one above the other, enclosed within a border. The top one read:

"The future is as bright as the promises of God"
M. NORVEL YOUNG
October 5, 1915 – February 17, 1998
Beloved Husband, Father, Grandfather and Friend
As an educator, he laid the foundation
for Pepperdine University.
As preacher & publisher he lifted the
vision of Churches of Christ.

As a Christian, he called us to accept
the grace he had received.
As a man, he acted justly, loved mercy,
and walked humbly with his God.

On the second, lower plaque was inscribed a Bible passage
from Romans chapter 8 in the New Testament:

"I have become absolutely convinced that neither death
nor life, neither what happens today nor what may
happen tomorrow, nor anything else in God's whole world
has any power to separate us from the love of
God in Christ Jesus our Lord!"

Helen said that Norvel had two burial plots set aside at Forest
Lawn Glendale, provided for him as a member of the board of
Forest Lawn. But when Norvel died and it came time to use one
of those plots, the chairman of Forest Lawn Memorial Parks,
Fred Llewellyn, who had been a longtime friend of Pepperdine
and of the Youngs, said, in effect, "I want to provide a more
appropriate plot for Norvel Young. He should have a more
prominent place." The generous Llewellyn then substituted the
two regular plots for two very expensive and very beautiful ones
high on the hill in a private garden looking out across the valley.
Not far from the gravesite is a commanding statue of George
Washington, one of Norvel's favorite heroes. It is a quiet and
dignified place. A place Norvel would like very much.

But he is not there. Not really.

M. Norvel Young left a cocoon behind, but he himself has flown
away on the wings of hope to another of his fabulous adventures. Once again, he is out in front of us, experiencing *The* "Great
Day to be Alive," as he always put it. At this moment, he is where
he knew he would one day be. Some may have missed it,
because of the zest he had for this world and everything in it ...
but all of the remarkable building he accomplished here was

not an end in itself. It was all in anticipation of the "City with foundations, whose architect and builder is God" (Hebrews 11:10).

HELEN ALONE

Following the Celebration of Life service in Firestone Fieldhouse and the interment at Forest Lawn, Helen flew to Texas the next week to attend the Abilene Christian University Bible Lectureship. The Lectureship had been an annual journey that she and Norvel had rarely missed in all their married years. In Abilene, at the 21st Century Christian breakfast program where many longtime friends had gathered, she spoke movingly of the life of her beloved husband.

On behalf of ACU, President Royce Money presented Helen with an official resolution that highlighted many of Norvel's contributions to his alma mater and to the Churches of Christ. This was to be the first of several such resolutions that Helen would receive on behalf of Norvel in the next few weeks. Among the others were resolutions issued by the House of Representatives of the State of Tennessee, the House of Representatives of the State of Texas and the California Legislative Assembly.

From Abilene, Helen traveled to Lubbock to attend a memorial service for Norvel at the Broadway Church of Christ on Sunday afternoon, March 1. She was accompanied by two of her daughters and their husbands, Emily and Steve Lemley and Marilyn and Stephen Stewart. The occasion was a triumphant homecoming. More than 40 years had passed since the Youngs had waved good-bye and driven west to Pepperdine College. But there were still many people in the area that remembered Norvel and Helen Young. More than 500 Broadway members and other friends attended the service and heard tributes from Floyd Stumbo, Harvie Pruitt, Ken Jones, Horace Coffman, Steve Lemley and Stephen Stewart.

Helen returned to her home in Malibu and remained very busy in March and April. She was asked by managing editor Glover

Shipp of the *Christian Chronicle* newspaper to write her personal reflections on her husband after his passing, to be part of a special tribute, titled "The Young Years." What she wrote, which was published in July 1998, is so insightful that we offer it here in its entirety:

> Several times I have been asked, "What was it like to live with Norvel Young?" I would laughingly say, "It was like catching hold of the tail of a comet and spending 58 years trying to hang on." But I did hang on, and what a blessed trip. We shared six great loves: each other, our family, the Lord, the church, Christian publications and Christian education.
>
> Through the years as I thought of Jesus' statement, "Only in his home town and in his own house is a prophet without honor" (Matthew 13:57), I tried to recognize Norvel's uniqueness and not let proximity crowd out appreciation. When I memorized Galatians 5:22, I realized that the person I knew who best exemplified those nine qualities was Norvel.
>
> I often told college women, "Marry someone you can admire and respect." I hear about husbands who preach good sermons on 1 Corinthians 13, but are rude, neglectful, silent at home. Norvel was better at home than in public. He was supportive, non-critical, encouraging. He had more faith in my ability than I had. He believed in his children.
>
> Norvel loved God with all his heart and he loved people. His warm, gregarious, impulsive spirit reached out to those of every color, language and class around the world. As Bill Banowsky asked, "Have you ever known a man who loved more people of more kinds more lavishly than Norvel Young?" He believed in students and prospective students and often helped them to reach their full potential.

He had a disarming, childlike self-confidence. He felt as much at ease telephoning Malcolm Muggeridge or Norman Cousins as his next door neighbor. He believed he was doing a person a favor to ask him to give a million dollars to Christian education.

He believed in women. In a day when many parents put more emphasis on the education of sons, he encouraged women to get all the education they could. He lifted their sights about what they could accomplish.

Norvel loved the church. He wanted it to grow and serve, not just where he was but everywhere. He used the phrase, "There's no competition between light-houses," and he believed it. He rejoiced with the church's growth around the world. He loved preaching full time for thirteen years and being an elder for thirty-five. He was sad when some seemed to have an inferiority complex about the church. He was never ashamed of it. He didn't enjoy a conversation that concentrated on what's wrong with the church.

He was criticized, but spent little time answering his critics. He usually answered by phone. He was not jealous or envious. He had a big spirit. He was never vindictive. He did not hold grudges. He didn't waste time on resentment. But he would not stop working on something he believed was right because of his critics.

Norvel was a dreamer and a builder. It is a rare combination. But he could plan, organize and execute to make his dream a reality. He was a doer. He was patient in working for a consensus of all involved. But he never gave up on a person or a project.

The hallmark of Norvel's life was joy. He loved life. He knew "The future was as bright as the promises of God."

He knew he was a sinner, but he knew he was loved and forgiven. He greeted people with "It's a great day to be alive." For him the glass was always half full. He had unbounding energy, zest and enthusiasm. Optimism was his way of life. He was always upbeat, always cheerful.

How could this be, when twenty-three years ago he experienced the most painful, personal tragedy – an accident in which he was at fault, in which two people were killed?

He was crushed – crushed for me and for our four adult children, as well as for himself. It was a devastating blow. My faith was very weak. But God held him up, as well as the children and me. God gave him the strength to confess his guilt, to repay his debt to society as best he could, to accept the forgiveness of God and to forgive himself. He found Christ his ever-present help in trouble. Turning back to life, we had a greater dependence on God, a life of constant, believing prayer, and a firm trust that God does work all things together for the good of those who love Him. Every day was a precious gift and life a joyful experience.

Norvel spent little time looking back. His heart was in the future and its possibilities. "The past is prologue," he would say. When he started talking twenty years ago about the party he planned for the year 2000, I admit I thought it was a fantasy. But he was serious, and although he will not be present in person, the rest of us plan to celebrate the new millennium and God's great goodness to us all. He is with the Lord he loved, and I look forward to a grand reunion.

More than 100,000 copies of that issue were circulated around the world. She also worked with Bill Henegar, Joyce Hutchison and others in the production of a seven-minute video that presented a visual memory of Norvel, with only music for audio background. The video was projected onto two large screens during a special tribute to Norvel at the annual Pepperdine University Associates Dinner on April 14. Pepperdine's indebtedness to Norvel Young was also the subject of articles in *Pepperdine People*, the university's magazine, and *Pepperdine Voice*, the alumni newspaper.

During the busy week of the Pepperdine Bible Lectures at the end of April, Helen hosted a house full of out-of-town guests, spoke for the AWP Banquet and for the 21st Century Christian and Power for Today Luncheon, then taught a class on the promises of God. President David Davenport delivered a soaring tribute to Norvel before a capacity crowd in Firestone Fieldhouse on the opening night of the Bible Lectures. The spring issue of *Pacific Church News*, a publication of Pepperdine's office of Church Relations, was available at many campus locations during Lectures week. Norvel's picture graced the cover and he was the subject of the lead article. Norvel was also on the cover of the May/June issue of *21st Century Christian* magazine, and he was the subject of Prentice Meador's editorial.

In the months after Norvel's death, Helen was encouraged by her children and by many friends to think about accompanying Jerry and Lori Rushford on their "Literary and Hymns Pilgrimage to England and Scotland" tour in May. She and Norvel had often considered joining the annual tour, but the timing had never seemed right. When Helen's good friend, Patty Atkisson, agreed to also go along and be her roommate, Helen decided that it was finally the time to make the trip. In her heart, she knew that Norvel would approve of the decision. He would want her to be a part of the pilgrimage of song while she was enjoying good health. This was not the time to stay home. And her children said, "Don't wait on anything."

It turned out to be the right decision. Surrounded by friends on a comfortable touring coach, with perfect weather in both England and Scotland, Helen thoroughly enjoyed singing the great hymns of faith in Anglican, Baptist, Methodist and Congregational churches across the country. She also relished the London production of *Les Miserables* and the Royal Shakespearean Company's performance of *A Midsummer Night's Dream* in Stratford-Upon-Avon.

Visiting the historic residences of people of literary consequence was especially enjoyable and educational for Helen. Although very tired when they reached Stratford, she and Patty Atkisson immediately jumped on a bus and rode out to Anne Hathaway's Cottage. Touring the homes of Jane Austen, Dr. Samuel Johnson, William Shakespeare, Sir Walter Scott, Beatrix Potter and William Wordsworth was a highlight of the tour for her.

The tour group of 28 people included some friends she had known for many years: Haven Miller and Anna Pearl Adrian Miller from Abilene, Texas (who had just married and were on their honeymoon), W. L. and Marilyn Fletcher of San Diego and Edwin and Joan Biggers of Tucson, Arizona. W. L. Fletcher and Ed Biggers were both members of the Pepperdine Board of Regents.

On Sunday morning, May 17, prior to attending the services at St. Giles Cathedral, the tour group worshipped together and celebrated the Lord's Supper in a private conference room of the George Hotel in Edinburgh. It was the three-month anniversary of Norvel's passing. And on this lovely Lord's Day in Scotland, Helen missed him terribly. They had traveled so many miles together, enjoyed so many scenes and experiences almost as one, single person. But now she was indeed a "single person." She was visibly emotional during the singing of the familiar old hymns and the sharing of communion. At the close of the uplifting worship experience as they sat in a circle, Helen told the group that she had been thinking of how much Norvel would have savored this moment. In fact, she had been thinking of how he would have enjoyed the camaraderie of this compatible group.

When Helen returned home at the end of May, she plowed through mountains of correspondence and began organizing photographs and other memorabilia from Norvel's long career. At the end of June she traveled to Nashville to attend both the David Lipscomb University Bible Lectureship and the 60th anniversary of *21ˢᵗ Century Christian* magazine. And she was added to the Board of Directors of that magazine and *Power for Today* devotional guide.

Summer came and it was August 17 at 3 p.m., six months after Norvel's death. Helen was seated in Smothers Theatre on the Pepperdine campus. The house lights gleamed down on a sea of orange across the front of the stage and across the orchestra pit area. It was dozens of orange-shirted Seaver College students who had taken two weeks of their summer to serve as New Student Orientation (NSO) advisors. Hung Le, associate director of campus life, stood at the microphone in front of most members of the entering class of nearly 750 students. He explained the year's NSO theme, "Forever Young," saying, "Rod Stewart didn't originate that phrase [referring to a hit music single of a few years ago], Norvel Young did."

Hung Le went on to say that the man who saved Pepperdine in 1957 had, many years earlier, proposed to a beautiful coed named Helen Mattox and told her, "Marry me and you will be forever Young." At that point, he asked the head advisors to escort Helen to the microphone. Two young women and two young men in orange tee shirts surrounded her and ushered Helen the 20 feet to the podium – to a standing ovation from a packed Smothers Theatre. Then Marcus Brown, graduating student body president, said a few words of warm thanks and honor to the special woman and her beloved husband.

One by one, several students offered her gifts: a bouquet of flowers, an orange NSO advisor shirt, a Bible in which a passage from Isaiah had been highlighted. Hung Le read the highlighted words: "The Lord is the everlasting God, the Creator of the ends of the earth. He will not grow tired or weary, and his understanding no one can fathom. He gives strength to the weary and increases the power of the weak. Even youths grow tired and weary, and young men stumble and fall; but those who hope in the Lord will renew their strength. They will soar on wings like eagles; they will run and not grow weary, they will walk and not be faint" (Isaiah 40:28-31).

Hung Le concluded by reading a special proclamation to Helen, officially naming her an honorary NSO advisor. There were hugs and more applause before she returned to her front row seat. Norvel most certainly would have approved of her participation with the college students he loved so much.

After his passing, Pepperdine's Chancellor Charles B. Runnels reflected on the life of Norvel Young. He said:

> I was blessed to work side-by-side with Norvel for more than three decades at Pepperdine and I was blessed to be able to count him as a great friend. He was always reaching out to others and giving of himself. It was later, after they got to know him and the University, that they would either apply to attend here or make a gift to Pepperdine.
>
> I think everyone will always remember his tremendous spirit. Norvel made friends with literally everyone he met. His motto was "Wow! It's a great day to be alive!" and it seemed it was his mission to make everyone feel that way, too. It is no wonder that he accomplished so much on behalf of so many other people. Dr. William Banowsky, who succeeded Norvel as Pepperdine's fourth president, perhaps summed up Norvel's influence best when he said, "Pepperdine University is the lengthened shadow of Norvel Young."

Pepperdine's Chairman of the Board of Regents Thomas G. Bost was impressed with the breadth of Norvel's work. He said:

> Through Norvel Young's leadership, the Churches of Christ enlarged their vision, particularly in the areas of missions and benevolence. He was probably the most significant leader of the Churches in the post-war era. He was active in relief and mission efforts; he helped found educational institutions and Christian publications; and he was a leader in civic affairs and an influential member of corporate and community boards throughout the Los Angeles area. Though he will be greatly missed, his work will impact and influence generations to come.

David Davenport, the sixth president of Pepperdine University, remembered Norvel's expansive dreams and forward-looking spirit. He summarized:

> It has always seemed that for as long as Pepperdine has been in existence, that Norvel Young was the heart of the institution. He had truly become thought of as our "Mr. Pepperdine." It was really his vision that transformed Pepperdine from a small liberal arts college to a larger university with multiple schools and campuses around the world. He always spoke with pride of the 830-acre Malibu campus he envisioned and helped make possible. He often described it with great verve as "smog-free, sun-kissed, ocean-washed, island-girded and mountain-guarded."
>
> It is rare for a leader to have such a sustained, almost life-long impact on a single institution. But Norvel found his two great passions at play here: the Christian ministry and higher education ... preparing the next generation. He was a great futurist with

a spirit that embraced everyone with whom he had contact. He is as well known in Bangkok and Berlin as he was in Los Angeles or his hometown of Nashville.

With his passing, our vision of Norvel's greatness will increase. His failings, which seemed so apparent at times, will diminish in our memory as the years go by. And it will become clearer and clearer that M. Norvel Young was crucial to the heart and soul of Pepperdine University, and to its meteoric rise in stature among institutions of higher learning ... as he was crucial to so many other wonderful works. Growing numbers of people will come to a deeper understanding of the legacy he leaves for the American religious movement he loved and sought to lift. His indomitable spirit will shine brighter for thousands as they remember his heroic trek from the pit of despair to grace-inspired triumph.

But as for Norvel, he is on to bigger and better things ... somewhere else. And his beautiful, inspiring, enabling partner, Helen, is close by.

LIVING LIGHTS, SHINING STARS

---

*H*ad he chosen to apply himself in the business world, M. Norvel Young would certainly have been a success – probably a wealthy captain of industry. We have mentioned that his father had been a successful businessman, but considered making money one of the "lesser" talents. Norvel undoubtedly would have outstripped the accomplishments of the senior Matt Young.

Had he chosen to enter medicine, who knows what break-throughs he might have introduced? His son, the junior Matt Young, is a prominent physician today, specializing in the treatment of serious burns. Norvel certainly could have attained a highly respected position in the medical community.

Had he chosen psychology, law, politics, or any of a number of other careers, M. Norvel Young surely would have emerged on top of his field. Because of his character. Because of his intelligence and drive and wit and grace.

As it was, he chose two careers and melded them into one. First of all, regardless of where he served, he was always a devoted minister of the gospel of Jesus Christ. But second, he also was a consummate educator. These two careers came together in the person of Norvel Young. Where one career left off and the other began is hard to say. Perhaps we should simply conclude that Dr. M. Norvel Young was a *Christian educator* who moved with ease in the church and in the academy – always teaching, always preaching, always helping and serving, always leading the way. And always moving his complex life in the direction of the carpenter of Galilee. It was obvious that Norvel was attracted to the brilliance of the Messiah, and in turn, his own life took on a certain dazzle, a reflection of the object of his gaze.

As the years go by, we will stand more in awe of the man, not necessarily because his intellect dwarfed us or his spirit intimidated us or his talents overwhelmed us. But because of his unique combination of love, inclusiveness, enthusiasm, optimism, grace and vision. *Especially vision.* There was no one quite like him.

F. W. "Billy" Mattox was Helen's older brother. And Billy obviously knew his brother-in-law very well. After more than 55 years of observing Norvel's life, Billy told him, "If Christians were being searched out and martyred today, you would be among the first to die, for your position is well known and you would be easy to find." When it came to Norvel's life and faith, it would be difficult to say it better than that. Because Norvel Young's "position" was indeed well known. And he was indeed "easy to find."

Of all his marvelous accomplishments, perhaps the most remarkable was discovering a mate who so completely complemented him. He and Helen Mattox seemed destined to live their lives together. In retrospect, it is simply inconceivable to imagine one without the other. She was his other half. Alone, he was only a half. But *together* they built churches, orphans homes, universities, periodicals, and a host of other wonderful works. *Together* they gave their world four wonderful children. *Together* they were a blessing to the lives of those whom they touched. And they blessed thousands of people whom they would never meet.

Helen was a rare combination of the beauty and grace of women of old and the intelligence and drive of the women of today. She, too, had choices of careers. She could have been an accomplished author, a successful entrepreneur or administrator, a speaker on the circuit, an educator, or a leader. She chose to be all of those things. And yet she refused to let any of them confine her or define her. For many of us, she elevated the concepts of *woman, wife, mother, servant,* and *professional* to new heights. She allowed Norvel to be great—she *enabled* his greatness, in a sense. And in so doing, she proved herself to be great indeed. The words "selfless" and "grace" inevitably come to mind at the thought of Helen Mattox Young.

Norvel and Helen moved in remarkable circles, among the wealthy and influential, among the celebrity and powerful. They entertained presidents, cabinet members, senators, foreign dignitaries, and a parade of important people. But they never took on any sort of aloofness or arrogance. Though the Youngs moved through life in a most regal manner, those with whom they interacted were warmed, rather than intimidated, by them.

Some men and women wonder what their legacy eventually will be. Others don't seem to care. As for Norvel and Helen Young, their legacy was secured long ago: A university in Malibu owes it continued existence to them; many people will be blessed through the Young children and grandchildren; churches, colleges, homes for homeless children, and so many other good works will prosper because of them. Norvel's final book aptly distilled his philosophy of life. And the title he chose for the book is a truly appropriate summary of his and Helen's life and ministry: *Living Lights, Shining Stars.*

We have alluded to an occasion in 1997 when Norvel was speaking to a group of colleagues and said, "There are givers and there are takers. We've always tried to be givers." He spoke with tears in his eyes and with a throat that was tight with emotion. He was emotional for two reasons: he knew his and Helen's journeys were well advanced; and he knew that they wished they could do much more to make the world a better place. Perhaps that is their most profound legacy: *to the end, they were givers.* And they made us – those who knew them – want to be givers as well.

Both Helen and Norvel loved to tell people, "The future is as bright as the promises of God." Did one of them originate the quotation? They couldn't remember. But it doesn't matter. They never were interested in getting credit for accomplishments, much less quotations. They just wanted to share with people, bless people, and give people hope.

The Young children put a poetic verse in large letters beside Helen's treadmill as a reminder that the future can be bright. It reads:

> I would not have you sorrowful or sad,
>   But joyfully recall
> The glorious companionship we've had,
>   And thank God for it all.

Norvel was famous for exclaiming, "It's a great day to be alive!" Very often, he would add, "in Malibu!" He did dearly love Malibu, after all. On the balcony of their hillside home, he and Helen spent many serene hours gazing out over shoreline breakers toward Santa Monica Bay and beyond.

"It's a great day to be alive" became more than a greeting or a conversation starter for those two lovely people. It was their declaration. It was their prayer. It was their word of gratitude and grace. A reminder. A blessing. A confidence. A philosophy of life.

After Norvel's passing, Helen replaced the familiar quotation by her husband's voice on their answer-phone. But she changed it only slightly. If you call her home while she is away, you will receive an answer-phone message in her own warm, beautiful voice saying, "This is the Helen Young residence. As Norvel would say, It's a great day to be alive! I hope you have a happy day."

ACKNOWLEDGEMENTS

Like so many thousands of others, we are deeply indebted to Norvel and Helen Young. This book is a very small payment toward that indebtedness. We appreciate the long hours of interviews that they graciously gave to us in early 1995. And we are grateful for the additional interviews of Helen in 1998 and 1999, as well as the many hours she spent hunting through photographs and papers at our request.

All of the children – Emily Y. Lemley, Matt N. Young, Marilyn Y. Stewart and Sara Y. Jackson – and their spouses were very helpful in supplying stories, memories and reflections. They also added to the book by reviewing the material for accuracy.

We are thankful for Pepperdine University, the institution that figured so largely in the lives of Norvel and Helen. The support of President David Davenport, Chancellor Charles B. Runnels, Executive Vice President Andrew K. Benton, Provost Steven S. Lemley, Executive Vice Chancellor Lawrence D. Hornbaker and others is greatly appreciated.

Great thanks go to the good people at 21st Century Christian: Winston Moore, Mark McInteer, Jim Bill McInteer and others. But especially we thank Barry Brewer, who saw the potential and the need for this book and helped initiate the project. Since this is the company and these are the people that Norvel loved so much, it is appropriate that the biography of Norvel and Helen Young be produced there. And it is most appropriate that Norvel's story be printed in his hometown. We appreciate their patience with the tight scheduling and their attention to detail and excellence.

We want to thank Richard VanDyke & Leigh Ray for their expert production services, as Richard formatted the entire book in record time and Leigh added her fine proofreading skills to the project.

People in Pepperdine's publications office contributed substantially to the production of the book. Rick Gibson designed the beautiful dust jacket and title logo. Amy Cook scanned all the photographs and put them in place with captions on the 32-page section. And Debbie Pikul designed the chapter headings and specified the various type styles.

The people of the Public Affairs area at Pepperdine were very supportive. Joyce Hutchison proofread manuscripts and gave advice in many areas. Anita McFarland did research and dozens of other chores. Ron Halls was helpful in a number of photographic projects. And Patti Atkisson and Bridget Smith helped with various communications.

Our wives always end up contributing heavily to any project with which we are involved. Lori Rushford spent hours proofreading and editing the manuscript of the book and attended to other important tasks. Laurette Henegar transcribed many hours of video interviews and also proofread manuscripts.

A final word of thanks goes to George and Reva Graziadio, who supported the biography of their dear friends, Norvel and Helen Young, in a very substantial way. Their faithful friendship has been proven in many ways included this generous gesture. We appreciate Claudia Arnold for coordinating internal distribution and facilitating communication.

Our hope and prayer is that this biography will adequately portray two heroes of our time. Many people, especially those listed above, have been coworkers in this labor of love.

As Norvel would say, "You just don't know how much good you are doing."

Index

A

B

C

F

G

H

K

L

M

T

Y